More comments on
Site Plan and Development Review

"*Site Plan and Development Review: A Guide for Northern New England* is the most comprehensive and readable book that I have ever encountered. Bound between its covers is a college course. It should be mandatory reading for every neophyte planning board member. (P.S. It wouldn't hurt the veterans to read it also.)"

– Kenneth L. Niemczyk
City Planner
City of Lebanon, New Hampshire

"Honestly, this book is great!... [It] should prove to be an invaluable resource to thousands of planners in northern New England who are charged to protect the region's great natural beauty and incomparable resource base. This work is highly informative, well-organized, and comprehensive. I have known the authors for the better part of two decades and I cannot think of two individuals who are more highly qualified in the practical application of land use regulation. This is due to their highly varied backgrounds in academia and state and local regulatory review programs. I know the readers will benefit from their extensive knowledge and direct experiences in the field."

– Michael Zahner
Executive Director,
Vermont Environmental Board

SITE PLAN AND DEVELOPMENT REVIEW:
A GUIDE FOR NORTHERN NEW ENGLAND

Robert M. Sanford
Dana H. Farley

Published by
Putney Press

For additional copies of this book or information about other
Putney Press publications, contact:
Putney Press
PO Box 430
Newfane, VT 05345
Phone: 802/365-7991 Fax: 802/365-7996

Dedication

This book is dedicated to the many hardworking and often under-appreciated professionals and volunteers—the people in the trenches—who review development plans in an effort to guide growth in New England, keeping it one of the most wonderful places to live.

It is a bad plan that admits of no modification.

– Publius Syrus (Maxim 469) 42 BC

TABLE OF CONTENTS

LIST OF FIGURES

FOREWORD

By Mark B. Lapping
Cumberland Center, Maine

Planning is an intellectually robust and demanding field. It is loaded with many "big ideas" about important things such as: How can we live more convivially with nature? What form should communities take and how might they look? How should towns and cities "work" in terms of meeting the needs of their residents as well as those who work there? Can we truly sustain this pattern of life and livelihood? And lots more. As significant and large as these matters are, community planning is one of those processes where the proverbial "devil" is truly in the detail. It is often the little things, the mundane things, which give us answers to the above questions even when the results are less than fully satisfying.

Certainly one of the most important elements of planning is the review and assessment of proposals to use the land in one manner or another. Is a piece of land capable of supporting homes or industrial parks given its intrinsic characteristics? Is a particular proposal consistent with what the larger community believes is appropriate for an area and is it consistent with local needs? Can a proposal for a development be improved so that it creates a "win-win" both for the developer and the community? What will likely be the long-term impact of a specific pattern of land use in terms of how it will affect local fiscal realities as well as environmental concerns? Answers to these very important questions are most often derived from the review of site plans and development proposals. This is, in essence, "the nitty gritty" of community and land use planning.

There are only a few books which discuss in great detail site plan and development review. Almost all of these have a strong landscape architectural orientation. This is not problematic in and of itself. As important as these considerations may be, however, we have been lacking the one comprehensive text that includes additional perspectives, particularly the concerns of planners and members of citizen-based planning boards and commissions. To my knowledge there exists no book that is regionally contextual in that it speaks to the realities of the practical aspects of site plan and development review in specific places and regions, such as northern New England.

We now have a book that fulfills both needs admirably. *Site Plan and Development Review* is both practical and theoretically tight. It provides its readers with an enormous amount of the information, data, tools, sources of information and concepts that will facilitate more robust and decisive site plan and development review processes here in northern New England. It is a model that ought to be emulated in other places and other regions for, after all, America is environmentally amazingly diverse and planning needs to reflect this reality.

– Mark Lapping is the coauthor of Partnerships in Communities: Reweaving the Fabric of Rural America; The Small Town Planning Handbook; *and* Rural Planning and Development in the United States; *and is the editor of* Contested Countryside, The Rural Urban Fringe *and* Big Places, Big Plans: Regional Land Use in Rural North America. *He has written over 150 other publications, and is Professor of Public Policy and Management at the University of Southern Maine.*

PREFACE

This book is an introductory reference to the drawings and concepts provided on site and development plans in Northern New England. We focus on the basic information necessary for those who review development projects to understand what the plans convey and what the accompanying documentation and studies mean. Fortunately, reviewers do not need to know how to prepare an impact study or site plan themselves, just enough about them to make a reasonable decision on whether to approve the project unconditionally, to approve it with conditions, or to deny it. Reviewers also need to know where to find any further information needed to make a decision or take an informed position on a development proposal. Good sources of information on specific land use laws and associated procedures already exist (e.g., Cindy Corlett Argentine's *Vermont Act 250 Handbook*, *Maine Land Use Control Law* by Orlando E. Delogu, and the New Hampshire Office of State Planning's *Data Requirements for Site Review: Guidance for Planning Boards*), but we see a benefit in a general reference guide tailored to the broad land use issues and concepts reviewers face when interpreting site and development plans in northern New England—a practical companion to existing legal, regulatory and procedural materials.

When we make decisions on what can be built in our communities, we are authorizing relatively permanent changes in the physical landscape as well as in the social and economic fabric. A new house in New England, for example, will typically last more than 150 years. Planners and regulators understand the instinct to allow developers and land owners as much freedom as possible to do what they want with their land, yet they must find ways to balance that freedom with the rights of community members to a clean and healthy environment. Further, each community has a vision of how its growth will unfold wisely, a vision that relies on land use regulations, comprehensive plans, and tools to apply in the review of development projects—a significant responsibility often exercised by volunteers with little or no formal training. Clearly, there are both strengths and weaknesses to this democratic process. With the right tools, review boards can make decisions that realize the vision of their communities; hopefully, this book can be one of those tools.

Those who sit on a local or state review board can use this book to get a quick handle on what is behind all the procedures and science to determine when to ask for more information. It should also serve those who represent non-profit organizations, citizens, and state officials—all of whom may act as "interveners," or as advisors in the development review process. Students of planning, design, and engineering can also benefit from this information.

In Part I, we describe the components of development plans and summarize the goals and processes in their review. In Part II, we devote specific chapters to the more common environmental impacts associated with typical developments. These chapters encompass air quality, noise, soils, septic systems, water, erosion, traffic, municipal services, aesthetics, historical and archaeological resources, plants, wildlife, energy, forestry, agriculture, and coastal development. Only passing reference is made to the myriad statutes, ordinances, and regulations that govern specific development review processes in northern New England. Our goal is to address impacts at a level of detail sufficient to facilitate interpretation of site plans and their accompanying narratives. Scattered among the chapters are 'Tales from the Trenches,' some contributed by colleagues, reflecting common experiences of reviewing development plans.

The end of each chapter has a section on where to go for more information, which includes the names of organizations, web site references, statutes, regulations, and publications related to the specific topic of the chapter. We have tried to select references that are easily located, and accessible sources from Internet sites that can be downloaded for free.

Robert M. Sanford and Dana H. Farley

Acknowledgements

While there is not space to acknowledge properly the many talented people who helped us, we do want to mention the following people who kindly contributed: Kate Albert, former Senior Planner, Southern Maine Regional Planning Commission (thanks for going through all those early drafts); Bill Burke, Vermont Environmental Board; Julie Campoli, Terra Firma Urban Design; Cynthia Cook, Adamant Accord; Beth Della Valle, planning consultant; the staff and faculty of the 2001 Maine Smart Growth Institute; Marianne Dubois, Maine Department of Environmental Protection (MDEP); Dr. Nancy Gish, University of Southern Maine (USM); Dr. Nathan Hamilton, USM; April Hensel, Vermont Environmental Board; Elizabeth Humstone, Vermont Forum on Sprawl; Faith Ingulsrud, Vermont Agency of Commerce and Communty Development; Ken Kaliski, P.E., Resource Systems Group, Inc.; Dr. Jack Kartez, USM; Dr. Samantha Langley-Turnbaugh, USM; Dr. Mark B. Lapping, USM; Ken Niemczyk, City of Lebanon, NH; Sarah Marshall, Terry DeWan Associates; Paul Miller, builder; Evan Richert, USM; Ellen Roffman, Putney Press (thanks for instant and durable faith); Robin Sanford, librarian; Dr. Richard Sanford, P.E.; David Sanford, P.E.; Julie Schmitz, Vermont Environmental Board; Dr. Jim Smith, USM; Christine Smith, MDEP; Dr. Arthur Spiess, Maine Historic Preservation Commission; the Springfield offices of the Vermont Agency of Natural Resources; Dr. Diane Zahm, Virginia Tech; Michael Zahner, Vermont Environmental Board; and the Town Planning Office of Gorham, Maine.

Special thanks go to John Bruno, P.E., Bruno Associates and Sandra Vitzthum, Architect, for their time and energy in developing the figures for this book; they participated without compensation other than their belief in the merits of this project.

Credits

The cover photograph is the property of Stephen Brooks. Interior figures are by Sandra Vitzthum Architect LLC, Bruno Associates, and Robert Sanford.

Part One:

CONCEPTS AND PROCESSES

Chapter 1
INTRODUCTION TO THE REVIEW
OF SITE AND DEVELOPMENT PLANS

What is a "swale?" remarked one of the authors to the other on our first day of site review training back in the 1980s. We were thrown into the trenches after two days and expected to employ basic land use terminology (a swale is a low-lying, linear area of land that provides drainage) and processes. The struggle to gain a foothold in the language and tools of land use regulation isn't made easier by tight time constraints and by the fact that many reviewers of development are hard-working volunteers who do this in addition to their regular jobs. We, at least, were paid professionals, but our own struggles to become conversant in the language of swales, setbacks, PRDs, and other specialized aspects of project review, spurred our efforts to help train others.

As hearing officers, a significant part of our duties was to instruct citizens and neighbors in how to participate in public processes. While we found adequate materials to explain legal procedures and particular land use and environmental laws, we realized that much of what is used to convey the basics of project review is cobbled together, stitched of various materials from here and there. We found a need for an introductory guide to the concepts, terms, and nuances of land subdivision and development projects as represented in applications for permits—a resource that would focus on understanding and reviewing drawings, narratives, and plans, while directing the reader to sources for current and easily obtainable references on the Internet, from government and in the professional literature.

The centerpiece of the review of land use development is the site plan. A site plan is typically drawn by a civil engineer and depicts the general layout of a subdivision or development project, the proposed access, roads, building footprints, sewer and water infrastructure, lighting and other features. Depending on the complexity of the project and the requirements of the review board, the site plan can be confined to one page or be accompanied by several pages of drawings with detailed information including natural features, topography, soils, and drainage.

Maine, Vermont, and New Hampshire have similarities in regulatory procedures, geography, and culture. In Vermont, development review is done at the local level and also at the state level for projects that fall under the jurisdiction of Act 250, Vermont's land use control law. New Hampshire does not have a comprehensive state-wide land use law, leaving regulation to the local communities. Maine has a land use regulatory process (LURC) somewhat similar to Vermont's Act 250, but applying only to unincorporated townships where there is no local government. In Maine, the Site Location of Development Law enables the Department of Environmental Protection to review site plans for development that may have a substantial effect on the environment. This book takes into consideration the commonalties among these states, as well as the distinctions, and is designed to assist volunteer review boards, professional planners, students, non-profit organizations, and citizens in making sense out of proposed land use developments.

When we refer to the term "review board" we mean those individuals constituting a planning commission, planning board, conservation commission, zoning board, Act 250 Commission, design review board—basically any kind of development review board. The newly appointed member of a review board quickly finds out that he or she has a huge responsibility to anticipate a variety of impacts, ranging from water quality, to archeological resources, to educational services. Review board members must distill large amounts of information, much of it complex and technical, in a short amount of time and arrive at decisions on development projects. Their decisions must meet appropriate planning, legal, and regulatory standards. A failure to fully evaluate a site plan and anticipate environmental impacts can result in haphazard, poorly conceived development that uses land inefficiently, causes traffic congestion, and jeopardizes important natural resources such as wetlands. Poor or no development plan review results in sprawled land use patterns, such as strip development, and environmental problems (e.g., stormwater mismanagement, pollution, excessive curb cuts, soil erosion), which are difficult to remedy after the fact. Those who review development plans must be mindful of the problems inherent in reviewing projects in a piecemeal fashion. Review board members have a right and an obligation to ask for and get needed information and to consider surrounding land uses.

When we look around an area that has seen fast growth and development pressures even those who are unfamiliar with the precepts of environmental review can sense whether "the rules" are working. Is traffic queuing up at intersections or at a standstill at predictable times of the day? Have sensible connections between commercial developments been made to encourage pedestrian use? Is there excessive lighting and glare in parking lots? Is stormwater run-off dealt with effectively on each site or does it flow and pool over property lines? Do residential subdivisions fail to provide adequate open space? Are houses lined along a prominent ridgeline? Are once large farm fields fragmented by scattered commercial or residential development?

The above questions must be answered on an individual basis through a case-by-case review. The answers depend in part on understanding the context of the laws and concepts governing the review of land use development.

Brief chronology of development plan review

Development plan review in America is descended from English common law, under the guiding principle *Sic utere tuo ut alienum no laedus* (Use your property so as not to harm others). Essentially, development plan review is the political review of a proposed change to the environment. As such, its roots begin at least a thousand years ago, back when politics and religion were more intertwined. A quick review of the beginnings of development regulation will help in understanding the reasoning and goals behind it.

In theory, development plan review begins with the seeking of permission from the gods, through their intermediaries, the priests, for permission to build sacred structures or in sacred places. Later, kings and queens integrated their divine mandates into decisions on where and what the public could build. Still later, having lost their divine rights, nobility made the rules using their own secular authority with support from the elite classes. The protection of resources for use by the king was sufficient justification for royal agents to intervene in public and private construction projects. For example, during the Dutch War of 1654, white pines were needed for Royal Navy masts. By 1704, royal surveyors were marking broad arrow blazes on potential mast trees all over New England and actions that could hurt these trees, such as removing them to create agricultural land or settlements, were prohibited (Cronan, 1983). Perhaps those evaluations of farm clearings for their potential impact on the king's trees can be considered early forms of development review.

Long before the British Royal Navy, the building professions had evolved in ancient city-states such as the Mayans and Egyptians along with religious proscriptions that dictated the appropriate appearances of public structures. Later, health and aesthetic considerations provided incentives for public regulation of structures. Plagues demonstrated the need to isolate structures as well as groups of people. An enormous fire in Boston in the late 17th century resulted in a number of laws mandating the use of brick or stone in buildings. It wasn't until the 20th century that this regulation of structures extended to regulation of the land itself.

Northern New England flirted with planning and zoning in the early 1930s through the encouragement of the federal government's programs for recovery from the Depression. Like other regions, New England made extensive planning efforts during World War II. Some of these efforts carried over into fairly comprehensive post-war town plans. The following brief chronology lists the major events leading to modern development plan review.

Chronology of land use regulation laws and events

1867   A San Francisco ordinance prohibits certain "obnoxious uses" in certain districts, the beginning of land use zoning in the U.S.

1885   A San Francisco ordinance excludes laundries from housing areas.

1895   Los Angeles ordinance prohibits steam shoddying plants (a process of recycling woolen materials and known for its noxious odors) within 100 feet (30.5 meters) of a church.

1899   The Massachusetts Supreme Court upholds a maximum height of building limitation in *Attorney General v. Williams* (178 Mass. 330).

1901   New York City Tenement House Law is passed, requiring construction on two lots with wide light and air corridors, and a toilet in each apartment.

1907   First official and permanent town planning board in the United States is created in Hartford, Connecticut.

1909   Building height limit zones are upheld in U.S. Supreme Court (*Welch v. Swasey* 214 US 91).

        Los Angeles passes multiple zoning ordinance, including regulation of undeveloped land—the first American use of zoning to direct future development.

1912   Horizontal restrictions on building locations are upheld by the U.S. Supreme Court (*Eubank v. City of Richmond* 226 US 137).

1915   In *Hadacheck v. Sebastion* (239 US 394, 405), the City of Los Angeles banned brick-making from certain areas to protect surrounding residential neighborhoods from noxious fumes.

        New York City Zoning Code is passed, the first comprehensive zoning code in the United States.

1920s   The U.S. Supreme Court held in a series of decisions that excessive or "overreaching" zoning regulations may result in a taking (the taking of private property for public use without just compensation) without violating the U.S. Constitution.

1926   In *Village of Euclid v. Ambler Realty Co.* (272 US 365), the U.S. Supreme Court upholds the constitutionality of comprehensive zoning.

1927   In *Zahn v. Board of Public Works* (274 US 325), the U.S. Supreme Court upholds the zoning of raw land for uses that need not necessarily be the most lucrative ones.

1940s   Federal regulations for war and post-war public housing bring federal review to the planning process. Mustering of resources for war demonstrates value of planning and forethought in development.

1966   In *Jenad, Inc. v. Village of Scarsdale* (18 NY2d 78, 271 NYS2d 955), the New York Court of Appeals holds that a municipality can require money in lieu of land allotment for parks in subdivision approval processes.

1970   The National Environmental Policy Act (NEPA) is implemented, requiring submission of environmental impact statements (EISs) for federal actions and other projects requiring federal review or approval. The EISs must be comprehensive assessments of environmental impacts ranging from air quality to energy conservation.

       Vermont's Land Use and Development Law (Act 250) goes into effect. Like NEPA, Act 250 requires comprehensive environmental impact assessments but unlike NEPA, Act 250 is geared towards a yes/no decision on development.

1971   In *Golden v. Planning Board of Ramapo* (30 NY2d 359, 334 NYS2d 138, 285 NE2d 291), the New York Court of Appeals supported control of development timing, slowing the rate of growth by the imposition of development performance standards.

1987   U.S. Supreme Court rules in *Nollan v. California Coastal Commission* (483 US 825) that permit requirements must have an "essential nexus" to the pertinent regulatory program and that there must be a "rough proportionality" between the development impact and the condition specified in the permit.

1992   In *Lucas v. South Carolina Coastal Council* (505 US 1003), the U.S. Supreme Court held that a "taking" had occurred when a state beachfront management regulation prohibited a property owner from building permanent structures on his lots.

The "takings" issue is perennial. However, most land use regulation makes a reasonable connection between public benefit and the use of private property and readily survives "takings" challenges. It is now routine for review of some kind to apply to most small projects; large development projects are usually subject to a more comprehensive review. The purpose of these reviews is to determine compliance with government regulations, which generally include social and environmental components. The environmental sciences and design professions have also advanced to incorporate a knowledge base that contributes to the review of development projects.

Approaches to development plan review

There are various types of review. Some of the most common types seen in northern New England are decisive reviews and advisory reviews. Decisive reviews are outcome-based. Advisory reviews may be nestled within decisive reviews and are sort of a

---

Tale from the Trenches

THE PROFILER

I asked a well-known and highly successful development consultant to speak to a class in site planning and design. In my capacity as an environmental regulator I had reviewed many projects submitted by various developers who had hired this consultant, and I hoped he would share a few words on strategy with the students. I was surprised to find that his company carefully researched each board member or commissioner who would sit in review of his clients' projects. He prepared brief profiles of each reviewing official and would use them in crafting an overall strategy for steering a project through the permit process. The students were quite amazed as well. He stated that it made sense when so much money and energy were invested in a project and that it was just good business. Many times in development review, the amateurs are reviewing the work of the professionals, and it is good to remember just how strategic the professionals really are.

check-in for the project and the involved parties. Everyone needs to know which type of review is applicable to the matter at hand so the range of outcomes matches expectations.

Decisive reviews result in a yes/no decision and are probably the most common type of development review process. The decision is usually accompanied by a permit (if approved) and often, a basis for the decision (the "Findings of Fact and Conclusions of Law"). If the project is denied, the Findings (written or orally read into the record) typically explain the rationale for the denial. In the decisive review process the facts and assessment results are more important than the process by which they were achieved. However, the reviewers should still use standard scientific and engineering methods. Decisive reviews are the primary form of municipal and state review. Local review boards carry out decisive reviews on subdivisions and developments. These reviews are not necessarily for small projects alone and can entail complex assessments similar to Environmental Impact Statements.

Great discretion can exist in the range and depth of environmental evaluations. Vermont's Act 250 land use permit program has application materials that require the applicant to consider the character and complexity of both the development and its proposed environmental setting. An Act 250 review for a large development such as a regional shopping mall would include formal environmental assessments under established procedures within various professions such as traffic engineering, wildlife biology and fiscal impact review.

Local review boards may also consider large and complex projects and have the authority under municipal bylaws and regulations to evaluate impacts, hire experts, and impose conditions. Issuance of a yes/no decision requires an understanding, if not a mastery, of all potential impacts within the reviewers' jurisdiction.

Advisory reviews

Advisory reviews are less formal than decisive reviews and are used to provide indicators of a project's feasibility or to inform a regulatory review board or other concerned organization. An advisory review can help acquaint the developer, the public, and the review board with the nature of the project and of the review process. Accordingly, an advisory review is usually a component of project planning, rather than the formal review or permitting process, and is not decision-oriented.

An advisory review can include a presentation before a regulatory body such as a planning commission, an advisory body such as a conservation commission, or it can be an "in-house" review among various consultants associated with the project. Many communities have formed design review boards that provide information and advice to regulatory bodies.

Regulatory bodies should establish procedures that address the range and degree of advisory reviews. Such procedures will help the review boards manage their time and will encourage fairness. The need for procedures becomes critical when the regulatory body has to render a permit decision within a judicial or quasi-judicial proceeding. The matter must be properly brought before the regulatory body to ensure compliance with the administrative procedures and regulations in the various states.

Social and cultural influences in development plan review

People exhibit great variation in their attitudes about the environment and about construction that alters it (Rapoport, 1977). Attitudes toward private property rights can affect decision–making by land use regulators and the degree to which conditions bind use of the land. However—and this can be a surprise to people who have never served on a review board—land use decisions in the public arena are bound by rules and procedures that have a leveling effect on predispositions; governmental processes are restrictive and require supporting reasoning for land use decisions to survive legal challenges. The vast majority of development projects are approved rather than denied, and most issues arise over the particular nature of specific conditions of approval. Differences among board members can be quite striking when conditions perceived as too onerous or restrictive are considered. This is when the composition of review boards, appointed by local or state officials, comes into play (and why most astute developers make a practice of examining who serves on these boards). In many cases, and despite the difficulties, political officials attempt to maintain balance when appointing citizen regulators.

Tale from the Trenches

THE DIFFICULT COMMITTEE

Most towns fancy themselves somehow different—more difficult or picky or political—than all other towns. I don't want to start my client relationships by popping their bubble and asserting that people are really the same everywhere, so I smile and humor my clients, and begin by trying to understand what their individual concerns are, and also by finding out who else in the town needs to be contacted. Usually by making sure that everyone is heard, and by going slowly to get consensus each step of the way, we arrive at design solutions that have broad support.

In one town though, a certain Library Planning Committee had truly been struggling with process, communications, and personal styles long before they hired their consultants. They were divided into almost angry factions, but through their own efforts they had stayed together and still all agreed that they wanted a beautiful and expanded library. I was very impressed with their determination to make the committee work. I learned from them that sometimes there has to be a very rigid set of rules about talking in group settings, and decision-making. For example, they went around the table as many times as it took to be satisfied, but never allowed debate or 'cross-talk' between two impassioned committee members. This defused their personal heat and kept everyone involved, even those who might prefer to 'check out' when the going gets rough. I have used this equal-air-time technique in many group situations since being exposed to it with the Library Planning Committee of that town. And they do now have a beautiful library.

Where to go for more information

American Planning Association. http://www.planning.org/

Argentine, Cindy Corlett. (1998). *Vermont Act 250 Handbook – A Guide to State and Regional Land Use Regulation*, 2nd edition. Newfane, Vt: Putney Press.

Lincoln Institute of Land Policy. http://www.lincolninst.edu/index-high.asp

Maine, State of. http://www.state.me.us/

Maine State Planning Office. http://www.state.me.us/spo/

Maine Land Use Regulation Commission (LURC). http://www.state.me/doc/lurc/lurchoe.htm

Michaud, Frederick L. *Planning & Land Use Laws*, Brown & Michaud: Augusta. Revised annually.

New Hampshire, State of. http://www.state.nh.us/

New Hampshire Department of Environmental Services. http://www.des.state.nh.us/

New Hampshire Office of State Planning. http://www.state.nh.us/osp/

New Hampshire Planners Association. http://www.nhlgc.org/Public_Documents/NHPA/nhpa_index.html

New Hampshire State Data Center. http://www.state.nh.us/osp/sdc/sdc.html

Northern New England Chapter of the American Planning Association. http://www.nnecapa.org/start.html

Planning Commissioner's Journal. http://www.plannersweb.com/

University of Vermont. http://www.crs.uvm.edu. http://www.uvm.edu/~uvmext.

Vermont, State of. http://www.state.vt.us/

Vermont Environmental Board. http://www.state.vt.us/envboard

Vermont Department of Housing and Community Affairs. http://www.state.vt.us/dca/housing

Vermont Agency of Natural Resources. http://www.anr.state.vt.us

Vermont Department of Housing and Community Affairs. *History of Planning in Vermont*, December 1999.

Vermont League of Cities and Towns. http://www.vlct.org/

Vermont Office of Secretary of State. http://www.sec.state.vt.us

Vermont Planners Association. http://www.rutlandrpc.org/VPA/
    VPAdefault.htm

Chapter 2

SELECTION AND REVIEW OF SITE LOCATION

Choosing the site

How do developers choose sites? How do they determine what can be done on them? Knowing how a site was selected for a development can help reviewers understand environmental impacts, which may be useful when requesting changes or mitigating the project. The factors in site selection reveal where there is room to negotiate.

The main orientations to site development are: 1) A project in search of a place; 2) A place in search of a project; and 3) Investors in search of a project and a place. Using any of these approaches or a combination of them, the developer will consider both the constraints and the opportunities in a site. Environmental factors such as steep slopes, wetlands, and agricultural soils can be constraints, as can be political factors such as strict zoning, anti-development stances, and overburdened local government officials. Site conditions, such as flat, well-drained soils, established municipal services, and supportive neighboring property owners, can also be opportunities. Depending on the orientation, the selection process may focus on site design opportunities, particularly if it is a project in search of a place, or on the site's environmental conditions.

Development consultants may use overlay maps to determine the suitability of a site. In this approach, maps of various factors such as slope, soils, zoning, and buffer zones for watercourses are compared. While this can be done by hand, it is increasingly done on a computer, using design packages or Geographic Information Systems (GIS).

Site analysis

After a general location is selected, potential sites in the area are analyzed. There is quite a range in the thoroughness and depth of site analyses, starting with an informal "look over" by the owner of a small business who might want to determine the best place to put a prefabricated building. For a larger or more critical development, the analysis could be a formal feasibility assessment with reports by engineers, architects, and biologists.

Under most site plan and development review regulations, the reviewer is primarily concerned with environmental and cultural (including economic and social) impacts. But how these impacts are treated in a site selection analysis depends on three factors that may be loosely grouped as natural, cultural and client factors.

Natural factors

Consultants and large-scale developers will usually have their own proprietary system of categorizing natural factors. An agency or local municipality may also have its own version for use in the permit process.

Cultural Factors

Cultural factors range from the built environment (e.g., roads, parks, neighborhoods) to the aesthetic and social values of the involved human communities.

Figure 2-1. Sample natural factors checklist.

Category	Conditions			Notes
Air quality	❑ poor ❑ occasional problems		❑ pristine	issues:_____
Depth to bedrock	❑ deep soil	❑ average	❑ outcrops	issues:_____
Seasonal high water table	❑ relatively low	❑ relatively high		issues:_____
Ground water quality	❑ monitored	❑ unmonitored		issues:_____
Wetlands	❑ acreage	❑ classification		issues:_____
Floodways	❑ 100 yr. flood zone		❑ mapped	issues:_____
Vegetation	❑ % forested	❑ % open		issues:_____
Slopes	❑ % average	❑ steepest		issues:_____
Surface water	type:_____			issues:_____
Agricultural soils	❑ acreage	type_____		issues:_____
Forestry soils	❑ acreage	type_____		issues:_____
Landforms	types_____			issues:_____
Wildlife habitat	types_____			issues:_____
Earth resources	types_____ ❑ mapped			issues:_____
Rare/endangered species	❑ known	❑ unknown	❑ absent	issues:_____

There are many types of matrices and schemes to represent the various natural resources and their impacts. Figure 2-1 shows a simplified general checklist, which usually has some kind of qualitative assessment for each factor, such as a checkmark or a rating to indicate degree or importance for the specifics of the project, or as a resource to be considered in an impact assessment.

The following checklist (Figure 2-2) provides an example of the variety of culturally related factors in developmental analysis. Some checklists and matrices combine cultural and natural factors.

Figure 2-2. Sample existing cultural factors checklist.

Category	Conditions			
Area land use	☐ urban	☐ suburban	☐ rural/agric.	☐ commerce/industrial
Scenic beauty	☐ locally rated	☐ significant viewsheds	☐ ridgelines	
Traffic patterns	☐ existing access	☐ proposed new access	☐ congestion issues	
Government regs.	☐ local	☐ state	☐ federal	☐ other
Socio-econ. data	☐ town plan	☐ relevant studies re: affordable housing, energy, historic		
Noise	☐ zoning	☐ background levels	☐ from project	
Hazardous materials	☐ pre-existing on site	☐ suspected		
Spatial patterns	☐ strip/ribbon ☐ cluster	☐ open	☐ low density	
Municipal sewer & water services	☐ available ☐ not available			
Solid waste services	☐ construction	☐ operation		
Water supply	☐ municipal ☐ on-site	☐ adjacent		
Septic capacity of soils	☐ tested ☐ untested	issues:_____		
Local climate	issues:_____			
Solar orientation	slope orientation:_____			
Utility services	available public utilities:_____ available private:_____			
Emergency services	☐ fire ☐ ambulance ☐ police			
Educational services	☐ children contributed by project	impact fee:_____		
Recreac. services	impact fee:_____			
Town/county/ regional plans	☐ compliance check			
Archaeological resources	☐ sensitive area			
Architectural/ historical resources	☐ certified local government	☐ sensitive area		
Transportation systems	☐ road ☐ public	☐ pedesrian/bike		
Political/legal boundaries	jurisdictions:_____			

17

Client factors

Client factors require consideration because they represent political, economic, and social realities, but mostly because the analysis is required by a particular client. The project will likely reflect the client's goals and values. It would be unrealistic to not expect some influence by the client on the type and scope of the analysis.

Some factors in the analysis may be the result of the needs and characteristics of the development (and the client). For example, a ski area needs a mountain. A yacht club needs a shoreline. Accordingly, these factors are constants rather than variables in the development equation. Some economic factors may also be relatively inelastic. There are population thresholds that must be met or exceeded to support the "central place" functions of various businesses. A fuel oil dealer might have a threshold community population size of 420 while a sporting goods store would more likely require a threshold population of around 1000. Accordingly, a developer will only look at areas with sufficient population to serve as central places for the intended function—a non-negotiable client condition. Figure 2-3 shows a checklist for client factors.

Figure 2-3. Sample client factors checklist.

Category	Conditions		
Demographic requirements	☐ rural	☐ urban	☐ regional
Regulatory requirements	☐ project requires permits from state or federal agencies:_____		
Economic resources needed	☐ investment project	☐ grants	
Amenities/cultural opportunities necessary for this project _____			
Special infrastructure requirements_____			
Natural resources needed_____			
Political support on hand_____			
Reputation/image_____			

The above checklists represent some or all the factors developers take into consideration when considering a site for its development potential. These factors may not necessarily be subject to review. A review board's authority to review any of these factors is entirely dependent on the statute, bylaw or regulation that governs its particular review process.

As a result of meeting these factors, a developer may have made environmental tradeoffs of a short-term or long-term nature. The trade-offs may be quite clear, such as in the selection of a hilltop with scenic views for a vacation home subdivision. The site may impact the views of others and the future houses may be energy-inefficient due to increased exposure to the elements. The site may be in a place that is too steep for the town's fire trucks and other emergency service providers. Yet there may be no other place that provides such panoramic vistas. If these factors are known, we can be more effective in working out compromises. It helps to have a full understanding of how the site was analyzed and what trade-offs exist.

Site location

Consideration of site location is essentially a planning matter. When planning fails by the designation of inappropriate districts or uses within them, regulators must carry the ball, usually on a piecemeal basis. When this happens often, and when it makes for a painful review process, it is time to change the local bylaws and regulations. By far, the bulk of planning occurs at the local level. State-wide environmental review processes in northern New England are not "planning laws" because they are almost purely reactive. Even Vermont's Act 250 is not a planning law: as a strictly regulatory process, projects are reviewed one development at a time, each located in various places within the environmental district (usually the county). It is easier to actually "plan" within the regulatory process on the local level because review board members know what has recently received local approval and what is in the pipeline. They are knowledgeable about local natural resources, and school and infrastructure capacity. Nevertheless, inherent in quasi-judicial regulatory review is the difficulty review boards find in keeping an eye on the bigger picture.

Site location is an important part of the development assessment, although review boards are usually limited to addressing it by considering the constraints and opportunities on a given site, including wetlands, agricultural soils, and the provisions in a town's comprehensive plan (also known as "master plan," as in New Hampshire). Inadequate consideration of location means a failure to address surrounding land uses. This can add to strip development, other forms of sprawl, and unwanted impacts such as traffic congestion, air pollution, and aesthetic degradation. Considering context, to the greatest extent possible, is an important aspect of determining permit conditions for landscaping, lighting, access points, "building envelopes," stormwater management, and other potential areas of concern.

The vision of a community as expressed through planning documents such as a growth management policy or a comprehensive plan may include goals that encourage patterns of development to strengthen the town center; provide facilities for pedestrians and bicyclists; keep agricultural land open and productive; and preserve historic districts. In cases such as these, consideration of a development project's location becomes critical. Approval of one more mini-mart along an arterial highway may contribute to a blurring of "the edge" between a town's built-up area and its open land. Approval of a commercial or residential project in an area that is distant from existing development may require the installation of new sewer and water infrastructure, which is very expensive to the community. The location of a development on a site that requires the demolition of a historic structure may prompt consideration of several alternatives such as moving or renovating the building, or denial of the project. However, the review board must have the statutory and regulatory authority to deny a project on these grounds or to impose mitigating conditions. This is not always the case.

The topics of "smart growth" and "sprawl" have become popular in recent years. But the problems associated with sprawl have long been understood within the planning community (Figure 2-4). Sprawl is development that spreads out of town centers into the countryside, usually in the form of strip commercial development and low-density residential development. There are statewide programs that educate about sprawl but very little legislation to address it (Act 250 in Vermont allows review of sprawl through application of Criterion 9(K), "Costs of Scattered Development").

Municipal planners are becoming more conscious of directing new development closer to the center of town. This principle of smart growth not only helps maintain vibrant downtowns, but also saves taxpayers money, and preserves natural areas, agricultural soils and open space outside the center. Zoning regulations and municipal

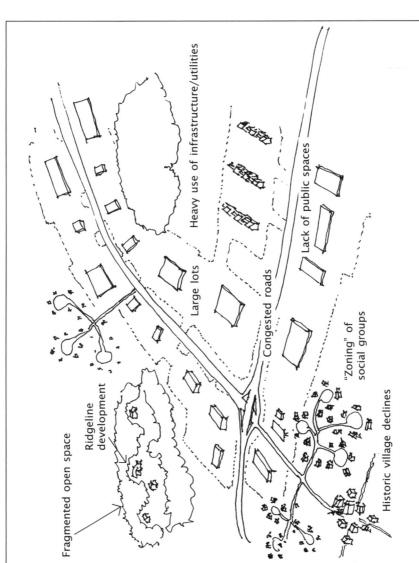

Figure 2-4. Characteristics of sprawl.

- Large-lot developments, fragmenting open space
- Automobile-dependent
- Densities lower than town and urban centers
- Extension of public infrastructure and services to undeveloped areas
- Low economic and social diversity in residential areas
- Lack of public spaces and community centers
- Repetitive, "big box" buildings without distinctive character
- Large paved areas: wide roads, large parking areas
- Lack of effective growth management policies
- Depleted sense of community

Fragmented open space

Ridgeline development

Heavy use of infrastructure/utilities

Large lots

Congested roads

Lack of public spaces

"Zoning" of social groups

Historic village declines

plans may reflect growth management principles, although this does not mean much unless they are rigorously applied in the day-to-day permitting processes. Some communities are happy to have any kind of economic activity and do not see themselves as able to afford the "luxury" of guiding growth. Of course, history has shown us that unguided growth can cost more in the long run; sprawl and unplanned growth deplete a community's infrastructure and can over-commit natural and social resources in the name of short-term economic return.

Patterns of sprawl development

Three patterns of commercial development are found in urban areas: central places, ribbons, and specialized areas. Central places generally consist of central business districts. Ribbons are strips of development formed along well-traveled routes. Specialized areas are perhaps best represented by shopping malls, but also include medical districts, automobile dealer and service areas, and other specialized markets and services. If we understand these patterns and how they occur, we will have a context in which to review urban development (an important implication, since urban areas in New England can consist of centers with populations of only 5,000). The environmental and economic successes or failures of all projects in urban areas are influenced by these basic patterns. Roads and other infrastructure services link the patterns; any change to the nature of a pattern will have a potentially greater affect on these services.

If we know the history of change in the downtown, as well as the goals for downtown development, we can more easily assess the consequences of projects in urban centers. Business districts in northern New England are generally in the fourth or fifth stages of the evolutionary path described in Figure 2-5.

Residential growth patterns have changed dramatically since the post World War II years. Instead of dense neighborhoods linked by grid-type street networks, public transportation, and sidewalks within walking distance of schools and amenities, we have dispersed into automobile-dependent developments in rural and agricultural areas, disconnected from schools and employment centers. Many village and city centers have been abandoned for suburban settings, leaving small centrally-located businesses faltering and store fronts

Figure 2-5. Commonly recognized stages in downtown business districts.

All downtown business districts are in one of these stages or in transition from one stage to another. Many downtowns will have buildings and other features left over from past stages.

1) Inception
2) Exclusion
3) Segregation
4) Retail decline
5) Revitalization

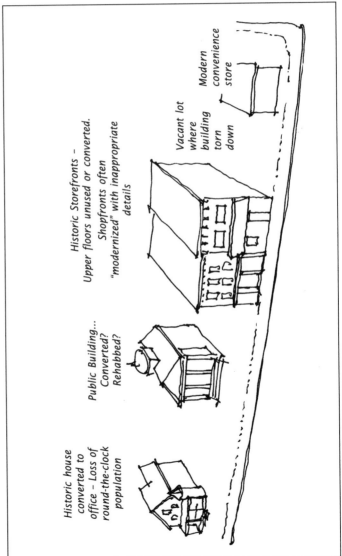

Historic house converted to office – Loss of round-the-clock population

Public Building... Converted? Rehabbed?

Historic Storefronts – Upper floors unused or converted. Shopfronts often "modernized" with inappropriate details

Vacant lot where building torn down

Modern convenience store

23

Tale from the Trenches
CLUSTERING
Our planning board now requires developers to submit two plans, one showing clustering and one showing a traditional development configuration. Once, we used the traditional plan because we wanted the buffer protection it would provide for a riparian area, but we almost always go with the clustering option. By making applicants show clustering we are encouraging efficient use of the land and conservation of resources and by allowing submittal of the traditional plan we are providing flexibility in the review process.

boarded up. As a result, there is often no visual distinction between our communities, only a blur of development from one to another.

To counter this trend, the "smart growth" movement has advocated a return to higher density living centers where children can walk to school and adults can shop and walk or take public transportation to work. Returning to traditional neighborhoods will involve changes in our statutes, regulations, and bylaws; coordinated open space planning; infrastructure sufficient to attract development where citizens want it to occur; affordable housing in town centers; public investment in downtown schools and post offices; administrative functions in town centers; and the adaptive re-use of historic buildings. While many of these "planning issues" are beyond the purview of regulatory review boards, it is good background information as context for the review of case-by-case projects. There are still many review boards in northern New England that perform both planning and regulating.

Modern patterns of industrial development have occurred in relative isolation from commercial and residential land use. Although often arising for entirely legitimate reasons, such as traffic safety, pollution and odors, this pattern is unnecessary, especially in the case of light industry. Segregating such uses into specifically zoned "industrial parks" can waste land, foster dependency on automobiles, and expend energy. Historical patterns of industrial development occurred where they were expedient: near ports and rail lines. But how do we guide new industrial growth and integrate it with planned commercial and residential growth?

Today, planners are considering new patterns of efficient industrial development that use existing infrastructure; manage stormwater wisely; integrate public transportation and mixed uses; use existing but still functional structures; take advantage of energy efficiency methods; improve the aesthetics of historic sites; complement the existing scale of buildings; and connect to existing retail, residential, and recreational uses. The Vermont Forum on Sprawl and the Vermont Business Roundtable note that, laudable as these objectives are, many cannot be achieved without changes in permitting, planning, funding, legislation, education, and training. The Maine State Planning Office and the Office of the Governor in New Hampshire echo this perspective.

Where to go for more information

Campoli, Julie, Elizabeth Humstone, Alex Maclean.(2002). *Above and Beyond: Visualizing Change in Small Towns and Rural Areas*, Planners Press, American Planning Association.

Daniels, Tom. (1999). *When City and Country Collide: Managing Growth in the Metropolitan Fringe*. Island Press.

Grow Smart Maine: http://www.growsmartmaine.org/newsletters.htm

Heart, Bennet, Elizabeth Humstone, Thomas F. Rowin, Sandy Levine, Dana Weisbord. (2002). *Community Rules: A New England Guide To Smart Growth Strategies*, Conservation Law Foundation and Vermont Forum on Sprawl.

Lacy, Jeff. (1990). *An Examination of Market Appreciation for Clustered Housing with Permanent Open Space*, Center for Rural Massachusetts.

Maine Rural Development Council. http://mrdc.umext.maine.edu/sitemap.htm

Maine State Planning Office. http://www.state.me.us/spo/

New Hampshire, Office of the Governor. http://www.state.nh.us/governor/sprawl.html

25

Planners Web. http://www.plannersweb.com//

Richert, Evan. (1997). Confronting the issue of sprawl in Maine. *Rural Connections, A Quarterly Newsletter of the Maine Rural Development Council,* Vol. 4, No. 2.

Smart Growth Network. www.smartgrowth.org

Smart Growth Network. Getting to Smart Growth: http://www. smartgrowth.org/pdf/gettosg.pdf

Society for the Protection of New Hampshire Forests. http://www.spnhf. org/what/sprawl.html

Sprawlwatch Clearinghouse. www.sprawlwatch.org.

Vermont Department of Housing and Community Affairs. http:// www.state.vt.us/dca/housing/

Vermont Forum on Sprawl. http://www.vtsprawl.org

Vermont Forum on Sprawl and Vermont Business Roundtable, *New Models for Commercial and Industrial Development.* http://www.vtsprawl.org., http://www.vtroundtable.org.

Chapter 3

THE DEVELOPMENT PLAN

What should be on the development plan?

Ranging anywhere from a single hand-drawn sketch on an 8½ x 11 piece of paper to an extensive series of site maps, architectural drawings, and engineering specifications, a development plan can be formal or informal, depending on its purpose and the applicable regulations. Local review processes usually have a preliminary review, often known as "sketch plan," in which the project is evaluated on a conceptual level and for which less extensive, detailed plans are required. Enough information should be on the development plan to show reviewers where basic components such as roads and utilities will be located, and how the proposed project will be placed on the tract and fit into the surrounding landscape. This task is made easier for developers by use of checklists and other guidance documents provided by most regulatory review processes.

Identified on the following pages are components commonly required or expected on development plans.

Tale from the Trenches

SIDEWALKS IN THE COUNTRY?

Some planners feel that there are developments that don't warrant or need sidewalks. I disagree. Pedestrians are never going away! Even if the subdivision is in the middle of nowhere, I ask the board to require a sidewalk because some day there may be a need for connection of pedestrian ways. Also for single development sites, I ask the board to consider the applicant putting in a sidewalk on all of their street frontages. Even if it doesn't hook up to any other one now, it may some day. And maybe sooner than we think. And the town won't be building new pedestrian ways any time soon. Roads are for cars – I don't care how slow they are traveling – they are cars, people are pedestrians!

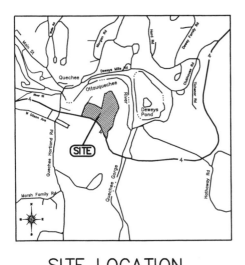

SITE LOCATION
SCALE: 1" = 2000'

Figure 3-1. Sample location map. Anyone not familiar with the project should be able to find it.

SURVEYED:	OTHERS
DESIGNED:	
DRAWN:	JLD, KH
CHECKED:	JMB
DATE:	2/28/03

PROJECT
ABCD

OVERALL SITE
PLAN
SHEET TITLE
SHEET NUMBER

C−1

© 2003

BRUNO ASSOCIATES INC., P.C.

FILE:
01244\1244−PL3

PROJECT: 010244
ABCD

Figure 3-2. Sample title block. The title block contains basic information about the plan, the project, the land, and the people who worked on the plan.

Location map

Any site plan submitted for review should have a location map (Figure 3-1). Often, the location map is an insert on the corner of the site plan itself. United States Geological Survey maps (usually a 7.5 minute series, occasionally a 15 minute USGS map), town highway maps, and street map are used, depending what provides the greatest clarity. Some reports include a cover figure with an outline of the state connected by a line to a circle inset of the USGS map showing the immediate vicinity of the project. In urban settings, a 1:5000 scale plan is common (see Scale, below).

Title block

All plans have "title blocks," usually containing a project title, plan title, location description, site address, name of landowner, name of developer/client, scale, and name and title of the people who designed and drew the plan (Figure 3-2). Depending on the type of plan, it may have a license number and stamp of a surveyor, engineer, architect, or landscape architect. Some title blocks include the title of the governing planning and zoning regulations.

North arrow

Usually, you will see two north arrows: one for true north and one for magnetic north. By convention, north arrows are located to the right or top of the plan. A compass usually points to magnetic north, not true north. The angle between magnetic north and the true north direction is the magnetic declination. This declination changes over time, thus making it necessary to adjust the orientation on older maps. It also explains why the date of the map is important. Magnetic north will be close to 15 degrees west of true north. A third north is called "grid north," referring to the grid lines, usually UTM (Universal Transverse Mercator, see page 34) on a map. Magnetic fields fluctuate over the earth; on a five year basis, angles of declination are recalculated from a new International Geomagnetic Reference Field (IGRF). A final type of north is a "plant" or assumed north placed straight up on the sheet regardless of where true north or magnetic north point is; fortunately, professionally prepared plans are very clear about which north is used.

Planning and zoning information

Development plans often give the title and section of applicable planning and zoning requirements along with some details, usually in an accompanying narrative, on the conformance of the project. For example, the engineer may prepare a chart with the name of the zoning district, the requirements for lot size, building lot coverage, required parking spaces and total lot coverage, as well as dimensional requirements such as front, side and rear yard setbacks, and frontage.

Area

An area in square feet or acres is usually specified for each tract, lot, structure, and large feature. A square measuring one acre is about 208 feet by 208 feet (43,560 square feet). A square mile is 640 acres. The metric system is used rarely in review of site plans, but it is found increasingly in scientific applications such as wildlife surveys, forestry management plans, and hydrogeology. Under the metric system, one hectare (ha) equals 2.47 acres (1 acre = 0.405 ha) and is equivalent to 10,000 square meters. A square meter equals 10.76 square feet. Common parcel sizes: 2 acres = 87,120 sq. ft.; 3 acres

= 130,680 sq. ft.; 4 acres = 174,240 sq. ft.; 10 acres = 430,560 sq. ft.

Scale

A map scale represents the ratio of a distance on the map to the actual distance on the ground. A basic engineer's scale is typically used to create and measure the scale. If two feet on a map represents one mile on the ground, the scale would be 2 feet = 1 mile. It would also be given as distance on the map divided by distance on the ground, which equals 2 feet/5280 feet (since one mile = 5280 feet). Dividing both numerator and denominator by 2 to simplify, the final scale is 1:2640 or 1 in 2,640. Confusion can result if the scale does not have units or if it has both English and metric units. Metric units are easier to convert. Development plans need to be at a sufficient scale to show clearly the details of the site and proposed construction. By convention, English units are still commonly used in the United States, which means you have to look at the units to determine the true ratio. Commonly, the local or state regulatory program specifies the required scale. Most small projects are drawn at 20, 30, 40, or 50 feet to the inch. To get the ratio for a scale of one inch to 50 feet, convert 50 feet to inches (50 times 12 = 600); therefore, the ratio is 1:600. Larger projects may use 100, 200, 400 or 1,000 feet to the inch, with different scales for infrastructure and individual buildings. A large project will have match lines to indicate where two sheets match up. However, there should always be one sheet that shows the entire tract at one scale.

Topography, contours, and slope

Contour lines represent lines of elevation on a map. The lines are the result of connecting a series of points of equal elevation above Mean Sea Level (M.S.L.) in feet or meters. The interval between contours is given on the map. The spacing between the lines denotes the topography. Numerous contour lines drawn close together indicate hilly or mountainous terrain. A gentle slope or relatively flat land is represented by widely separated contour lines. Usually, every forth or fifth contour is an index contour drawn as a slightly wider line to help in counting contours. If the contour map seems complex and the site is hard to visualize, it may help to combine and color the contours on the map by group. For example, all elevations over 400 feet could be a dark color and the colors could gradually lighten for groups of lower elevation contours.

The site plan should show the existing topography, generally at a two-foot contour interval, unless it is a large tract (Figure 3-3). For large tracts, a five-foot or more contour interval could be used, although two-foot contours should be shown for the areas that will be improved (e.g., roads, septic systems, buildings). Local ordinances commonly require specific contour intervals. Spot elevations of specific features on a map are usually indicated by a dot on the map with the elevation listed next to it. Slope ratios derived from these contours are important in engineering, especially road design, erosion control, drainage, and site stability.

Figure 3-3. Contours and land features on a site plan. Even at a larger scale there is a wealth of information and plans can be difficult to interpret.

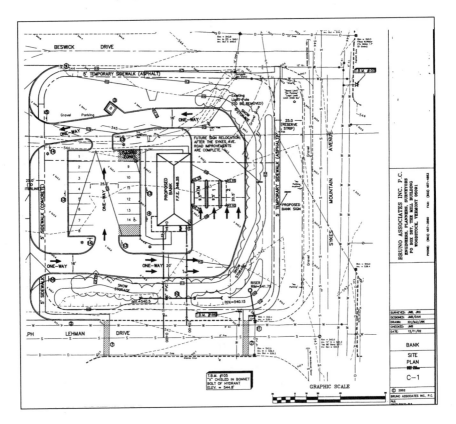

Lot and tract identification

Boundaries should be shown clearly for the entire tract, for each proposed lot, and for any involved land (access road, easements, rights-of-way, and impact mitigation land). The reader should be able to tell the difference between existing and proposed boundary lines. On-site and adjacent easements and rights-of-way should be shown and labeled. Each lot needs a number for reference. The legal definition of lot varies by the review process. For example, under some jurisdictions and conditions, a roadway or a green-belt may be considered to be a separate lot; under others, the reviewers focus on the developable lots.

Existing features

Features are the non-portable components of a landscape. Streams, wetlands, barns, wells, stone walls, and old cellar holes are all features, as are forest boundaries, fields, and other indicators or products of land use. Ordinances, statutes, and administrative rules may specify the features that must be shown on a site plan.

The proposed project

Sometimes there is a problem in defining a proposed project. Essentially, a proposed project consists of all improvements planned for one or more related sites. The development plan should show all these improvements, including buildings, roads, driveways and parking areas, landscaping, utilities, signs, dumpsters, tanks, lights, water supplies, and septic systems. Mitigation measures such as stream buffers, agricultural easements, and protected deer wintering habitat may also be part of a project.

Off-site improvements

The site plan materials should include any off-site improvements, which will likely be a requirement in specific ordinances. If, for example, the developer intends to mitigate traffic impacts by adding a turning lane to a town road, the land should be treated as part of the project, with enough information for effective review given on the site plan. Off-site improvements might include construction, buffers, landscaping or other mitigation within an adjacent easement or leased area; all should be shown.

Date and revisions

The date of preparation should be on the plan. Any plan prepared by a surveyor, engineer, architect, or landscape architect, has a small area designated on or near the title block to show the dates for any revisions as well as initial preparation. We should be able to tell what additions were made and who made them (e.g., "added turning lane, 1/25/04, RMS/DHF"). This important aspect of accountability helps regulators track the changes to a project and formulate approval conditions. It may be tempting for a person to ask, "Just let me drawn in this subdivision line," but there can be real problems — legal and ethical — when a client or other non-professional alters a survey. However, one of the benefits of give-and-take at a hearing is in penciling negotiated solutions onto a plan; later, a professional can make the formal revisions necessary for adequate record-keeping and official versions.

Adjacent property and owners

Adjacent property is any tract of land bordering the project site. Many review processes require the inclusion of property owners across the street from the project site. Failure to include an adjacent property owner, and his or her address, may cause a subdivision or development application to be considered "incomplete." In cases where the project site borders a condominium project, often the name and address of each unit owner must be provided to the review agency. The names of adjacent property owners should be listed on their tracts, as should the type or predominant feature of the tract (e.g., "National Forest" or "Route 5"). If you see "n/f" in front of the name on an adjacent property, it refers to "now or formerly" and is just the surveyor's way of indicating that the sources of names came from other maps or town records, and thus might have changed by the time the plan comes up for review.

Envelopes and reserve areas

Designated "envelopes" on a site plan provide a general idea of building locations, a useful feature for subdivisions and developments where no specific building, parking, or septic systems areas have yet been designed or proposed. Some applicants do not want to designate envelopes, preferring to leave this to the prospective purchaser—an acceptable strategy if there is sufficient environmental information to support a location within the subdivision. An alternative is to identify the setbacks and other "no build" areas. The goal is to reduce the likelihood of construction occurring within setbacks and to give a better picture of how the built-out project will look. It also aids in planning. Some developers are happy to designate specific building envelopes, finding it a useful marketing and planning tool.

A reserve area is an area set aside for future development or to accommodate changes in use. Reserve parking areas might be designated for special events or in case of growth within the project. Areas reserved for future expansion or overflow parking should be designated on the plan.

Project coordinates: USGS maps and reading UTMs

USGS maps contain a host of information, including vegetation (green color), water (blue), revisions from aerial photography (purple), and densely built-up areas (gray or red). Large features and landmarks on the map are labeled, as are highways and communities. On the edges of USGS maps are two sets of markings: a coordinate grid, and latitude and longitude.

Many municipal regulatory review processes require that applications include project coordinates. The New England states each have a government Geographic Information System (GIS) office that tracks and makes available mapping information to locate projects and to facilitate local planning with layers of mapped information. The metric system is generally used (1 meter = 3.280 feet). Commonly, USGS 1:24,000 scale topographic maps serve as the basis for the location of projects. If the USGS map is not ancient (i.e., printed within the last 30 years or so), it will have blue grid tick marks (actual grid lines were printed on some maps for a short time after 1978) representing a rectangular map projection system known as Universal Transverse Mercator (UTM). These marks represent distances of 1000 meters (1 kilometer).

A hand-held GPS unit can check an interpolated position in the field. The top set of number on the GPS will start with the applicable zone location. UTM divides the earth into 60 horizontal (longitudinal) zones of 6 degrees each, with a letter of the alphabet to designate the vertical element (range of latitude) for each zone. For example, 19 T is a zone in the northeastern United States. A good GPS unit under the right conditions should be within several meters of the true location.

The traditional, angular coordinates familiar to us (latitude and longitude) can, like UTM, specify any location on Earth. Each degree (1/360th of a full circle) is divided into 60 "minutes" (1/60th of a degree), and a "minute" is divided into 60 "seconds." Latitude is measured north or south of the Equator, which is equidistant from the poles. Longitude is measured east or west of the Prime Meridian, which passes through the North and South poles, and the Greenwich observatory near London. Operating with changes in latitude and longitude require converting with degrees, minutes, and seconds. The cumbersome nature of this, coupled with the rise of GPS and GIS, has bolstered the popularity of UTM coordinates, making it easier for municipalities to keep track of project locations.

Match lines

Match lines are depicted on the site plan where one sheet of plans joins another. Letters of the alphabet on the edges of the sheets usually mark the lines. It may seem sacrilegious to fold or cut them but the easiest way to see how the whole project looks is to fold the sheets along the match, cutting excess overlap where needed, and put the sheets together. One set of stamped plans can be saved for the record but everything else can be folded, spindled, and subjected to any other treatment that improves project understanding.

Plans, plats and surveys

Plans, plats, and surveys are defined in State enabling legislation for municipal site plan, subdivision and development ordinances. Chapter 16 of Maine's Land Use Regulation Commission (LURC) defines plat as a map or site plan of a subdivision showing the location and boundaries of individual parcels of land divided into lots and customarily drawn to a scale. Title 27 of the Vermont Statues defines "survey plat" as a "map or plan drawn to scale of one or more parcels, tracts or subdivisions of land, showing, but not limited to, boundaries, corners, markers, monuments, easements and other rights." A plat is a special type of site plan or subdivision map that depicts the arrangements of buildings, roads, landscaping and other services for a development use. Plats and surveys denote different legal status than plans; they are included in the deed.

A survey refers to two things: the process of determining boundaries and areas of tracts of land, and the map or plan prepared as a result of that process. Licensed surveyors usually prepare the surveys accepted for site plan review purposes.

Public rights-of-way and easements

The site plan should show public rights-of-way (ROW) such as public streets that may traverse or border the development project. In many northern New England towns this ROW is a 60-foot width containing sewer and water lines and room for road widening. Easements, legal designations of conveyed or allowed rights of use, are shown on plans. Telephone and electric lines easements are common. Increasingly, as towns generate greenway and recreational path plans, easements are depicted for bicycle and pedestrian paths.

Specialized plans

A large project might entail many sheets of specialized plans presenting aspects of the project in greater detail than that readily comprehendible on a single plan. The range and content of specialized plans vary among engineering firms and depend on the specifications of the individual project. Some of the more common types of plans are summarized below.

Overall plan: Similar to the site plan, an overall plan contains topography, general lot lines without the precise survey points, natural features, roads, and access points associated with the proposed project.

Utility plan: The utility plan shows the location of water and sewer improvements, including force-mains and pump stations, and underground electric and telephone lines.

Grading and erosion control plan: This plan may be drawn separately or be shown along with a plan with other features. It generally shows locations where sediment must be trapped before entering a watercourse and the devices used to impede erosion. These features commonly include silt fencing, and hay-bale or stone dams around catch basins and at intervals in swales and ditches. A separate page with details and sketches of the specific devices often accompanies the erosion control plan. The erosion control plan is described in more detail in Chapter 8.

Stormwater management plan: Stormwater management plans are increasingly important as concerns mount about the quality of northern New England's water and as new U.S. Environmental Protection Agency regulations come into effect. Nearly all state and local regulations require some plan for how stormwater will be managed as part of site planning. The stormwater management plan typically provides details on the collection, retention, and treatment of stormwater. Site grades are shown, as are the direction of drainage flows and the design of any detention basins. Chapter 7 addresses stormwater management in greater detail.

Road and utility profile: This plan depicts current and proposed grades for the installation of roads and utilities. It shows the finished grade of the centerline of the proposed road and where the utility lines will be located in relation to the road and other site features. As with many of these plans, a bar scale is shown for reference at the bottom of the page. The plans typically include a flat version of the road and an exaggerated vertical scale.

Specifications: A set of plans is usually accompanied by several pages of details that show drawings and notes on specific components of the plans. Items commonly noted include: sewer/water separation, pump stations, catch basins, road access and grade, forcemain cleanout, inlet protections, road cross-sections, entrance sign details, typical sidewalk details, stabilized construction entrance, lighting fixtures, temporary silt fencing, stone or hay-bale check dams, stormwater outlet details, and planting specifications.

Landscaping plan: The landscaping plan shows the locations of existing and proposed vegetation, as well as structures, features and other topographical information. Information about proposed vegetation should contain the scientific name and the common name, as well as a symbol for each species, the caliper size, the quantity, and the height at planting. No-cut zones should be shown, as well as limits of clearing to the sides and rear on the individual lots. Some landscaping plans will detail areas of selective clearing, especially if the site is to be shielded from a feature such as a lake. For example, the plan may contain a note that prohibits cutting of any tree greater than 2 inches dbh (diameter at breast height). Landscaping is discussed in Chapter 11.

Lighting plan: The lighting plan shows the locations of exterior lights and is on a separate sheet or the landscaping plan. Lighting fixtures and other lighting details may be shown on the side of the plan or submitted as "cut sheets." A narrative of the lighting scheme may be included with the application materials. Lighting may be placed along the street, or on the individual properties to illuminate garages, doors or landscaping. Signs depicting the name of the business or residential neighborhood may also be lit. Lighting is discussed in Chapter 11.

Architectural elevations: Architectural elevations prepared by an architect are often attached to the complete set of site plans (see Figure 3-4). For small projects, the owner or engineer may provide the elevations instead of a licensed architect. Elevations are renderings of the project's physical appearance as seen from the east, west, north and south viewpoints. The elevations often include

Figure 3-4. Section plan and architectural elevation.

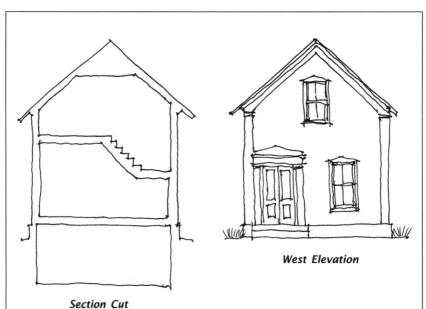

West Elevation

Section Cut

information about building colors, materials, features and height. In many cases, elevations are essential indicators of whether or not the project "fits" in its locale (see Chapter 11). Stylized drawings—perspective drawings—are another way to show structures and landscaping.

Section plan: A section plan is a vertical view of a building or structure, usually at the same scale as the architectural elevations. The view is a slice through the building intended to show relevant features and details. The direction of section lines or arrows is usually shown on the plan to help interpret the sectional view. The review processs may require the inclusion of building height, internal structural features and dimensions, and information about how the structure relates to the grading or contours.

Guiding principles for reviewing the development plan

The formal review of development follows specific regulations and procedures created under state enabling legislation. After a municipality or other organization has reviewed a number of plans it usually develops a set of practices and principles (formal and informal) based on common sense and practicality, including axioms along the following lines.

Lead responsibility: One person should assume the lead responsibility for seeing the review process through to completion. This is true for both the applicant or developer and the review board. If the chairperson of the review board does not take this responsibility then the task should be delegated to another member or to professional staff.

Site visit: A pre-hearing visit to the site by the review board is important for development projects of any size. Physically viewing the site can assist reviewers in understanding the context of the project, the existing vegetation, topography, possible access points, and the relation of the project to adjoining property. If the project will generate noise or odors, this may be the time to take measurements and conduct tests. At the expense of the applicant, balloons may be floated to help reviewers gain a sense of the height of a proposed structure. Other demonstrations of potential impacts can be conducted. Even if everyone already knows the site, and the visit reveals no surprises, it is a good public relations measure and helps preserve the credibility of the review process.

Progression: The review process should progress in a timely manner to a logical decision. Repeated reviews of the same project do not necessarily result in a better decision. There are trade-offs in taking too much or too little time; the reviewing team should be aware of these trade-offs and keep the process moving forward. Ordinances and administrative rules often include time constraints and deadlines by which regulatory bodies must act.

Design first: The reviewers should not be the designers; the review process should not begin until there is actually a project to review. This practice gives the reviewers something to react to and avoids shifting the role of regulators or reviewers to de facto consultants. It may be tempting or flattering to be asked to help create or shape a project, but unless you are the developer or designer, it is a good idea to resist, thereby avoiding misunderstandings and problems (Figure 3-5).

Compromise: How do we cut the Gordian Knot? Is it in the best interests of the community to find the proverbial "middle ground" when, in fact, the project should be denied outright (or is it fine as presented and should be approved outright)? Despite the allure of finding common ground between the town, the developer, and neighbors and conditioning the project approval in such a way that everyone is happy (or just a little bit disgruntled), the best decision is not always in the middle. In such cases, a compromise may do a disservice to the spirit in which statutes, regulations, standards, and procedures were written by community members and state officials. Conversely, many projects are improved by creating consensus through the give-and-take of the permit process. The bottom line should be whether approval conditions are true to the underpinnings of the comprehensive plans, laws, and regulations that govern the process.

Condition overload: Development projects, especially complex ones, may require dozens of conditions of approval. Reviewers should avoid burdening permits with so many conditions that enforcement becomes an administrative impossibility. The project proponents should put as much information as possible on the plans so that engineers and contractors can refer to it in the field and

Figure 3-5. The design-review relationship. A good design improves the efficiency and speed of the review process. Similarly, an effective review process helps inform the design; both designer and reviewer benefit from a coordinated effort, although neither need do the other's job.

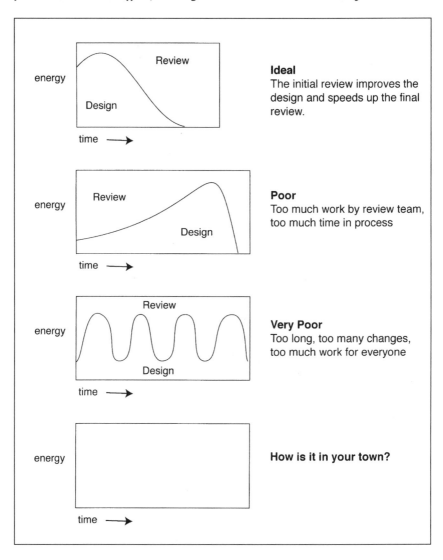

compliance can be achieved by simply implementing the plans. If a project requires excessive conditions, perhaps the project should either be significantly revised or denied. A multitude of conditions may also point to a flawed review process.

Technical resources: Know what technical resources are at hand for you—maps, staff, and equipment— to review the project. Are there sufficient details in the project application and plans to enable you to review it or to indicate what additional help you need? Where do you go to get technical information? What resources are available to the public? What types of technical information cannot be obtained without hiring a consultant or requiring a specific site assessment? Review boards may be hesitant to pay for the services of outside experts (or to ask applicants to do this), but it might be the best way to obtain needed information and to clarify complex issues for the reviewers. For most review procedures, the applicant holds the "burden of persuasion" and thus may need to bear the cost of providing some technical resources.

Boiler-plating: All professions impress other professions (and the public) through boiler-plating (the use of standard repeated items and materials in fresh presentations or products). Boilerplate material has its place in saving people from "re-inventing the wheel"– saving time and money, but should not replace designs for on-site conditions and should only be incorporated into permit conditions if appropriate to the site. For example, suppose hay-bale check dams are shown on the plans around an entire perimeter of stockpiled topsoil on a flat site. Incorporated into permit conditions, odds are good that the people in the field will not actually install the check dams because they see this measure as inappropriate. Even if they do comply, they have reasonable cause to be suspicious of other permit conditions, eroding the credibility of the review process.

Scoping: The act of sorting out what is important in describing a project and its impacts, is crucial in promoting effective and timely review of development plans. Begin with an overview of the entire project and sift down to the crucial issues, which will have a context for interpretation by the time you get to them. Many reviewers use procedures such as writing down key words, first impressions, and making matrices; this can also be applied to understanding the process of review, not just the project itself.

Deal with the difficult: Confront the controversial issues square on. Try not to pass along an unsolved problem. For example, if you conclude that a road should be paved by the time of full build-out, then set up a specific means to ensure this happens. Violations are reduced and credibility is improved if difficult problems are not postponed. Many ways exist to close open-ended requirements and resolve tricky issues. Discuss and explore options such as bonds, contingency reviews, performance deadlines, performance standards, sinking replacement funds, contingencies, and transfers to homeowners associations. These concepts and tools have power to solve many problems if properly applied.

The full build-out impact myth: In essence, this refers to the tendency to see projects and associated impacts in terms of completion or full build-out. First, ask "What is it going to look like while it is being built or before those landscaping trees mature?" Construction impacts can be worse than the impacts of the completed project. Every project should be viewed as having at least four stages: planning, construction, operation, and closure or post-operation. Some conditions are appropriate or necessary for one stage but not another. This scenario is obvious in the case of a gravel pit or other earth resource extraction project. That said, large, multi-phase or high impact projects such as ski resorts merit requesting a master plan at least on a level sufficient to allow the review board to ascertain future areas of growth and potential impacts.

The seasonal trap: Architectural renderings sometimes show projects during the prettiest time of year. Site plan reviewers should take seasons into account. How will the project look in the dead of winter? What will the effects of spring runoff be? If you need landscaping for screening, then you might want a variety of trees that include species with early budding, late fall holdover, and evergreens. If the landscaping does not have to provide screening, then flowering shrubs rather than evergreens may be appropriate. The seasonal trap applies to other categories of impact, such as traffic conditions during foliage season or ski season, or to how parking lots function with large piles of snow.

Long-term versus short-term: Projects that have long-term impacts might appear more attractive in the short-term than they should. Be aware of what impacts, costs, and benefits will accrue regardless of whether they are short-term or long-term. For example, strip development has short-term benefits but eventually increases the cost of infrastructure, more so than development in designated growth areas or central business districts. The costs of strip devel-

43

opment might be hidden until a traffic bottleneck develops. Then it might be too late or exceedingly expensive to fix things. Examples abound where the short-term view prevailed despite the long-term environmental, social, and economic costs of poorly placed growth.

Regulatory feedback: Make sure your procedures allow you to do what the regulations require you to do. Are you meeting the requirements of the enabling legislation or statutory authority? Does the level of authority match the level of responsibility? Is this also sufficient for you to do a good job for your community, the applicant, and the environment? Is good science being used to make decisions? Be an advocate for change, if needed, in the regulatory process.

Details: Are sufficient details provided to allow reviewers to fully evaluate the impacts? Sometimes details are left out accidentally. Sometimes they are left out because the developer does not want to commit too early. On the other hand, some individuals and organizations require excessive detail. Seek a level of detail sufficient for the project to be adequately and competently reviewed.

Tale from the Trenches

THE BARREN SHOPPING PLAZA

We were members of our town's planning commission when a developer proposed enlarging a shopping plaza. The parking lot had no amenities or flow control and several fatalities had occurred in addition to numerous fender benders. The developer, whose family controlled many business interests in town, was reluctant to make any changes and kept resubmitting the site plan to the commission, with little or no modifications, and reiterating his requests. It was an exhausting process for all concerned. We had previously rewritten our town plan and had solid planning and zoning regulations to support our concern about traffic and aesthetics.

Finally, when he realized he was not going to get his approvals, he allowed his consultant to submit the requested traffic control islands, plantings, and pavement markings. A few years later, the bustling shopping plaza, with its healthy economic climate and attractive, safe parking lot, bore truth to the benefits of good design. We learned the value of holding to our planning regulations in requesting good design. Had we given in, the project would not have been as successful for both the developer and the town.

Use other processes: The typical project crosses the desks of more than a few agencies, government offices, and non-government organizations. Many review systems thrive on shared input—planning commissions value the input of their conservation commissions; state and local processes can be coordinated. Discover where processes overlap. Promote the efficiency of reviews that reinforce each other and do not drag out the process.

Where to go for more information

American Society of Civil Engineers, 1801 Alexander Bell Drive, Reston, VA, 20191. http://www.asce.org.

Arendt, Randall G. (1996). *Conservation Design for Subdivisions: A Practical Guide to Creating Open Space Networks.* Island Press, Washington, D.C.

Daniels, Thomas L., John W. Kellerman and Mark B. Lapping. (1995). *The Small Town Planning Handbook,* 2nd edition. American Planning Association, Chicago.

Eyerman, Mark and Brian Kent. (1997). *Site Plan Review Handbook: A Guide to Developing a Site Plan Review System.* Maine State Planning Office. Augusta, ME.

DeChiarra, Joseph, and Lee E. Koppleman. (1978). *Site Planning Standards,* McGraw Hill: New York.

Ewing, Reid. (1996). *Best Development Practices,* American Planning Association, Chicago, IL.

Maine Office of GIS. http://apollo.ogis.state.me.us/

Maine State Planning Office. (1992). *Comprehensive Planning: A Manual for Maine's Communities.* Maine State Planning Office, Augusta, ME.

Massachusetts Office of Geographic and Environmental Information http://www.state.ma.us/mgis/utmcoord.htm

Nelessen, Anton Clarence. (1994). *Visions for a New American Dream,* Planners Press, American Planners Association, Chicago, IL.

New Hampshire Geographically Referenced Analysis and Information Transfer System (NH GRANIT). http://www.granit.sr.unh.edu/

New Hampshire State Data Center, New Hampshire State Planning Office. http://www.state.nh.us/osp/sdc/sdc.html

New Hampshire Office of State Planning. http://www.state.nh.us/osp/

OnLine Conversion. http://www.onlineconversion.com/

Vermont Center for Geographic Information. http://www.vcgi.org/

Vermont Forum on Sprawl. (2001). *Growing Smarter, Best Site Planning for Residential, Commercial & Industrial Development*, Burlington, Vermont: Vermont Forum on Sprawl.

Vermont Municipal and Regional Planning and Development Act, Title 24, Chapter 117, (with additional sections including *Act 250* and the *Downtown Development Act*). Reprinted from Vermont Statutes Annotated and 2000 Cumulative Supplement, Lexis Publishing. http://www.state.vt.us/dca/housing

US EPA. (1994). *Environmental Planning for Small Communities, A Guide for Local Decisionmakers*, EPA 625/R-94/009, Washington, DC: EPA Office of Research and Development.

US Geological Survey. http://www.usgs.gov/

US Geological Survey. Topographic Map Symbols. http://mac.usgs.gov/mac/isb/pubs/booklets/symbols/reading.html

Part Two:

COMMON CATEGORIES OF IMPACT

Chapter 4
AIR QUALITY

A broad range of air quality impacts can be addressed in various site plan review processes: noise, odor, light, particulate matter, radiation, vibration, thermal, and chemical vapors. These impacts are generated by many things: traffic heading toward a mall; gravel pit blasting; vapors emitting from a furniture-making facility; night skiing at a ski area; and myriad other types of projects and sources. Most impacts under these categories are treated by local and state review boards as aesthetic concerns until the impacts reach a level at which they become pollution or a health hazard. This chapter presents a brief summary of terms and concepts used by review boards when evaluating the potential air pollution impacts of development projects. Noise and light impacts are discussed in Chapters 5 and 11.

The federal Clean Air Act (42 USC § 7401 et seq. [1970]) refers to pollutants as "hazardous air pollutants" (189 carcinogens and other chronic pollutants) and "criteria pollutants" (NOx, CO, SO2, PM, lead and a few others). Pollutants may also be called toxic air pollutants, or air toxics. Most municipal and state development review boards are authorized to address at least some aspects of air pollution to varying degrees. Due to the technical nature of air pollution assessment, municipal and state review boards may rely on or seek expert opinion from the state's office of air quality.

Commonly, developers are asked to describe any air emissions, odors, or sources of noise associated with the project, as well as the measures proposed to control them. The fuel source of any heated building must be described, including its efficiency rating. Developers must indicate how dust will be controlled during and after construction. The review of large projects (defined, for example, in tons per year of an emission, BTUs per hour, or by physical size, such as a new parking lot for 1000 or more cars) can get quite technical, especially in complying with the Clean Air Act.

At the municipal level, air quality impacts may be addressed through performance standards included in the zoning regulations. For example, the Shelburne, Vermont zoning regulations require that all development meet standards for vibration, noise, smoke, odors, heat, radioactive radiation, dust, vapors, gases and other forms of air pollution. Some standards are numerical, as in the case of measuring smoke density, or are expressed as a shade on the Ringelmann Chart (various shades of gray are formed by a series of lines and used for eye comparison with visible smoke and assigned a value. For example, a 1 is 20% opacity, a 2 is 40% opacity; the chart can be found on various Internet sites). Other standards may be more general, referring only to impacts as measured from the property line: Section 1660.b of the zoning regulations in Shelburne states: "No vibration shall be produced which is transmitted through the ground and is discernible without the aid of instruments at or beyond the lot lines" (a qualitative standard not directly related to health or nuisance). Nashua, New Hampshire, uses a general concern about air quality as one of the factors in its performance overlay district (Ordinance #2002-11). Wide variety exists in how air quality is reviewed in northern New England, but all municipalities share an awareness of acid rain, vehicle exhaust, ozone, and other air pollutant problems even if it isn't possible to address external sources such as acid rain in local reviews.

Outdoor air

In reviewing air quality, the example of acid rain from pollutants in the Midwest reminds us that the atmosphere does not just get rid of pollutants, it puts them someplace. Unfortunately, that place may be in northern New England. Ideally, a development review process deals with potential pollutants at the source and does not simply pass them along. Knowledge of general principles of wind behavior may be helpful in predicting the paths of those pollutants that do escape. Local climate patterns influence the behavior of air pollutants, as do wind speed, temperature, and direction. Stable wind conditions and inversion patterns may be documented for a high-emission project. Some assessment reports address "prevailing wind," and other wind behaviors (for example, wind tends to go up a valley during the day and come back down at night). The speed of wind is related to inversions; high wind speed prevents strong inversions.

Smoke, odors, and other stack emissions reveal the influence of air conditions through visible dispersion patterns (e.g., loops, cones, and funnels) resulting from a combination of atmospheric conditions and emission characteristics. Any assessment of air quality impacts should include how emissions behave in an area under the most adverse circumstances, an approach called "worst condition analysis." The level of impact should be tolerable even under the worst conditions (usually defined as not exceeding a standard more than once per year).

In reviewing air quality impacts from development projects, consider the effects from three stages: construction of the project; discharges from operation of the project; and discharges from storage, closure, and other times of inactivity. In addition, there is usually increased traffic associated with a project. Terms used to quantify emissions and impacts include parts per million, milligrams per cubic meter, and kilograms per hectare. Grains per dry standard cubic foot and grams per million calories heat input describe emission rates. Units must be clearly presented as part of the quantification process but reviewers can also require that this information be converted to qualitative terms for a decision-making process. Sometimes the impacts will be reported in terms of how they meet various air quality indices. A statement that the air contains so many parts per million for a pollutant should be accompanied by a statement on whether or not the air quality will, for example, conform to state standards for the prevention of significant deterioration.

Although northern New England has few modern development proposals that create emissions like those of the industrial Midwest, it does have pollution, mostly from automobiles and urban environments. Benzene and other motor vehicle emissions are higher in cities, as is zinc from combustion processes, and nickel from oil-burning. Other pollutants from atmospheric reactions, such as sulfates and ozone, are generally in equal concentrations above rural and urban areas. These pollutants arise from sources emitted to the air from varying locations and, once formed in the air, may soon move to a completely different state or country.

Odor

Odor, interestingly enough, is one of the strongest triggers of memories and emotion, more so than sight or sound. Our sense of smell cannot always detect gasses, such as carbon monoxide, but it does serve as an alarm system for potential harm. Consequently, people can detect concentrations so small that they can hardly be measured in laboratories. Potential odors, even slight ones, should be a component of commercial and industrial development review; when odor becomes a problem it generally is a big one.

Odor sensitivity varies greatly from person to person. Acclimation is a big factor; some people who live near chemical plants may even lose the ability to detect an odor obvious to visitors. Of course, a community may not tolerate the thought of simply allowing an odor and accommodating it over time. Some cities, such as Portland, ME, have put odor detection and monitoring into a regulatory scheme. A development plan review process should provide for the assessment and consideration of odor impacts.

Tale from the Trenches

THE FRAGRANT PROJECT

When I worked as an assistant city planner, people used to come to my office to complain about the bakery. I went down to check it out and it smelled like fresh-baked bread. Yet when I lived in a paper mill town, there were few complaints about the rotten-egg smell of the mill. I guess that is because it was the smell of money for the town. It made me wonder what people would say if the bakery employed more workers. It is interesting what people can get used to, and what they won't get used to.

Odor should be described in standardized terms so that people can understand its potential impacts. The Henning scheme (Figure 4-1) provides a recognized classification (Moulton, Turk, and Johnston, 1975). Odors from a project may not match these examples, but standardized terms become valuable in dealing with permit compliance. After the project is built it may become important to know whether or not a project has the type and degree of odor impacts anticipated in the review process. Put simply, "Did they know it would smell this bad?"

Figure 4-1   Henning Odor Classification Scheme.

Odor Name	Example	Project
spicy	cinnamon	bakery
flowery	jasmine	greenhouse
fruity	apples	orchard
resinous	turpentine	paint store
foul	rot, hydrogen sulfide	paper mill
burnt	tar, scorched material	chemical plant

Steps are available to reduce odors generated by development projects. Smell can be mitigated by the use of mechanical equipment and filters. Biochemical neutralizing processes exist. Berms and plantings may be added to a project site to help reduce the perceived impacts of odor. A proposed building location could be changed. Emissions can be limited by time of day and season; this may help address prevailing wind and climate patterns or it may reduce the amount of people exposed to the odor. Other scents can be added to diversify or counteract the smell.

Emissions

State and federal reviewers evaluate emissions such as NOx, ozone, Volatile Organic Compounds (VOCs), SO_2, and other toxics. Local officials can compare the results of state reviews to see how the project emissions compare with the local or regional comprehensive plan and the documented ambient air quality conditions.

Particulate matter

Dust, smoke, fumes, and all kinds of particles emitted into the air fall under this category. Particulate matter may be described as a quality—soot, smoky haze—or in quantitative terms like "micrograms per cubic meter." Particulate matter is generated by all combustion processes in varying amounts, and by the entrainment of dust in the air over dirt roads, construction, demolition, and quarrying.

Dust and debris result from the processing and transport of materials during construction of a project and during its operation.

53

For some projects (like gravel pits), the two are the same, but for others, such as residential subdivisions, the construction impacts may be different than impacts associated with full build-out.

A construction road serves as a good illustration of methods to mitigate dust (Figure 4-2). Three types of actions can reduce dust: 1) things that can be done to the road; 2) things that can be done to the equipment using the road; and 3) ways to control the terms of use. These mitigation measures can be drawn on the plans or discussed in a narrative.

Figure 4-2. Options for dust control on construction roads.

- Apply calcium chloride or other chemicals.
- Apply water.
- Limit use during commuter hours.
- Limit use during dry spells.
- Limit use during windy days.
- Limit size of equipment using road.
- Limit number of trips by using alternate routes.
- Reduce debris on vehicles – water baths, shakers, hand-sweeping, wheel-wash stations, etc.
- Reduce width and length of road to minimum.
- Add mulch along edge of road.
- Pave or gravel road as soon as possible.

Wood smoke

Wood smoke is a potential emission from residential developments or wood-heated commercial businesses. The visible portion of wood smoke is mostly unburned fuel. Consequently, there is less smoke when stoves are efficient. Wood stoves emit smoke, soot, carbon monoxide, and about a hundred other chemical gases, including many carcinogens. Large residential subdivisions, especially in the "second home" market may have enough wood stoves to cause air quality problems in small valleys with frequent winter air inversions. One preventative measure is to ensure the houses or condominiums have efficient stoves identified as "EPA-certified" to meet "Phase II requirements."

Radiation

Radiation is a potential environmental concern when it involves radon or electromagnetic radiation (EMR). Other radiation hazards are beyond the scope of typical development plan review. Fortunately, these are usually scrutinized through federal regulations.

Radon

Radon, a naturally occurring radioactive gas, is now the second leading cause of lung cancer. It has no taste or smell, and is invisible. It seeps from soil through cracks in building foundations and can be brought into the home or workplace from wells. The gas attaches itself to aerosols, dust, smoke, and other particles suspended in the air. Radon is very site specific—it can be very high in one house yet absent in adjacent houses. Radon-sensitivity maps may be available from the state or town offices, or downloaded from an Internet site. These maps show the towns that have had relatively high radon, however they are not accurate enough for site-specific use.

Radon has always been around us in the Northeast. The EPA estimates that today at least eight million homes have elevated radon levels. Levels are measured in pico Curies per liter (pCi/l). Anything above four pCi/l may be a cause for concern. The EPA also uses "working level" (200 pCi/l = 1 WL) as a measurement unit for the decay products of radon. The presence of radon is an issue for new construction as well as for rehabilitation projects. The Maine Department of Human Services estimates that 1/3 of all homes in Maine have four or more pCi/l (MDHS web site, 2002).

There are three approaches to radon mitigation: 1) reduce the pressure pushing the gas into buildings; 2) reduce pathways used by the gas to enter, and; 3) ventilate the gas that has already entered. Pressure in the soil under the building and in buildings can be regulated. Cracks in basements can be sealed. Basements can be ventilated. Radon levels should also be monitored to ensure for the life of the project that the levels are safe. If the project involves high background radon levels, then the mitigation and monitoring systems should be aggressive and well-documented. All states have state radon coordinators and experts as well as advice and procedures for dealing with radon.

Electromagnetic Radiation (EMR)

Government agencies, the American National Standards Institute (ANSI), and other non-governmental organizations have developed guidelines for exposure to radio frequency radiation. The increase in towers, cellular telephones, and other communications devices has fueled public concern about the potential health effects of EMR as well as potential interference with signal transmission. In addition to federal regulations, municipalities have started to adopt telecommunications ordinances and establish separate review boards.

Review of Telecommunications Towers and Facilities

With the proliferation of telecommunication towers and facilities in recent years, located anywhere from hilltops to barn silos to church steeples, review boards have grappled with evaluating their impacts. Towns across northern New England have begun to adopt ordinances specifically for reviewing these facilities. Vermont's Environmental Board, which administers Act 250, the state land use law, has adopted special procedures for their review. While telecommunications towers can have aesthetic and other impacts, their electromagnetic emissions are often considered an air quality issue.

When towns establish a telecommunications ordinance they often name a board (sometimes the zoning board) to review the applications for towers and facilities. Local ordinances are most often written so as to be consistent with the federal Telecommunications Act of 1996. Local ordinances usually have at least the following features: 1) a list of the kinds of facilities that require a permit and which are exempt; 2) review criteria; 3) a statement of project requirements which address aesthetic impacts; location; construction of access roads, screening, fencing and signs; tower design and finish; lighting; commercial advertising; noise; air navigation; and height; 4) an enforcement section; and 5) a definition section.

Local ordinances may also include provisions for hiring independent consultants because of the technical nature of evaluating and measuring the transmission of radiofreqeuncy energy. Human exposure must be in compliance with the Rules and Regulations specified in 47 C.F.R. Part 1 – Practice and Procedure, Subpart I-Procedures Implementing the National Environmental Policy Act (NEPA) of 1969.

Vibration

Minor earthquake tremors occur in northern New England—
every year some tremors are felt—but not to a sufficient degree
for special consideration in the design and review of most projects.
Noise and mechanical shaking of equipment are the primary sources
of vibrations. Low frequency noise vibrations, largely from explosives, cause rattling of windows and china. Mechanical vibrations
result from transportation—usually large trucks or railroad cars—
associated with a development. Other sources of mechanical vibration include specific processing equipment and factories.

Vibration is an issue in development review when the project
involves the commercial extraction of earth resources, as in the case
of a quarry (Figure 4-3), or for the preparation of a foundation.
These activities may vibrate windows and structures on nearby
properties. Another concern is the effect on wells. Water loss and
contamination are the most commonly expressed concerns of adjacent
well owners. A seismograph can be used to indicate how blasts
radiate from the epicenter, but it cannot detect whether the blast
is a cause of a well depletion. Reviewers may require that well tests
be conducted and structures inspected before blasting takes place
so that the effects of blasting, if any, can be documented. In
addition, many review boards use the U.S. Bureau of Mines standards
to control the vibration and noise impacts of blasting. Noise issues
related to vibration are discussed further in Chapter 5.

*Figure 4-3. Sample mitigation evaluation matrix for dust, noise, and vibration
at a quarry operation.*

Mitigation	Explosives	Equipment	Trucks
hours	x	x	x
notification	x		
route/location	x	x	
blasting mats	x	x	x
monitor effects	x	x	x
mediation	x	x	x

Thermal

Heated air discharges can be a concern in village centers and urban areas. Heat vents for ovens in downtown restaurants can cause unpleasant heat sensations, as well as odors and combustion byproducts. Heat discharge can affect adjacent plant growth. Exhaust discharges from air conditioning can be a fire hazard. Most urban areas are hotter than the surrounding countryside due to the "heat island" effect. Health codes and other regulations usually require review of heat vent locations, which should be examined for all commercial and industrial projects.

Chemical vapors

Chemical vapors can be loosely sorted into sources of direct occupational health hazards regulated by OSHA, and atmospheric discharges that pose long-term or indirect threat, such as chlorine- and bromine-containing chemicals accused of destroying ozone. Direct occupational health hazards may occur when formaldehyde and other compounds "off-gas" from synthetic building materials. Toxic materials in the air may contribute to "sick building" syndrome. We hear more about this problem as people move into more artificial surroundings and become aware of environmental hazards.

Even if a proposed development includes processes and emissions not directly regulated by the review board, there is no harm in inquiring about them. The reviewers should ask about indoor work conditions and atmospheric discharges, especially if halons and chloroflourocarbons (CFCs) are released during proposed manufacturing processes. On-site health risks from air pollution are as relevant as the "global commons" of general air quality; both raise issues of health, ethics, economics, and politics. Maine, Vermont, and New Hampshire products generally have a "green" image. Some communities may want to capitalize on that image in promoting appropriate new industry.

Indoor air quality

The time to address potential indoor air quality problems is before a structure is completed, or if it is already built, before a conversion is approved. If there is bad outdoor air quality we can expect problems with indoor air quality. However, good outdoor air quality doesn't tell us anything about indoor air quality (radon exists inside and outside, but disperses readily outside; see above). OSHA and other non-local avenues address indoor air quality. However, some municipal ordinances regulate indoor air quality as do some state agencies. If a structure is unoccupied by humans, then by definition it does not have an indoor air pollution problem.

About 30% of buildings in New England have air quality issues. Indoor air pollution was a problem in factories fueled by the Industrial Revolution. Hearths and stoves created the problem even earlier. Labor and health laws cleared some of this up in the 20th century, but the energy crunch of the 1970s, coupled with artificial building materials, gave rise to modern indoor air quality issues. To save energy, many buildings of the 1970s had poor ventilation and reduced window space. We "tightened" our buildings. Revolving doors and separate lobbies had the effect of reducing air exchanges. These measures save heating and cooling expenses but erode air quality.

The generally accepted regulatory goal in managing indoor air quality is to satisfy 80% of the people. Some people can tolerate anything and others are highly sensitive to any external irritants. Given the wide range of individual responses, it is not feasible or practical to protect everyone. There are two types of indoor air quality problems commonly addressed: sick building syndrome and building-related illness.

Sick Building Syndrome (SBS)

Symptom of SBS include headaches, respiratory tract problems, and lethargy. Despite no specific association with an identifiable contaminant, the symptoms are real. A major indicator of SBS is when workers feel better at home. Association is the problem; removal of the affected people from the environmental setting (the building) alleviates that problem.

Building-Related Illness (BRI)

In cases of BRI, specific symptoms – asthma, allergies, respiratory tract illnesses – are linked to a particular cause or source. The classic example is Legionnaire's disease, which first came to prominence when bacterial infection from water in a cooling system

59

led to pneumonia among conventioneers. The main indicators of BRI are: 1) the illness doesn't go away when people leave the building, and 2) the illness requires medical treatment.

Evaluating indoor air quality

Indoor air quality is very complicated but can be evaluated by looking at comfort level, exposures, and work conditions—preferably as part of the initial planning of the project:

1) Comfort level—temperature, humidity, fresh air. These are the three biggies; if we can solve them, people are generally happy.
2) Chemical and particulate exposures—dust, poor housekeeping, cleaning chemicals, improperly stored or handled chemicals.
3) Biological exposures (water)—common sources include condensation in ducts, toilets, pipes, and organic material. If there is wood in these areas then there will be particularly high amounts of mold and bacteria growth. A carpet not dried out within 24 hours will have mold forming in it.
4) Psycho-social factors—lighting, noise, quality or degree of ergonomic design, vibration, job satisfaction, job stress. High job stress is associated with increase in reports of SBS. Low job satisfaction, low control over workspace and seasonal affective disorder (SAD) are all associated with reports of SBS.

Measuring contaminants is hard; hundreds could be tested. However, there is a simple indicator of indoor air quality—the CO_2 exhaled by people in the building. The level of CO_2 can indicate if there is enough fresh air input or proper exhaust. If the levels are high, that might mean too many people or poor exhaust. High CO_2 levels imply that chemical contaminants are high. The solution is either more outdoor air or more circulated air. CO_2 has health effects when it rises to 5,000 parts per million (ppm) range. We seek to keep it below 1,000 ppm as a safety factor and to provide enough air for circulation. In an office building, the CO_2 levels start out low in the morning, have a little peak just before lunch, then drop a bit and have a second, larger peak towards 5 PM; morning tests do not give a true picture.

The best way to promote good indoor air quality is through good design and planning before the structure is built.

Where to go for more information

Creative Methods, Inc. http://www.creativemethods.com/airquality/

Environmental Protection Agency. http://www.epa.gov/airnow/where/
A radon zone map can be found at http://www.epa.gov/iaq/radon/
zonemap.html. For information on air quality standards and air quality
planning, see EPA's http://www.epa.gov/oar/oaqps/

Maine Bureau of Air Quality. http://www.state.me.us/dep/air/

Maine Department of Human Services, Maine Radon Homepage. http://
www.state.me.us/dhs/eng/rad/hp_radon.htm

New Hampshire Department of Environmental Services, Air Resources
Division. http://www.des.state.nh.us/ard_intro.htm

Northeast States for Coordinated Air Use Management (NESCAUM).
http://www.nescaum.org/about.html

Vermont Air Pollution Control Division, Agency of Natural Resources.
http://www.anr.state.vt.us/dec/air/

Chapter 5
NOISE IMPACTS

Standards and interpretation

One cost of development is an increase in noise. Noise (from the Latin word for "nausea") can be considered simply as unwanted sound, a definition the EPA uses. Like many other pollutants, noise has psychological and sociological, as well as biological effects. Noise levels are linked to stress and crime. In some communities, background noise levels are doubling every ten years. At its best, noise is an aesthetic benefit, as in the case of a babbling brook (white noise); at its worst, it is a form of air pollution that causes severe physical impairment. The Noise Control Act of 1972 and the Quiet Communities Act of 1978 (PL 95-609) set federal noise policies, but most outdoor noise issues occur at the local level and must be handled by local processes. Some planning boards do not evaluate noise impacts unless they are an obvious concern such as those associated with a quarry or gravel pit. Yet noise is consistently high on the list of issues people raise after a project is completed.

Noise is sound in the form of pressure waves measured in decibels on one of three scales, A, B, and C, ranked respectively for low, intermediate, and high intensities. The "A" scale is used most frequently for regulation and environmental assessments and is assumed unless a different scale is specified. Although the "A" scale simulates the subjective response of the human ear, it is not as sensitive to impulse noise, such as a shotgun report, and is not particularly effective in measuring high-intensity, low frequency noises such as giant car woofers. In contrast, the "C" scale is as responsive to low-pitched sounds as it is to mid- and high-pitched sounds. Consequently, communities across the country are converting to the C scale for ensuring compliance with noise ordinances.

In comparing decibel levels (Figure 5-1), note that decibel levels increase in a logarithmic rather than an arithmetic manner. For example, suburban street noise (70 dB) is not ten percent louder than ordinary speech (60 dB)—it is ten *times* as much sound energy. It will be perceived by a listener as at least a doubling of loudness (energy level is not quite the same as loudness level).

Figure 5-1. Sample decibel levels.

10-20	rustling leaves
20	rural nighttime
30	rural residential neighborhood while the kids are at school
34	soft whisper
40	refrigerator
55	typical window air conditioner
60	conversational speech
65	nine typewriters, busy restaurant
69	vacuum cleaner ten feet away
80	passing car ten feet away
86	printing press plant
90	jack hammer
92	heavy city traffic, large diesel truck at 25 feet
98	lawn mower
104	car alarm
107	air hammer, siren
110	rock band in a bar
120	pain begins to occur

Pursuant to the federal Occupational Safety and Health Act (OSHA), the Environmental Protection Agency (EPA) sets permissible noise exposure levels based on an assumption that, after exposure, people have a quiet place to go to while they recover from the noise (Figure 5-2). Some state and local governments, and many European countries, have more stringent standards.

Figure 5-2. EPA/OSHA standards for permissible noise exposure.

Hours per day	Decibels (A scale)
8	90
6	92
4	95
3	97
2	100
1.5	102
1	105
0.5	110
0.25	115

(Source: 29 CFR 1926.52(d)(1))

The U.S. Department of Housing and Urban Development (HUD) sets noise preference levels (NPLs) for its projects (Figure 5-3). Some local governments use these levels as a guide. Noise preference level depends on the time of day; most people expect and prefer that sounds quiet down at night. The EPA developed a day-night level (L_d) by using a formula that accounts for the increased annoyance of nighttime noises.

Figure 5-3 HUD noise preference levels.

clearly unacceptable	exceeds 80 dB for 1 hour per day exceeds 75 dB for 8 hours per day
normally unacceptable	exceeds 65 dB for 8 hours per day produces loud repetitive sounds
normally acceptable	does not exceed 65 dB for more than 8 hours per day
clearly acceptable	does not exceed 45 dB for more than 30 minutes per day

Local zoning districts and subdivision regulations may also have noise standards. Colchester, Vermont, has a 70 dB maximum threshold for residential districts and 75 dB for commercial districts. Brattleboro, Vermont, specifies 70 dB for all districts. Concord, NH, has "use districts" for evaluating noise impacts and establishing noise levels. Westbrook, Maine, allows 75 decibels at six hundred (600) cps measured at any boundary line for industrial zones. While most town ordinances apply to "continuous state noise," such as traffic or music, the town of Essex, Vermont also includes in its ordinance an "instantaneous maximum" noise limit of 80 dBA at the property line. This standard applies to noise emanating from land uses such as gun clubs. The Maine State Planning Office provides guidance, including a basic sample review standard of 55 dBA in the day (between 7 a.m. and 7 p.m.) and 45 dBA in the night for projects abutting residential or neighborhoods or institutions (Maine State Planning Office, 2000).

Sound pressure waves do not become noise until they are heard. The act of perceiving noise is influenced by psychological as well as acoustical factors. Noise that does not affect health is "annoyance" noise, a complex phenomenon with acoustic and non-acoustic components. The acoustic aspects of noise include loudness, inter-mittency, duration (impact v. steady state) and spectral composition (frequency). Duration may be represented in community noise standards in the form of "sound level equivalents" (Leq), an averaging of the sound level for either one minute or one hour. Sound frequency is measured in Hertz, and is closely related to "pitch."

Non-acoustic aspects of noise center on the way the noise is perceived, its sensory and emotional effects, the time of day the noise occurs, and interference with activities. The duration and intermittency of noise must also be considered in addition to loudness. Impulse noises, such as gunshots, are often judged to be "noisier," or more unwanted, than non-impulse noise having the same total integrated energy. People vary greatly in the degree to which they are affected by noise—attitudinal factors play a big role.

Noise studies are often omitted in local site plan review processes. Information about noise may be helpful to the community as well as to the reviewers. Sources of variation in noise include the following:

Visibility of noise source. The image of the noise source influences perception. A large exhaust stack may be perceived as an unsightly symbol of neighborhood blight, thereby making the sounds of exhaust seem more irritating or louder. For people opposed to its presence in their community, the sight of a medium security prison may trigger a strong reaction to associated noise. The perception need not always be negative; a noise source could be a reminder that much-needed jobs are being brought to the community.

Fluctuations in sound level. Noise fluctuations can be a result of changes in the source itself, movement of the source, or changes that occur between the source and the listener. The human ear is drawn to fluctuations in noise, perhaps due to an innate attempt to locate the noise and interpret whether or not the change signals a potential threat. The net result is that fluctuations call attention to the source.

Sudden or startling noises. Like fluctuations, these noises are real attention-getters. Whistles and fire alarms take advantage of this characteristic but other sudden or startling noise sources may require mitigation.

Pure tone frequencies. Discrete frequency tones resonate and insinuate themselves, calling our attention even at 10 to 15 decibels below a noise preference level. Electrical utilities and factory whining sounds may produce pure tone frequencies.

Noise that interferes with sleep. Tolerance for noise depends on where the noise occurs within human schedules. People tend to like their evening hours at least 10 decibels below daytime noises. A conservative estimate of sleep hours accommodates a wide range of sleep patterns.

Noise that interferes with communication. Noise that disturbs spoken conversation or interferes with cellular or other electronic communication can occur directly or through electronic interference. The latter may be regulated by the FCC and is generally beyond local regulatory authority.

Low frequency vibrations. Rattling windows call attention to sounds that might otherwise be missed. Disturbance from low frequency vibrations heightens sensitivity to quarries and other sources.

Noise associations. Noise associated with unpleasant events or that conveys displeasing information is grating to the ear. Perhaps the best examples are the sounds of breaking glass and crumpling metal; both can sound like a car crash.

Low background ambient noise. A quiet background enhances aesthetic enjoyment of the environment. Accordingly, there may not be the same degree of noise acclimation found in urban areas. Community expectations for noise may be higher than levels set by federal agency standards, a consideration when reviewing projects that rely on federal standards.

Assessment of noise impacts in development applications

Environmental impacts of noise can be assessed in several ways, including an on-site experiment, by demonstrating a noise source similar to what can be expected from the proposed development. For example, a rock crusher could demonstrate the noise expected from expansion of a gravel pit. These tests might not be practical for a new pit or for a condominium development, which may benefit from assessment through modeling or expert opinion.

Modeling is done by comparing one project with a similar one or by setting up a noise source substitute. The substitute should be reasonable. In a case before the Vermont Environmental Board, a car horn was used to demonstrate the potential noise of a rock crusher. Interestingly, the board found that there was no "scientific correlation between the sound emitted from the horn of a 1984 Plymouth and the noise that may result from the Project"; apparently, a car horn does not sound like a quarry. (Vermont Environmental Board decision, Lemieux #3R0717-EB Findings of Fact, Conclusions of Law, and Order, Page 3, March 1, 1995.)

Sources of expert opinion on noise include sound engineers as well as equipment operators and project or construction managers. People who have lived near similar facilities merit a certain degree of expertise. Only a few states (none in northern New England) have formal licensing of professional engineers in acoustics.

Traffic noise impact has its own literature. One regulatory technique is to develop a Traffic Noise Index (TNI) based on weighted physical measurements of peak noise (the level exceeded ten percent of the time) and background noise levels (the level exceeded 90 percent of the time). Noise indices can be used for situations other than traffic.

Evaluating a noise impact study

Noise studies have achieved a standard format after years of concern about airports, highways and other external noise sources. Similar to lighting levels, "isochrome" graphs can be used to show noise levels at specific distances from an airport or other significant source. A good way to understand a noise study is to retrace the steps typically undertaken in preparing a noise report, starting with a definition of the project, then the gathering of background data. The study should address noise monitoring and mitigation.

The study likely assesses background or community noise levels, probably using decibels. Units of perceived noisiness might also be calculated from frequencies and loudness (e.g., the *noy*, and *sone*) but

Figure 5-4. Sample options for noise mitigation at a gravel pit with a crusher or screener and with an increasing extraction rate.

Changes to project
- Insulate crusher jaws.
- Use rubber-lined belt for screener.
- Process materials off-site.
- Change size or type of crusher, screener, or truck.

Changes to site
- Recess crusher/screener base to reduce elevation.
- Periodically move crusher to reduce trip distance to and from the excavation site.
- Use berm or stockpile as sound barrier.
- Plant pine trees.
- Relocate noisy operation further away from neighbors.

Changes to operation
- Pick a shorter time for more intensive operation.
- Limit hours, days, and seasons.
- Reduce number of vehicles/equipment operating at any one time.
- Replace standard backup beepers with motion sensing "smart alarms." Both are acceptable to OSHA.
- Use "scoop-bed" trucks that do not have tailgates.
- Re-route or reschedule truck trips.
- Change non-noise related aspects of the project to improve image.
- Use "white noise" generation devices.
- Monitor noise levels before and after changes.
- Implement a neighbor notification policy that includes mediation.

these should also include the basic information, including decibels, from which they were derived.

Consider whether the noise study answers a reasonable array of questions. What are the potential sources from a project—are they from transportation, industrial processes, construction, cooling systems, households, people, animals? When does the noise occur and under what conditions? Who is exposed to the noise? Are they elderly, children, operators, passengers, bystanders, neighboring houses or work places? What is the length of exposure and the proximity to the source? How will the noise be reduced?

To speed up the review process, the project application should describe proposed measures to reduce or mitigate noise impacts. The range of responses depends on the project and the site. In many review processes, approval is conditioned upon restrictions in design or operation. Figure 5-4 shows some options for a quarry.

Ensuring that noise levels will be acceptable

Noise level readings can be taken at the site perimeter at appropriate times during construction and at full operation. Sound meters typically cost several hundred dollars—a minor expense compared to the legal and administrative hassles associated with a recurrent noise problem. They can be used by anyone and provide immediate feedback. Internet sites that link to suppliers and evaluators of sound measuring devices are listed at the end of this chapter. Some municipalities specify standards for noise meters (Concord, NH requires meters to meet ANSI S1.4-197 Type I and IEC 179, a common specification for meters). There are other ways to evaluate noise in a qualitative fashion. A simple "walk-away" noise test can be done informally, as described below, without the use of a meter.

The "walk-away" noise test is a simple procedure to evaluate existing overall noise levels (Schultz and McMahon, 1971). It can be used during a site visit to establish a noise level baseline after construction of a new project or it can be used at an existing facility contemplating an addition. The test requires only two people with average hearing and average voice levels, a 100-foot tape measure and some unfamiliar reading material. One person reads while the other backs slowly away until he or she can hear only a word or two over a period of ten seconds or more. The distance is measured at that point and the people should switch roles; average the distances after several trials (Figure 5-5).

Figure 5-5. HUD "walk-away" test.

Distance for acceptable understood speech	Category
more than 70 feet	clearly acceptable
26-70 feet	normally acceptable
7-25 feet	normally unacceptable
less than 7 feet	clearly unacceptable

(Source: Schultz T.J and N.M. McMahon, 1971 HUD Noise Assessment Guide-lines, Washington, D.C., US Government Printing Office.)

Where to go for more information

Berger, Elliot H., Larry H. Royster, Julia D. Royster, Dennis P. Driscoll, and Marty Layne, eds. (2000). *The Noise Manual,* 5th edition. AIHA Press. http://www.aiha.org/

Federal Aviation Administration (FAA). http://www.aee.faa.gov/noise/index.htm

Federal Highway Administration (FHA). http://www.fhwa.dot.gov/environment/htnoise.htm

Institute of Noise Control Engineering (ISNCE). http://www.inceusa.org/

Maine State Planning Office. *Noise Technical Assistance Bulletin #4,* May 2000.

Noise Pollution Clearinghouse. http://www.nonoise.org/

Occupational Health & Safety Administration (OSHA). U.S. Department of Labor. http://www.osha-slc.gov/SLTC/noisehearingconservation/

Zwerling, E.M. (2000). *Regulation of Amplified Sound Sources. Proceedings of Noise-Con 2000.* Acoustical Society of America/Institute of Noise Control Engineering. Newport Beach, CA.

Chapter 6
SOILS AND SEPTIC SYSTEMS

Soil resources and soil suitability

Under site and development review, two main aspects of soils are considered: the properties and values of the soil as a resource (topsoil, gravel, ore), and the suitability of the soils on the site to accommodate the project (on-site septic systems, resist erosion, support buildings). Soil quality describes the fitness of a specific kind of soil to maintain air and water quality, support plant and animal productivity, support human habitation, and preserve human health (U.S. Department of Agriculture, 1996).

Large non-residential projects and multiple-unit residential dwellings undergo technical review by state engineers and soil scientists; the job for the rest of us is merely to interpret and apply that review. However, many small projects undergo only local review, increasing the responsibility of municipal officials. Small projects outnumber large ones and tend to have greater cumulative impacts. For example, in northern New England individual houses contribute far more to groundwater and surface water contamination than do large subdivisions or non-residential structures that are typically hooked up to municipal wastewater treatment plants. On-site septic systems serve many projects in northern New England because municipal treatment facilities are less common than in more urbanized areas of the northeast.

Directly measured soils properties of horizonation, texture, structure, color, redoximorphic features, horizons, and effective depth provide clues about other characteristics, such as permeability, leaching potential, heavy metal immobilization, infiltration, and expansion. The soils map may reflect the potential uses of soil for forestry, agriculture, on-site septic disposal and extraction. If the project requires an on-site wastewater disposal permit, an official from the state or town visits the site to look at the soils. Large or complicated projects usually also require a visit to the site as part of the site plan or development review process. If the site visit is timed right, exposed soil test pits are visible, giving reviewers an excellent chance to see first-hand the soil properties.

Soil impacts are usually summarized in a project application, typically as part of erosion control information, and in the form of an application for a subsurface wastewater disposal or septic design approval. (See Figure 6-1 for a sample soil review checklist.) Small communities that do not have in-house staff for this review commonly contract it out to a reputable local engineering firm, the local Natural Resources Conservation Service (NRCS, formerly the Soil Conservation Service) office, or defer to state review. The qualifications for soils expertise include training as an environmental or civil engineer, licensed site technician, or soil scientist. Site evaluators are qualified only to make judgements on where to site a septic system; engineers are qualified to design site septic systems and erosion and sediment control plans. Licensed or certified soil scientists should do all other soil evaluations. Some states license locally,

---

Figure 6-1. Sample checklist for a soil engineering report.

__ Data regarding the nature, distribution, strength, and erodibility of existing soils

__ Data regarding the nature, distribution, strength, and erodability of any soil that is to be brought to the site

__ Conclusions and recommendations for grading procedures

__ Conclusions and recommended designs for temporary soil stabilization/erosion control devices

__ Designs and details for permanent soil stabilization after construction is completed

__ Design criteria for corrective measures when necessary

__ Opinions and recommendations covering the stability of the site

__ Subsurface conditions, including soil profile

__ Soil boring results

__ Summary of geology of site

__ Test units data from borings, trenches and other excavations

__ Source of soils report, and qualifications

---

or rely on a national certification available through the Soil Science Society of America. Review boards and others involved in public decision-making can insist that soil information be communicated in clear, understandable terms. Below are some general concepts to help understand site evaluation reports pertaining to soils.

Soil horizons

The soil layer is defined as a type of horizon based on the soil properties; a combined stratigraphy of horizons is called a soil "profile." Soil horizon classification can be fairly difficult, however the typical profile usually starts with a thin top layer of organic material (O horizon) and might continue to an A horizon, a B horizon, and a C or bedrock horizon. Soil profile descriptions tell the reviewer about the horizons, reflecting the soil properties and indicating the suitability of the soil for its intended use. A sketch of the soil profile will likely be provided as part of any application for an on-site septic system.

Texture

Soil texture refers to the relative proportions of particle sizes in the soil. The group of smallest particle sizes is called "fine earth" and consists of sand, silt, and clay, in order of decreasing size. Technically, the definition of soils is < 2mm, so only the fine earth is soil and the rest is something else: "coarse fragments" (gravels up to three inches) or cobbles (three to ten inches). Significant amounts of coarse fragments lead to a soil description of "gravelly" or "cobbly" in test pit data. Coarse texture consists of sands, loamy sand and sandy loams with less than 18% clay, and more than 65% sand. Medium texture soils are sandy loams, loams, sandy clay loams, silt loams with less than 35% clay and less than 65% sand; the sand fractions may be as high as 82% if at least 18% clay is present. Fine texture classes are the clays, silty clays, sandy clays, clay loams, and silty clay loams with more than 35% clay.

Structure

Soil structure refers to the grouping (aggregation) of individual fine earth particles into larger as units called "peds," a result of soil formation through physical and chemical activities of plant roots, organic matter, and clay formation. Structure is defined by size and type, and is described in grades (strong, moderate, weak, and "structureless"). A well-developed (strong) structure has good aeration from large pores and the enduring peds. Water finds space between the pores; agricultural soils need adequate spaces for air and water.

Color

Soil color helps indicate the condition of the soil, as well as mineral composition. The color terminology of hue, value, and chroma, presented in Chapter 11, Aesthetics, apply to describing soil color. Generally, a dark color indicates organic matter. Yellows and browns show combinations of air and water usually suitable for agriculture or construction. Gray colors indicate reduced amounts of air and large amounts of water, as would be expected for a wetland. Color chips help the soil scientist determine the precise color (usually using a Munsell soil color book).

Redoximorphic features

Redoximorphic features (mottles) are spots of one color within a soil layer of a different color. Fluctuations of the water table cause redoximorphic features to develop. Iron "rusts" when it is exposed to oxygen after being wet, and the result is a reddish mottle in the soil matrix. Chemical weathering also affects different minerals in the soil, which can tend towards reds, grays, or yellows.

Redoximorphic features raise immediate concerns about the suitability of the soils for septic systems due to the presence of water. However, redoximorphic features might not be the result of recent water fluctuation: ancient changes may be recorded in "relic soils" that now are well-drained. The peds may also have coatings that are not due to the reduction and oxidation of iron. This is why the soil scientist will break open the peds. If the mottle is due to water table fluctuation, the color change should be apparent within the newly-broken clump.

Three terms describe the abundance of mottles: "few" (less than 2%), "common" (2-20%), and "many" (over 20%). The size of the mottles can be "fine" (less than 5 mm), "medium" (5-15 mm), and "coarse" (larger than 15 mm). The contrast between the mottle color and the soil layer color may be faint, distinct, or prominent.

Soil depth

Soil depth is described as shallow, moderately deep, or deep. Septic systems and agricultural uses depend on adequate depth. The soil starts at the organic top and extends down to bedrock, weathered bedrock, or where lime and silica have leached down to form a cement-like barrier. If the depth ends at 20 inches, the soil is considered shallow. A moderately deep depth is between 20 and 40 inches. If there is soil below 40 inches, the soil is "deep."

Soil maps and soil survey data

Soil maps are part of a soil survey, which also includes a description of each soil, as well as tables of physical and chemical data on the soils. Soils maps are at different scales—commonly 1:20,000 or 1:24,000; the largest scale is 1:5,000,000. The smallest scale, (1:1000) is used for a detailed inventory of the soils on a parcel. Soil survey data are maintained by the Natural Resources Conservation Service of the USDA. Most of the soils of northern New England are mapped, although some mapped counties have outdated information. To determine the current status of soils mapping for your state, see the references at the end of this chapter. Some states require high-intensity soil mapping prior to any sub-division application.

Other soil resources

Expect information about topsoil, sand, and gravel in the soil data and profiles. If the tract contains significant amounts of these resources, then they should be mentioned in the site assessment report. Most large developments will include the commercial extraction or on-site re-use of these resources if cost-effective. However, occasionally this information is not known or is not addressed in the plans and the review board may need to raise the issue.

Soils and septic systems

Projects that connect to municipal wastewater systems do not depend on the soils to treat septic wastes. For other projects, the soils are the medium for the chemical and biological treatment processes. In both types of projects, regulatory engineers usually review the design of the septic system or the wastewater connection lines. Not all projects are reviewed by the state and many towns have only nominally trained people to do this review. The review board member should have a rough idea of wastewater systems concepts in order to understand potential problems, and to understand the language and requirements in technical reviews. Even if the project will not have an on-site system, it might have a drinking water supply vulnerable to neighboring systems. Conversely, a project's on-site septic system may pose a threat to neighboring water supplies. In northern New England, with its shallow soils and steep slopes, a significant portion of disease outbreaks are traced to drinking water contaminated by sewage from septic systems.

On-site wastewater treatment systems require unsaturated aerobic conditions for success. Aerobic soils are necessary to support microorganisms that can digest the wastewater pathogens. The unsaturated soil conditions allow the sewage to flow by capillary action along the surfaces of soil particles. This flow increases contact between the sewage and the soil and thereby increases the retention and degradation of pollutants. It also assures the presence of aerobic microbes.

Wastewater contains metals of varying concentrations. Heavy metals persist in the environment and can pose a risk depending on their concentration and location. Wastewater also contains four principal pathogens: bacteria, protozoa, helminths (intestinal worms) and viruses. Bacteria and viruses tend to be the smallest in size and therefore have a greater potential to reach groundwater. Many pathogens die within a few days. Most are dead within 60 days and a very few hardy organisms can survive for several years. Pathogens should be kept within the system until they are dead.

Some bacteria and viruses move so quickly through the soil that a process must be designed to destroy them before they are transported into groundwater. The process of adsorption involves a chemical reaction that bonds the bacteria or virus to a soil particle. There, microorganisms can attack it. However, in sandy soils with heavy rains, the virus or bacteria can go back into suspension in the water and be transported to unwanted places.

If the water table is high, the soils are much more likely to have saturated, anaerobic conditions that enable bacteria and viruses to survive longer than normal. Percolation tests are needed to help determine if the soils can support effective wastewater treatment. Percolation tests determine permeability, but do not evaluate saturation. Before the field tests are done, the engineer or technician will consult existing soils documentation. Vermont, New Hampshire, and Maine provide soil classes using NRCS data to sort soils by the properties that affect septic design. Exclusive of other factors such as wellhead protection areas, these classes give a general idea of the potential of the soil to accommodate conventional, mound, and alternative septic systems. Systems can use dosing, sand filters, and other techniques governed by state or local regulations and plumbing codes.

Maine uses three soils suitability classifications under "shallow to bedrock":

I. less than 10" – extremely severe limitations, systems not permitted.
II. 10-14" – very severe limitations – replacement systems allowed if no alternative, no new systems permitted.
III. 15-48" – all systems permitted, but separation zone requirements.

In New Hampshire, ledge at less than 48" is flagged as needing a special lot size for septic system accommodation. All lot sizing in New Hampshire is based on soil type. There must be three or more feet of soil above bedrock; if ledge is found at less than four feet in depth, a test unit must be dug at each corner of the proposed disposal area to prove it does not get any shallower.

Vermont requires a minimum depth of 18 inches to bedrock. Regulations addressing seasonal high water table limit effluent to six (6) inches below soil surface. Slopes on lots can be up to 30 percent. In 2002, Vermont introduced the concepts of prescriptive, enhanced prescriptive, and performance-based designs.

Isolation distances for septic system components are an indicator of potential risk. Conditions in the field can vary greatly and the risk might actually be much greater (or less) than the isolation distances indicate. The governing regulatory agency will usually have specific minimum distances (Figure 6-2).

Figure 6-2. Sample recommended minimum isolation distance table for septic systems.

Horizontal distance in feet	leachfield	septic tank
drilled single-family well	100	50
well for two or more houses	125	50
gravel-pack or shallow well	150	75
spring	150	75
water (pond, lake, stream, river)	50	25
drainage swale or ditch	25	—
public water lines	50	50
foundation, footing & curtain drains	25	10
service water lines	25	25
slopes over 20%	25	10

Depending on the results of the soils testing, a designer selects an in-ground or mound system. The system may use a variety of innovate techniques but, generally, reviewing bodies tend to favor conservative system design.

Mound systems

Mounds are an option for sites that cannot support in-ground disposal systems—the normal preference due to reduced cost and visibility—because the soils are shallow, the water table is high, or there is an impermeable soil layer that acts as a barrier. Usually, regulations describe the conditions under which a mound system is required. Some sites may be too steep and the soils too shallow for any system at all. This problem is likely to increase as we continue to fill up the best soils with residential housing and prime-choice sites become unavailable.

The mound system requires a pile of sand and stone fill latticed with perforated pipes—the treatment portion of the system (Figure 6-3). A septic tank receives the waste from the structure, allows the sludge to settle out, and passes the liquid (effluent) to a vented pumping chamber. A pump in the chamber sends the effluent into the mound. A pressurized distribution system enables the pipe perforations to discharge equal amounts of effluent through the pipe network. If the distribution is not equalized, the effluent accumulates too much in one area and may surface out of the mound.

Good planning requires a designated area for a replacement mound system in case the first mound fails. No construction is allowed on top of the mounds, including seemingly innocuous things like swing-sets.

Figure 6-3. Sketch of a mound system.

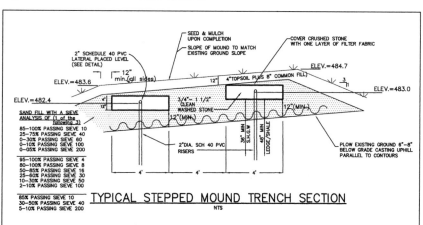

Conventional septic system

In-ground systems are usually several thousand dollars cheaper than mound systems and are less noticeable. Both primary and replacement systems should be shown on the plans (Figure 6-4). The test pits should occur at the actual location of the system, not just elsewhere on the tract. Like the mound system, the in-ground system and replacement area should be protected from impacts related to construction or use of the site. This risk is greater for the in-ground system because, being relatively flat, it may look like a good place for parking or for building a shed. Some municipalities require at least two test pits per lot to show that the site can support the system.

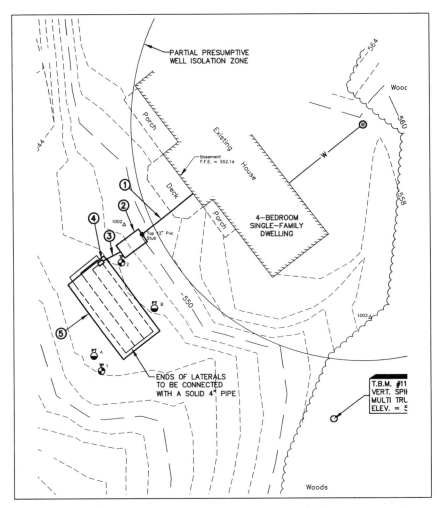

Figure 6-4. Diagram of in-ground system design. Note well isolation zone, protecting the proposed water supply. A replacement area is nearby.

Septic system as a private utility

If the project involves a shared wastewater disposal (or water supply) system, then the site plans should show easements and contain language preserving the rights of the shareholders to access and maintain the system. Sample covenants and deeds of incorporation may also be provided in the project application along with provisions for shared access, maintenance, and eventual replacement of private utilities such as septic systems—handy for ensuring environmental compliance.

Soil mechanics/physics

An engineer or other qualified environmental professional should assess the properties of the soils to determine if they can physically support a proposed structure. Issues such as earthquake stability and radon may also be discussed in the context of soil properties.

Soil contamination

The trend towards encouraging redevelopment of central areas, including "brownfields," along with an increase in applicability of environmental laws has led to more site assessments (also called Phase I, Phase II, and Phase III assessments). If the contamination problems can be remedied, reuse of these areas is an efficient application of "smart growth" land use.

The ability of soils to support a project is more than just a literal interpretation of soil mechanics. Viability of a site for development depends on the documented (or discovered) history of the soils in terms of contamination. Determination of the environmental risk depends on the nature of the contaminates and their physical properties in the soil. For example, a contaminate may be "bound-up" in the soil and thereby be fairly inert. Another contaminate might become air-born on exposure and desiccation (e.g., asbestos). Some contaminates, such as iron, are more of an aesthetic concern and do not pose a significant health risk.

Soil contamination occurs from natural causes as well as from construction, manufacturing, and other human activity; all should be reported in the site assessment data. Contamination from human activity may be an accidental byproduct, as in the case of a leaking underground storage tank, or it may occur from intentional activities such as the illegal disposal of hazardous waste. If the contamination is intentional, it may be discovered by accident, by investigation, or through an environmental assessment as part of the site development and selection process. Sometimes, accidental contamination can be anticipated by learning the history of the site. For example, if the site is in a former 19th century industrial belt, heavy metals are a reasonable expectation, as are accumulated organic and chlorinated organic compounds.

The high concentrations of iron along parts of the Connecticut River reflect contamination through natural causes. Metals contamination can persist through a manufacturing process—lead and cadmium are frequently found in New England soils in concentrations up to 200 ppm for lead and 7 ppm for cadmium. These metals are taken up by trees as they grow. Some of the trees are made into paper, the paper biodegrades, and the metals appear in the leachate. Although some reduction occurs, it is almost as if these metals were merely renters.

Any contamination in the site should be remedied under a plan revealed to state and municipal reviewers, including the method, funding, and schedule. The plan may recommend excavation, removal, and treatment of the soils; soil vapor extraction can remediate soil contaminated with polyaromatic hydrocarbons (PAH).

Construction debris can be used as fill if it has been examined and approved through a qualitative assessment that screens out potentially hazardous materials scattered among the larger, harmless-looking rubble. Fortunately, each state has a department or agency that generally regulates such material and related uses.

Where to go for more information

Brady, Nyle C. and Ray R. Weil. (2001). *The Nature and Properties of Soils* (13th Edition). Prentice Hall.

Geobopological Survey. http://www.geobop.com/paleozoo/Soils/NewEngland/

Maine Association of Professional Soil Scientists. http://www.mapss.com/

National Small Flows Clearinghouse. www.estd.wvu.edu/nsfc/nsfc_homepage.html

National Soil Survey Center. http://www.nssc.nrcs.usda.gov.

Natural Resources Conservation Service. (1992). *Stormwater Management and Erosion and Sediment Control Handbook for Urban and Developing Areas in New Hampshire*. Rockingham County Conservation District. Concord: NH Department of Environmental Services, Soil Conservation Service (now the Natural Resources Conservation Service).

Natural Resources Conservation Service. http://www.nrcs.usda.gov; Soil Survey Division, http://www.statlab.iaasstate.edu/soils.soildiv.

Natural Resources Conservation Service, Maine. http://www.me.nrcs. usda.gov/

Natural Resources Conservation Service, New Hampshire. http://www.nh. nrcs.usda.gov/Soil_Data/

Natural Resources Conservation Service, Vermont. http://www.vt.nrcs. usda.gov/soils/soil_home_page.htm

New Hampshire Association of Consulting Soil Scientists. 15 Muchado Drive, Barrington, NH 03825-3818

New Hampshire Office of State Planning. (1999). *Data Requirements for Site Review: Guidance for Planning.* Concord, NH: NHOSP.

NRCS & SSSA. (2002). *Soil Planner 2002: State Soils and Protecting Important Farmlands.* Natural Resources Conservation Services, Soil Science Society of America.

Rural Community Assistance Program (RCAP). http://www.rcap.org/

Russell, Howard S. (Abridged and edited by Mark B. Lapping). (1982). *A Long Deep Furrow: Three Centuries of Farming in New England.* Hanover NH: University Press of New England.

Society of Soil Science of Northern New England, USDA, Natural Resources Conservation Service, 27 Westminster St., Lewiston, ME 04240-3531

Soil Science Society of America. http://soilslab.cfr.washington.edu/S-7/.

Vermont Agency of Natural Resources. (1987). *Vermont Handbook for Soil Erosion and Sediment Control on Construction Sites.* Waterbury VT: Department of Environmental Conservation.

Chapter 7
WATER RESOURCES

Thousands of small bodies of water dot the countryside of northern New England, along with large lakes and rivers. These beloved features, coupled with shallow soils and steep slopes, make surface water resources an issue in most development projects. Less recognized, but equally important, are the myriad aquifers. Groundwater is affected by the same topographical conditions that bring runoff to surface waters. The simple fact that groundwater is hidden makes it even more difficult to assess the impacts of proposed development.

For management purposes, water bodies can be divided into four types: 1) rivers, streams, and small ponds; 2) ponds with more than ten acres of surface area; 3) coastal and tidal waters; and 4) groundwater. Class ratings within each type assist in water quality planning and management. State agencies make an effort to ensure that the standards are not degraded, but the bulk of the work in conserving

Tale from the Trenches
TINY STREAM, TINY TROUT
The project involved placing utility poles along about two miles of country road. There was a small, intermittent stream along part of the road. The stream was no more than about six inches deep and two feet wide. I wrote a proposed permit and assumed there would be no need for a hearing. When the district fisheries biologist told me that the stream had fish in it, I was surprised, but not nearly as surprised as the developer. The stream contained native Brook Trout *(Salvelinus fontinalis)* that got no longer than five or six inches even as adults, yet it was a thriving population. The project might have destroyed this delicate balance. Fortunately, we were able to relocate the proposed poles away from the stream. I learned that every watercourse is important and that wildlife can be everywhere, even in a little stream that might easily be overlooked.

water resources falls to municipalities in the case-by-case review of small projects, where most of the impacts occur.

There are four categories of potential impact to surface water resources from development: aesthetics, appropriate land use, water supply, and water pollution. Groundwater resources involve primarily the latter two categories. The four categories are not mutually exclusive, but do provide a way to organize potential impacts – a critical task in performing comprehensive site plan review.

Surface waters

States classify surface water resources as AA (scenic and suitable for public water supply with some filtering), A (potable, with some filtering), B (suitable for swimming and other uses including drinking if filtered and disinfected), or C (recreational boating, wildlife, industrial use, and irrigation of crops that will be cooked) under the federal Clean Water Act. This classification does not necessarily tell us how to manage water resources, or how to review potential impacts for all projects, but it does reflect water quality. The classes inform planning decisions and development review.

Water resources as aesthetics

The aesthetic value of lakes, ponds, rivers, streams, and wetlands in rural New England is well-known. The visibility of these resources contributes considerably to tourism, economics and quality of life. However, the end of the 19th century reliance on water for power caused many communities to turn their backs in neglect on the rivers that flow through them. Now, many firms and organizations consulting on urban revitalization and economic development recommend that communities re-examine these rivers. As a result, many communities have plan review and examine development with rivers and other water bodies in mind (Figure 7-1).

Aesthetic considerations of water resources include visual quality, public access, smell, color, turbidity, adjacent noise levels, vegetation, wildlife, and privacy. A campground on the shore of a lake may be a visual intrusion as well as a pollutant. The campground may lead to more boat traffic, littering, and other aesthetic impacts. Aesthetics is discussed further in Chapter 11.

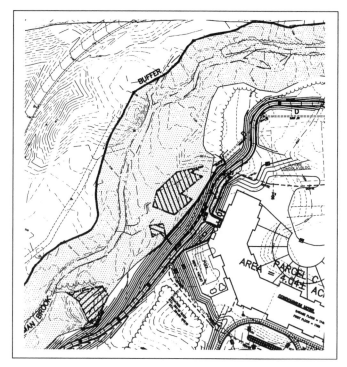

Figure 7-1. Portion of site plan showing a buffered watercourse. Language in the project proposal describes the buffer and how it will be maintained.

Water resources and appropriate land use

Development review takes place within an overall planning process. If the previous components of planning have been successful, we can tell if a proposed project is an acceptable land use for the area. However, there may be cases where no initial planning process occurred. Consequently the development review procedure is charged with reviewing all water quality issues, as well as assuring general compatibility with adjacent land uses. Factors to consider include the context of adjacent use, the degree to which the project is clustered away from riparian buffer zones and natural areas, and effects on shoreline access. Is construction of the project at the expense of a more appropriate land use and if so, how is that considered? How does the project fit with historical land used patterns?

Water supply

Projects affect water supplies through direct withdrawal of water and through discharges, contamination, erosion, and other consequences of operation. The major reasons for withdrawing significant amounts of water are for construction activity, drinking water supply and other domestic uses, and manufacturing or other operational processes.

If water is used in construction or in some manufacturing processes, it need not be potable. However, prior to discharge it may require treatment ranging from swales and infiltration to septic systems and leachate collection. The type and degree of treatment necessary to prevent water pollution requires technical review, usually at the state level. However, local reviewers are entitled to read and question engineering plans about drainage and wastewater treatment.

Water quality issues related to water supply include pH, taste, contamination, and quantity. These issues are usually described in environmental assessments for developments and in permit applications for water and wastewater services/utilities.

Pollution

An application for development review may describe the biological, chemical and physical conditions of existing water resources. These conditions provide the backdrop to environmental changes arising from a project. Depending on the nature of the proposed development, and the surface waters in the vicinity, information may be provided on many aspects of water quality, such as: suspended solids, dissolved oxygen, toxic materials, color, odor, temperature, and turbidity. Other physical characteristics of the body of water such as flooding and desiccation patterns might also affect pollution levels. Background information on water quality should be documented in technical terms such as "parts per million," and be translated into more easily understood terms, like "clean-smelling" or "clear." Sources of potential water pollution are described as "point source" (e.g., a discharge pipe) and "nonpoint source" (e.g., when runoff of rain or melting snow picks up pollutants and carries them to surface water or to where they leach into groundwater, see Figure 7-2). Point sources should be indicated on site plans.

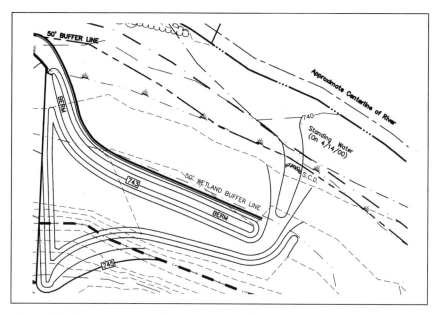

Figure 7-2. Treatment of surface water runoff before it enters receiving waters. The design directs flow and guides filtration.

Pollution levels affect bodies of water in three ways: public health, aesthetics, and ecology. Public health impacts are based on relationships between toxicity and use. For example, if a project is near a lake, the project review should include any recreational values of the lake (e.g., boating, swimming, and fishing), along with other functions of the lake (e.g., water supply, habitat). Large lakes, such as Sebago Lake in Maine, have active management schemes that restrict use (the lower end of Sebago supplies the Portland area with drinking water).

People expect rural northern New England to be a relatively pristine place; its bodies of water should smell and look clean. Contaminants, such as iron, have an aesthetic (visual) impact long before there is a public health risk, although other more dangerous pollutants (e.g., mercury) lack direct visibility.

Pollution raises ecological concerns in addition to user-related aesthetics and health. Pollution is associated with a reduction in key indicator species as well as a general decline in species diversity. The decline may start with a low-profile microorganism evident only to aquatic biologists, but it may progress to game fish, and affect overall lake ecology. Most commonly known pollutants or degraders of environmental quality, such as the spread of Eurasian Milfoil and other invasive species, have ecological impacts by definition, even if these are not yet completely understood.

Every year, in response to a federal mandate of the Clean Water Act, the states publish water quality assessment reports [305(b) report, available at the state water quality department and through various Internet links]. This report documents the progress made in inventorying and improving water quality—useful when reviewing proposed development near surface waters or aquifers.

Although federal and state regulations govern health issues, the likelihood of future contamination problems can be reduced if the local development review process identifies and remedies potential sources of contamination. Future site conditions should continue to meet applicable health standards.

Ecological balance and process

A development project can influence the ability of an aquatic environment to hold its own, to maintain stasis. Pollutants and other introduced elements may have a combined, synergistic reaction that is difficult to predict. Some chemical compounds change the form or availability of other substances. For example, chlorine added to water causes the release of bound-up mercury. Other environmental impacts initiate catalytic processes, as in the case of lowering oxygen in a stream, which increases the amount of oxygen needed by fish, thereby further lowering stream oxygen levels. Temperature and pH levels also act as catalysts for certain reactions. Conductivity and resistivity help track the amounts of solids and chemicals in water, improving our ability to understand potential change.

All ecosystems are subject to a homogenization process in which hardy invader species of plants and animals out-compete local species and gradually replace them, reducing species diversity. Eurasian milfoil, water chestnut, and zebra mussels are common invaders. Over 36 lakes and ponds in Vermont have already been infested by Eurasian milfoil, which can hitch a ride on boat hulls and propellers. Maine's efforts to stave off this invader appear to be successful, although about ten bodies of water are contaminated by

> *Tale from the Trenches*
> ## THE MANICURED BUFFER
> Concern about fisheries habitat had led us to require the developer to create a 50-foot buffer strip separating the new resort restaurant from the river. The buffer was to be kept naturally vegetated and undisturbed. This would reduce the surface temperature of the river in summer and help keep the trout happy. Alerted by a state fisheries biologist, we arrived for a post-construction site inspection and found the buffer to be nicely mown. The resort manager, experienced in urban areas, but not in rural New England, seemed pleased with how well groomed the project lands were. He thought the permit conditions were being met because no construction had occurred in the buffer. The manager seemed reluctant to give up the manicuring but finally understood after we explained the wildlife management goals behind buffers (and the need for literal compliance with permit conditions). We learned that not everyone has the same idea of what "natural" or "undisturbed" means.

a less aggressive species, variable-leaf milfoil. New Hampshire, also actively monitoring for invaders, has Eurasian milfoil in the Connecticut River and in a few other water bodies.

Principal types of surface water

Maine has about 5800 lakes and ponds totaling close to a million acres (Moosehead Lake alone is 74,890 acres). New Hampshire has about 177,280 acres of lakes and ponds and about 41,800 miles of river. Vermont has more than 225,000 acres of lakes and ponds, and over 5,000 miles of major rivers and tributaries. If a project involves disturbing the shoreline of rivers, lakes, and certain size ponds and streams, state or federal permits will likely be required. In other cases, little or no review occurs beyond the local level.

Maine law does not distinguish between lakes and ponds. Instead, Maine considers all inland waters with ten acres or more surface to be public property of the State, based on law extending back to 1641, when the wording of "Great Pond" was defined in a colonial ordinance (there are further distinctions, including an exemption if the pond is under 30 acres and was created by a dam). Maine has 2,787 Great Ponds. New Hampshire also designates ten-acre or more bodies of water as Great Ponds belonging to the public; it has over 800 lakes and Great Ponds.

Lakes

Vermont has 295 lakes of 20 acres or more in size. There are some large lakes in northern New England, including Lake Winnipesaukee (72 square miles) and Squam Lake in New Hampshire, Sebago Lake and Moosehead Lake in Maine, and Lake Champlain (the "sixth Great Lake") in Vermont. Lakes are permanent, and are often stratified with no light reaching the bottom; they are different from ponds in many ways. Ponds are shallower, with warmer temperatures and different amounts of dissolved gases, which means different nutrient cycles, habitats, and niches. The official name of a lake or pond may be deceptive because it might not reflect the true ecological definition.

Permit applications for shoreline development and other projects in a lake watershed should address the lake's existing condition, as well as how the project affects any state management plan for the lake. For example, chlorophyll-a, phosphorus concentrations (reported in ug/l) and Secchi disk transparency readings (in meters) may be submitted to indicate the capacity of the water to accommodate adjacent development. The ability of a body of water to accommodate pollutants depends in part on the existing nutrient conditions and on the physical, chemical, and biological responses of the lake to nutrients and silt. The rate of eutrophication is accelerated by nutrient loading from effluent, runoff, or erosion, all of which can be affected by adjacent development.

Some natural resource management agencies favor a "carrying capacity" approach, borrowed from ecology, to measure physical characteristics of water resources, simplify them with human use types and descriptions, and to derive a range of values for use management. The result is the capacity of a lake to accommodate development in a watershed, reflected in state recreation management goals and objectives. Big issues include access, crowding, speed limits, water-skiing, motors, jet-skis, sailboats, and other non-power craft.

Projects near lakes may affect them in one or more of the following three ways: location, discharges, and economic activity. For example, a project located on access roads or main roads can affect lake access. A project that has a stormwater collection system or injection wells can create impacts traveling off the site through surface or underground waters. Projects that influence economic activity on a lake can do so directly, as in the case of a boat dealership, or indirectly, by contributing to an increase in tourism, population, and sprawl. Lakes are difficult to escape; about 50% of Maine is in a lake watershed.

Reservoirs

Reservoirs are man-made bodies of water that control flooding, provide irrigation, or provide hydroelectric power. Although their properties and management issues are similar to those of lakes, artificial control of the water prevents the reservoir from carrying out all of the functions and processes of lakes. A power company or other entity that controls the water level in a reservoir will generally have an active role in the review and permitting process for development along it.

Ponds

Ponds are small natural or artificial bodies of water (see above regarding "Great pond"); most are an acre or less in size. Ponds are created in many commercial and residential projects for aesthetic reasons, to supply water for fire-fighting, or to contain and infiltrate storm water. Ponds built in streams or wetlands cause greater environmental harm than those built elsewhere, and are more likely to require specialized environmental permits and approvals.

The most popular type of artificial pond is a small farm or single-family residence pond excavated to below groundwater (Figure 7-3). The excavated soil may be used to reinforce an embankment around the pond. Excavated material should be kept out of wetlands and other bodies of water. Ideally, the site provides at least two acres of watershed drainage for every acre of pond at a depth of one foot (this is called one "acre-foot," and corresponds to a volume of about 43,560 cubic feet or 1,307 cubic meters). Deep ponds are good for fish, but are less favored by waterfowl who need the type of plants that grow best in shallow water (e.g., reeds, arrowhead, cattails, wild rice). The review process should include procedures

Figure 7-3. Diagram of pond construction. A constructed pond uses clay or silty clay at the bottom, or a plastic liner. These features should be profiled and detailed on a plan. The water supply, depth and size of the pond should correspond with its intended function.

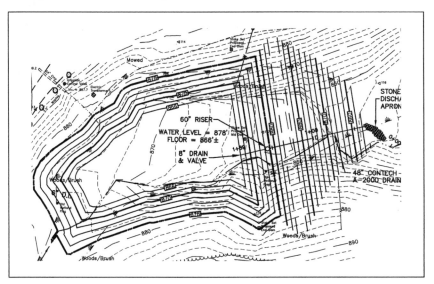

Figure 7-4. Sample checklist of potential problems and issues with ponds.

__ Local predation patterns. Will larger birds and animals eat the stocked fish?

__ Possibility and consequences of human and wildlife disease

__ Leech control

__ Siltation issues

__ Algae bloom from excessive nutrients, low dissolved oxygen turbidity

__ Public safety and access, need for fencing and posting

__ Agriculture—access for cows, horses, sheep and other animals

__ Skating and winter use

__ Owner liability for accidents

__ Control of nuisance plants such as purple loosestrife *(Lythrum salicaria)* and Phragmites reed *(Phragmites communis)*

__ Maintenance and removal of hazardous debris, annual cleaning

__ Rescue: plank near pond for emergency use if someone falls through ice, other measures as appropriate for management of the pond. Chemicals, nuisance plant removal, dredging, bank stabilization, stocking, and beaver control are a few of the factors for consideration. The plans might address safety issues such as access control and the removal of discarded machinery and hazardous material. Figure 7-4 presents a sample checklist that can be used in reviewing ponds.

Wetlands

To some people, all wetland areas are merely "swamps." However, there are all kinds of wetlands, including shrub swamps, wooded swamps, bogs, marshes, vernal pools, mud flats, flood-plains, and wet meadows. Floodplain areas, beaver flowages, slough, pot-holes, and other areas that hold water can also be wetlands. Knowing the type and nature of the wetland on a site helps in understanding the im-pacts of development plans and mitigation. Dif-ferent wetlands have their own soil and plant characteristics and distinct water conditions. For

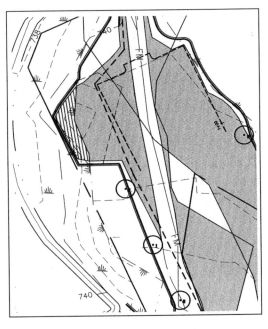

Figure 7-5. Annotated section of a development site plan with wetland. Protective buffers are at left side of plan.

example, bogs contain organic soils, with sphagnum cover. The distinctive pitcher plant found in bogs indicates still, shallow water.

If the wetland is "significant," or potentially significant, state permits may be required for certain activities in the wetland. The Army Corps of Engineers regulates some wetland activities. Projects subject to state or federal regulations have more information available for local review processes, but many small wetlands are only subject to local jurisdiction. Perhaps the biggest issue in reviewing wetlands is simply being able to recognize them, especially in the case of seasonally flooded meadows.

National Wetland Inventory Maps (NWI maps) show approximate locations of known wetland areas. The NWI maps generally have a ten percent or more error rate and omit some wetlands, especially small ones. Wetlands will often be described on site plans as "mapped" or "unmapped," or as a particular "class." Mapped wetlands usually receive a certain degree of protection by the state (Figure 7-5).

Many wetland areas appear to be dry fields most of the time, making identification and classification difficult (to say nothing of the frustrated owners who may not want to believe they have a wetland in the way of their project). Even the boundaries of obvious wetlands can be unclear as the soil gradually becomes drier. Accurate delineation of a wetland requires a soil scientist or other wetland expert. In general, three parameters describe wetlands: the water conditions (hydrology), soils, and the plant community. All three are examined as part of the wetland evaluation process.

Wetlands hydrology (the flow patterns and mechanics of water) is discernable through soil examination, monitoring wells, surface water conditions, vegetation, and records of flooding and high-water marks. Some wetlands may appear to be physically separate from each other but have underground hydrological connections.

If the project involves wetlands mitigation, look for planting details. When prolonged flooding or saturation reduces the oxygen to the point that only water-loving vegetation such as lily pads will prosper, the vegetation is described as "obligate wetland plants." If the saturation level is not too severe, some non-wetland plants ("facultive wetland plants") can thrive in wet areas. Plants that cannot survive in wetland areas at all are called "obligate upland plants."

Wetland soils (hydric soils) are saturated or flooded long enough during the growing season to develop anaerobic (lacking oxygen) conditions in the upper part of the soil layer. Usually, one or two weeks of saturation during the growing season is enough to create wetland soils. The microorganisms under these conditions further reduce the amount of oxygen. Peat and muck result when the decay of vegetation is slowed to almost a standstill as a result of anaerobic conditions. This build-up creates organic soils. Mineral soils are also found in wetlands (see Chapter 6).

Mitigation of impacts is determined by a wetland's values and functions. Wetlands are not simply a deterrent to development or

Figure 7-6. Wetlands mitigation checklist.

__ Does the site contain wetlands?

__ Have the wetlands been mapped?

__ Are the wetlands regulated? If so, by whom?

__ Are the wetlands linked to other wetlands?

__ Are the wetlands marked in the field?

__ What values and functions are provided by the wetland?

__ How will the project affect those values and functions?

__ Is the project placed to minimize impact?

__ Is the operation of the project compatible with the wetland?

__ Are mats and similar protective devices proposed for use during construction?

__ Is the weight of construction equipment in/near wetland minimized?

__ Is construction limited to the dry season?

__ Is there a plan to minimize vegetation removal?

__ Will topsoil be stockpiled for later use in backfilling and landscaping?

__ Are there details and plan for installing temporary measures and then monitoring and fixing them as needed?

__ Are there specified seed and mulch details and procedures?

__ Will construction plans be kept on the site?

__ Is the identity of the project supervisor clear?

__ Is there a plan for removal of materials and erosion controls when no longer needed?

__ Do the construction methods minimize impacts by reducing duration of construction?

__ Will a wetland be enhanced through techniques such as hand-weeding purple loosestrife? (A labor intensive method that is seldom effective, handpicking may work for tiny areas.)

__ Are there restrictions on uses that will help reduce impacts for the life of the project?

__ Will wetlands and buffers be flagged in the field?

__ Is there a suitable reclamation plan?

agriculture. Whether natural or man-made, they help control erosion by containing floods, stabilizing shorelines, and regulating stream flow. Wetlands, especially seasonal ones, improve water quality by diluting, filtering, and degrading sediment, bacteria, and other pollutants. Groundwater is replenished by filtered water from wetlands. Wetlands are arguably the most ecologically valuable wildlife habitat in northern New England. A healthy wetland produces its own creatures that eat mosquitoes and other pests, keeping the system in balance.

Mitigation options include techniques to minimize wetland impacts, the installation of buffer zones, enhancement activities, the managemement and protection of other wetlands, and impact fees (Figure 7-6). A developer may propose—or a regulatory agency may use—standard buffer widths, such as 100 feet or 50 feet. However, an individual evaluation of the adequate buffer size, based on the wetlands values and functions, the terrain, and the nature of the proposed project, may be good policy.

The plans should describe the type and degree of marking used in the field to delineate the wetland and to protect it during both construction and operation of the project. Planting plans and nuisance-weed removal projects can help wetland functions or at least reduce adverse impacts. Some uses of the wetland might mesh with the wetland function. For example, a vernal wetland providing emergent vegetation for bears in early spring may be safe for winter use by humans because that function is not impaired by trails for winter cross-country skiing.

Rivers

New England's rivers are legendary, and public policies reflect the high value we assign them. New Hampshire's Comprehensive Shoreland Protection Act (CSPA) includes most major rivers and river segments. The reference line for streams and rivers under the jurisdiction of the CSPA is the ordinary high water mark, defined as the line on the shore, parallel to the main stem of the river, established by the fluctuations of water. The high water mark is used in various states as the basis for measuring buffers and de-termining distances. Some rivers and river sections are actually "fourth order" streams and therefore not subject to the CSPA.

Protection for these rivers and river segments falls to local river management advisory committees and municipalities.

Most of Vermont's 5,264 miles of rivers and large streams are Class B waters suitable for multiple uses. As in Maine and New Hampshire, most urban areas have a major river or several small streams flowing through them. When mills stopped running on waterpower, rivers declined in perceived importance, becoming receptacles for tires, shopping carts, and septic discharges. By 1970, 60% of Vermont towns with sewer systems were discharging raw sewage into rivers. Other New England states were no better. The Clean Water Act and other federal and state environmental laws marked a reversal of this trend. Now, all municipal wastewater treatment systems provide at least secondary treatment and many town regulations provide guidance in reviewing projects on or near rivers. But there are still contentious water quality issues. Forgotten buried tanks continue to leak contaminants into ground water and eventually to rivers and streams. Antiquated septic systems continue to send untreated or partially treated septic waste into surface waters. Municipalities are the front line for review and protection of rivers.

If a proposed project is near a river, the watershed and water quality issues of the river should be documented. Review of local planning documents may help in understanding how the project complies with natural resource objectives, especially watershed management plans. A drainage basin (watershed) is the entire land area that collects water, sediment, particles, and dissolved materials in streams and brings them to a river and then to the sea. Most of the regional planning commissions in northern New England fit nicely into a particular watershed. Increasingly, watersheds are becoming a basic unit of planning and management for natural resources.

The shoreline is an integral part of the river. Without a shoreline, the river becomes a canal, a mere transporter of water. If there is no buffer, the shoreline is in danger. Perhaps the most critical issue in reviewing projects adjacent to rivers is the need for buffer zones. As complex environmental systems, rivers have many important functions and processes that should be protected from the impacts of development. For example, air quality, adjacent land uses, vegetation communities, wildlife, and a host of other development-

---

Figure 7-7. Sample buffer widths and water quality protective functions.

Distance	Function
50-100 feet	Soil erosion control for average or better slopes.
25-100 feet	Protective natural shrub vegetation along banks.
50-100 feet	Protect aquatic ecosystems.
200-600 feet	Wildlife management for hunting, migration, animal dens, foraging, nesting.
50-100 feet	Swimming and boating enjoyment.
100-200 feet	Privacy, wildlife viewing, canoeing, picnicking.

---

related actions affect oxygen, nitrogen, phosphorus, and other exchange processes.

The buffer zone should be derived from the potential and actual functions of the river. If a site-specific buffer has not been derived, then a general protective buffer might be appropriate. One approach is to determine width on the basis of soil erodability and slope. Another approach is for experts to determine all the functions of the buffer and derive a width necessary to achieve those functions (Figure 7-7).

Local reviewers may not have the resources for individual assessments, so standard buffers may be the only feasible choice for timely land use decisions. Whenever a buffer is chosen, it should be accompanied by a description of allowable activities within it. For example, some people might see a buffer only as an area in which no construction can occur and will mow or cut trees on the buffer. Yet such activity can almost totally negate the protective effects of the buffer.

Streams

New England's hundreds of tiny streams, totaling many thousands of miles, perform important recharge, pollution-flushing, aesthetic, habitat, and other functions. Small streams a few inches deep and a few feet wide can reveal significant amounts of native brook trout, aquatic insects and other life. Streams in villages and other urban areas continue their natural functions and become even more critical for water quality treatment and containment of stormwater runoff. Engineers can readily design plans to protect

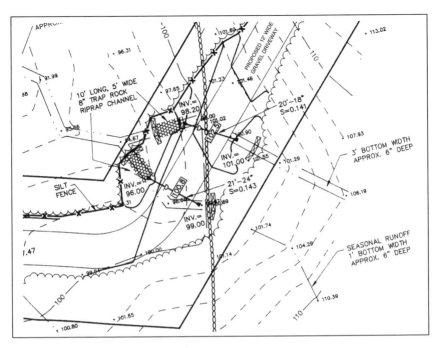

Figure 7-8. Typical stream crossing.

streams, using them to enhance the site, rather than viewing the streams as obstacles (Figure 7-8).

Some regulatory and planning schemes consider streams from the perspective of management zones: stream, middle, and outer. If possible, the stream zone extends 25 feet on either side of the stream bank, about the minimum distance needed to actually have a stream rather than a mere drainage swale or canal. Most cities allow only footpaths, storm-water utilities and other essential utility services in this inner zone. The middle zone is another 50-foot width of wetlands, floodplain, and steep areas that require protection to keep things from entering the stream. The outer zone is urban greenspace protected from septic systems, buildings, and other large disturbances. Most urban streams in northern New England have a truncated stream zone. Development is allowed in the middle zone, and there is no outer zone.

Urban runoff affects streams, particularly runoff from snow storage, parking lots and unmanaged drainages. Site design can prevent this through berms, grading, plantings, designated snow storage and removal schedules, and other measures.

Figure 7-9. Example of principal sources of groundwater contamination.

- Pumping well
- Gravel pit
- Waste lagoon
- Road salt stockpile
- Landfill
- Sewer/septic
- Hazardous waste injection well with leaky casing
- Agricultural spreading of pesticides and fertilizer
- Fuel & solvent tanks above & below ground
- Industrial supplies & waste, municipal waste
- Illegal or improper storage or disposal of materials

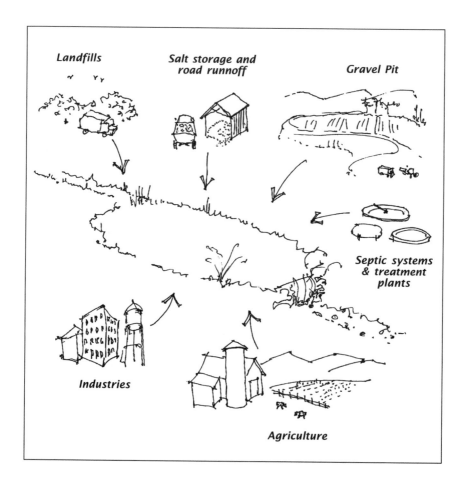

Groundwater

Over half the population of northern New England gets its drinking water from groundwater aquifers. Most of these aquifers are extremely susceptible to contamination (Figure 7-9). Fortunately, aquifers receive legislative protection, including groundwater classification systems, ambient groundwater standards, Best Management Practices (BMPs) for potential contamination sources, groundwater discharge permitting, withdrawal permitting, public education, and enabling language to assist municipal management of potential groundwater contamination.

Our aquifers occur in two main types: bedrock, and "unconsolidated deposits" of stratified drift or glacial till. Both are recharged by precipitation that percolates through upper layers of the soil profile until it reaches saturated soils. Recharge areas are identified and mapped for protection. Groundwater has discharge areas which surface in wetlands, streams, rivers, ponds, and lakes.

Groundwater flows so slowly that the rate is measured in feet per day or feet per year. This trait, coupled with other characteristics of flow, causes pollutants to spread gradually towards a discharge area. The flow time raises issues associated with monitoring and remediation. For example, a contaminant can enter the ground 200 feet from the Connecticut River, but might take anywhere from a week to 50 years to reach it, depending on the properties of the contaminant and on whether the soils are silty clay or more permeable sands and gravels. Existing conditions can be determined through a series of monitoring wells, but it is hard to detect an immediate cause and effect. Eventually, a contaminant can reach and eliminate a drinking water supply. MTBE, a fuel additive, is soluble enough to travel quite quickly. Clearly, applications for large projects or high-risk projects that could affect groundwater must include sufficient hydrological information to create engineering solutions that avoid contaminating water supplies and bodies of water. The monitoring plan must allow sufficient warning of potential contamination.

Major factors that contribute to the permanence of groundwater contamination are the lack of turbulence, lack of oxygen for decomposing bacteria, and cold temperatures that retard chemical reactions to break down contaminants. By the time the problem surfaces in a well or stream, it is usually too late for treatment other than preparation for the arrival of the rest of the plume. Potential risk cannot always be averted by modifications to a project. A groundwater supply may contain naturally occurring contaminants such as radon. In some cases, filters and other remedies can treat water. Elevated nitrate levels (a risk to young children and pregnant mothers) can be treated with filters. Otherwise, it is simply more effective to find another water supply or plan for connection to a municipal system. Prevention is best (Figure 7-10).

Figure 7-10. Sample checklist of contamination prevention measures.

__ Inventory of water resources in vicinity - underground and surface

__ Storage of hazardous materials

__ Use and removal of hazardous materials

__ Monitoring wells, schedule, reporting procedures for reporting and responding to spills

__ Inventory of existing conditions

__ Removal, treatment of existing empty tanks, contaminated soils

__ Listing and procedures for acceptable pesticide and fertilizer use for lawns, grounds, power line and road corridors, and fields

__ Drinking water well tests

__ Mapping of aquifers, springs and wells

__ Mapping of recharge areas and protection zones

__ Construction debris

__ Grading and location of roads

__ Stormwater discharge treatment systems

__ Vehicle washing areas and procedures

__ Berms or containment dams for potential groundwater threats such as spilled fuel

---

Identification and protection of aquifer recharge areas

Aquifer recharge areas for drinking water are known as "well head protection areas" (WPAs). These areas are mapped for surface water sources and for wells. Aquifers that are not currently used for water supply should be protected for future needs and to comply with the federal Clean Water Act. All of the New England states have wellhead protection programs in place. Protective zones are developed using site-specific hydrological information or general models. For example, the Vermont Department of Environmental Conservation developed a radius of 1000 feet for interim protection area delineation on non-community water supplies using an infiltration rate of 0.58 feet/year and a 25 gpm continuous pumping rate.

Maine WPAs have fixed radius circles of 300 feet to safeguard "non-transient" community systems and "non-transient non-community" systems serving less than 250 people. A system serving larger populations has a WPA radius somewhere between 300 feet and 2,500 feet.

New Hampshire uses a 150 to 400 foot "sanitary radius" for small public water supplies. The aquifer area may be much larger than the WPA, a consideration in reviewing potential impacts to the aquifer.

Salt

Roads, sidewalks, driveways, and parking areas require snow storage and removal and some means to melt ice, usually through salt and salted sand. A large project might have on-site storage of salt or salted sand, which should be kept on an impervious (concrete or paved) surface, covered, and away from wells, floodplains, and surface waters. Sodium from salt can cause a health risk if it gets into sources of drinking water.

We do not yet know the total effect that salt contamination has on our surface waters over the years. Salt attracts animals, which can then be poisoned through over-consumption—especially birds and other small animals—or struck by automobiles. Salt and salted sand should be spread only as needed for safe use of the project.

The loading areas for salt stockpiles should be impervious and subject to a cleanup procedure for spills.

Snow storage

Large projects involve snow storage and removal, particularly those with large parking lots or staging areas. Snow from parking lots contains salt, sand, trash, used oil, and other pollutants. If the snow is to be stockpiled on the site, then it should be in a designated place where it will not get into surface waters—a small stream or pond is quite vulnerable to the impacts of impure melting snow.

Commercial water withdrawal from surface waters

Ski areas, adapting to changing environmental and market conditions, withdraw water to make snow (Figure 7-11). Streams and rivers near ski resorts are in mountainous areas with steep slopes, shallow soils, and fragile structure vulnerable to ecological disturbance. Other commercial and agricultural projects—especially salmon aquaculture and blueberry farms—also withdraw water, sometimes in the face of controversy.

Figure 7-11. Options to reduce the amount of water withdrawn from streams and rivers for snow-making. These options may be applicable to other types of projects that withdraw water.

1) Step-down measures to decrease the pump rate when stream flow rate begins to drop.

2) Proactive measures to improve fisheries habitat in compensation: in-stream structures, stream-side vegetation, stream-bank stability, fishing/access easements, enlarging buffer strips and comprehensive buffer/stream management.

3) Construction of snow-making ponds to hold water, reducing the amount needed from the stream.

4) Gauging of the timing and cycles of water withdrawal, avoiding late summer and winter months.

5) Use of water-conserving pipes and pumps; use of effective monitoring and repair, reducing waste.

6) Maximum use of other sources. Gray water, stormwater, and other collected sources can supply snow guns.

7) Ski slope management strategies that preserve snow cover.

A minimum flow rate is needed to sustain the ecological functions of flowing waters. This rate can be determined by various methods. The federal government typically uses Aquatic Base Flow (ABF), by which rates are described in units of cubic feet per second per square mile (csm). The U.S. Fish and Wildlife Service, while recognizing the need for individual determinations of minimum flows, requires a flow rate of at least 1.0 csm for projects under its jurisdiction. This rate could be used as a starting point, but local conditions may dictate a higher minimum allowable rate.

Water withdrawal is described in terms of gallons per minute. Withdrawal rates vary, but may be in the range of several thousand gallons per minute. For development review, the issue is to determine the effects of the withdrawal rate on the flow rate and to optimize flow while meeting the needs of the project. If the water is too low, ice harms fish habitat and food sources. Fluctuating water levels also harm shorelines, dislocate plants from their roots, and scour the substrate. Fish become stressed from crowding when flows are excessively low. Key species, such as brown trout, are sensitive indicators of environmental change. Brown trout require shallow, fast water (riffles) for spawning and pools to survive the hot months of low flow in late summer.

Although key species are useful indicators of aquatic habitat quality, they do not necessarily reflect the quality of the riverine environment for all the forms of life—macro-invertebrates, insects, amphibians, fish, birds, mammals, reptiles, and plants—affected by water withdrawal. A consequence is that some development mitigative measures may be proposed to enable survival of key species, yet still not adequately mitigate for the impacts to other species (see Chapter 13).

"Optimal" flow rates are recommended to maintain the necessary flow rates for the least amount of risk to the habitat. A project that proposes water withdrawal should include optimal flow rates in its environmental impact assessment.

Where to go for more information

Connecticut River Joint Commissions. http://www.crjc.org/

Groundwater Protection Council. http://www.gwpc.org/

Maine Congress of Lakes Association. http://www.mainecola.org/

Maine Department of Environmental Protection, Bureau of Air and Water Quality. http://www.state.me.us/dep/blwq/

Natural Resources Council of Maine. http://www.maineenvironment.org/

New England Interstate Water Pollution Control Commission. http://www.neiwpcc.org/

New Hampshire Department of Environmental Services (DES). http://www.des.state.nh.us/.

New Hampshire Lakes Association. http://www.nhlakes.org/

A listing of New Hampshire rivers with management plans. http://www.des.state.nh.us/rivers/rivplans.htm

New Hampshire Rivers Council. http://www.nhrivers.org/

River Network. (1999). *The Clean Water Act: An Owner's Manual.* Portland, OR: The River Network.

Rural Community Assistance Program. http://www.rcap.org/

University of Maine Cooperative Extension, Water Quality. http://www.umaine.edu/waterquality/

U.S. Department of Agriculture, Soil Conservation Service. (1982). *Ponds - Planning, Design, Construction.* Washington, DC: USDA; GPO.

U.S. EPA Office of Ground Water and Drinking Water. http://www.epa.gov/OGWDW/

U.S. EPA, Surf Your Watershed. http://www.epa.gov/surf/

U.S. EPA Wetlands Information Hotline. www.epa.gov/OWOW/wetlands/wetline.html

U.S. Geological Survey. http://pubs.usgs.gov/products/books/index.html#circular

U.S. Geological Survey. Water Resources of New Hampshire and Vermont. http://nh.water.usgs.gov/

Vermont Natural Resources Council (VNRC). http://www.vnrc.org/water.htm

Vermont Natural Resources Council (VNRC). (1990). *River Regulations.* Montpelier VT: VNRC.

Vermont Water Quality Division, Agency of Natural Resources. http://www.anr.state.vt.us/dec/waterq/wqdhome.htm

Vermont Water Resources Board. http://www.state.vt.us/wtrboard/index.htm

Chapter 8
SOIL EROSION AND STORMWATER MANAGEMENT

Soils and erosion control

Responding to gravity, soil works its way downhill, into waters, and eventually to the sea. Soil travels mostly by surface water, but also by wind. Our job is to slow it down. Except in rare parts of some flood plains, soil erodes much faster than it gets replaced. Logging, mining, agriculture, and construction can all cause serious erosion. The thin soils, steep slopes, and numerous surface waters of northern New England make erosion a major concern.

Land subdivision may not directly involve construction, but it is usually the beginning of some type of earth alteration. Consequently, subdivision plans, as well as plans for commercial or industrial development, are usually reviewed for erosion impacts. Grading and soil erosion control plans are often included as separate sheets in larger projects, along with detail sheets depicting erosion control devices and their installation. Many municipalities and state reviewers do not accept development applications unless they include site-specific soil erosion control plans.

Federal regulations that apply to erosion control include the Clean Water Act, the Coastal Zone Management Act, National Pollutant Discharge Elimination System (NPDES) permits, and the Intermodal Surface Transportation Efficiency Act (ISTEA) requirements. Each state in northern New England has its own erosion control legislation and guides for creating (and reviewing) erosion control plans. In Vermont, for example, conformance with the prescriptions in the "Vermont Handbook for Erosion and Sediment Control on Construction Sites" are almost always made into boilerplate conditions in development approvals. State departments provide various specifications for sediment barriers, mulch composition, stone check dams, seed mixes, plantings to control erosion, best management practices (BMPs), and a host of other details and erosion control procedures.

Registered professional civil and environmental engineers prepare most stormwater and erosion control plans. Site technicians, foresters, soils scientists and other environmental professionals might also prepare these plans. Non-engineers may become certified as professionals in erosion and sediment control through registration with CPESC, Inc. (Certified Professional in Erosion and Sediment Control, Inc.).

The erosion control plan

An erosion control plan consists of much more than temporary devices such as silt fences and staked hay bale dams to reduce runoff during construction. The engineer begins with a comprehensive look at the site to derive measures that minimize the extent of the disturbed area, create erosion-resistant construction entrances, and stabilize as much exposed soil as possible. A good erosion control plan contains a location map, a site plan showing existing conditions, a grading plan and construction timetable, an erosion control site plan and timetable, and a narrative describing temporary and permanent erosion control measures.

Project application materials should describe the topography of the site and the proximity of sloping lands to water bodies. Local regulations usually specify specific contour intervals that guide applicants and reviewers when evaluating the potential for soil erosion ("two foot" and "five foot" are common specifications). The grading plan should show existing grades as well as all cut and fill areas and proposed final grades. It is the responsibility of the applicant to indicate what temporary erosion control measures will be taken during construction, such as silt fences, daily mulching, sediment basins, diversion ditches, etc. Permanent soil erosion control to stabilize the site after construction include paving, stone-lined ditches, rip-rap, grassed swales and seeding mixtures. If exterior site work occurs during winter months then the plans should include special winter erosion controls.

Although large projects have separate erosion control plans and details, smaller projects simply show erosion control devices and a narrative on the edge of the overall site plan or septic design plan.

For enforcement purposes, the review process typically includes some means of signing or marking the plans as exhibits for the file of record. Exhibits are often referenced in permit conditions. For a variety of reasons, erosion can occur despite the conditions of approval. These reasons include: failure to integrate the soil erosion plan into construction plans; flawed design; lack of site-specific conditions; catastrophic or unanticipated weather; or neglect. Proper development review reduces the odds of soil erosion.

We have reviewed many erosion control plans that merely incorporate the state manual by reference and little more. Research into erosion control programs around the country has found that many projects (more than half in some areas) had significant erosion control problems. Measures were never carried out or were never inspected or monitored despite discharges and other indications of erosion control failures (Brown and Caraco, 1997). Around the nation, many local erosion control programs exist only on paper (Brown and Caraco, 1996). However, northern New England cannot afford to have only paper programs. Significant local attention is paid to the prevention of erosion and the importance of reducing sediment loading to surface waters. If local plan reviewers lack the time or expertise to review plans, then problems are likely to occur at the site. Without an inspector, these problems can be missed or become costly to correct. Figure 8-1 depicts items to look for when reviewing erosion control plans.

Erosion control can be achieved through use of vegetation, installing structures and devices (including land form alteration), or some combination of the two (see Figures 8-2 and 8-3). Figure 8-4 lists items to consider in the use of vegetation for erosion control.

Structural methods include gentle re-grading of slopes, use of benches, berms, swales, and other constructed land features to interrupt and redirect flows. Level-spreaders, lined channels, sedimentation or retention basins, weir-covered drain inlets, sediment-filtering layers, culverts, floodgates, retaining walls, gabions, and rip-rap can be employed along with a host of other devices and mechanisms. Every intended device and technique for erosion control should be described in the plans so that the reviewer knows what they look like, who will use them, what maintenance they require, and how they work (Figure 8-5).

115

Figure 8-1. Checklist for erosion control plans and details.

__ Identify qualified individuals or firms.

__ Show site-specific, not generic, erosion control measures.

__ Show the limits of construction disturbance.

__ Minimize area of construction disturbance.

__ Stabilize swales and streams.

__ Refer to state/municipal erosion control standards, details, and objectives.

__ Phase construction to reduce amount of exposed land.

__ Mark and describe buffers (e.g., "undisturbed, naturally vegetated").

__ Show all staging areas for soil, equipment, temporary parking, and construction.

__ Designate topsoil stockpiled and surrounded by erosion control dams.

__ Describe how buffers, staging areas, critical areas, utilities, etc., will be flagged in the field.

__ Accommodate and protect steep slopes.

__ Depict typical erosion control devices, including silt fences, stone check dams, inlet protection, stabilized construction entrances, berms, swales, and mulch.

__ Provide a timetable and schedule for the application of erosion control devices.

__ Include winter erosion control plans (if site work continues after October 1).

__ Describe monitoring, especially during and after storm events.

__ Provide a routine maintenance schedule for erosion control devices.

__ Provide a system for reporting problems, inspections, and compliance with erosion control requirements.

__ Include contingency plan in the event an erosion control device or treatment fails.

__ Propose performance bond, irrevocable letter of credit or escrow agreement for large projects, or for sites where erosion control is a crucial aspect of the project.

__ Address removal of erosion control devices when they are no longer needed.

__ Provide plan and details for final site treatment, including rapid seeding, mulching, installation of permanent storm water drainage system and other devices for long-term erosion control and site stability.

__ Contain language for covenants or other agreements to maintain erosion control devices, storm water control systems, and other utilities.

Figure 8-2. Portion of a typical soil erosion control plan. The ritually executed hay bale with a stake through its heart has been ubiquitous on construction sites with gentle slopes. However, utilization of staked hay bale dams are no longer considered "Best Management Practices" (BMPs) because they are often installed improperly or in inappropriate areas, enabling silted runoff to bypass them easily. Stone check dams are a preferred alternative. Figure 8-2 shows a section of a typical erosion control plan. Figure 8-3 shows a stone check dam and other erosion control plan details.

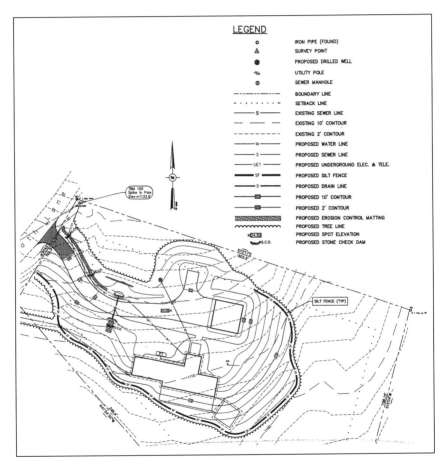

The Maine Department of Environmental Protection (MDEP) describes sediment barriers (a berm down-gradient from disturbed earth) in a manner suitable for erosion control plans and conditions. The guideline (Interim Guideline: Erosion Control Mix-Sediment Barriers, MDEP, 2000) suggests the use of sediment barriers in these instances:

117

Figure 8-3. Stone check dam and other erosion control details.

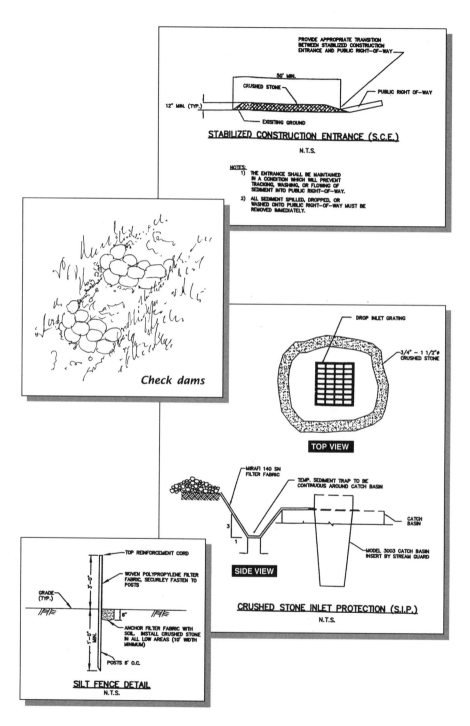

Check dams

Figure 8-4. Factors to consider in control of erosion through vegetation

- Minimal striping of an area to be cleared for construction.

- Temporary diversion of stormwater runoff.

- Ground preparation, such as tilling, application of topsoil, and fertilizer.

- Planting scheme; usually fast-growing indigenous species are preferred.

- Mulch or other stabilizing measure to protect and nurture.

- Compliance and repair scheme.

- Perspective or plan showing final appearance.

- An adjacent wetland and/or water resource is at risk from pollution or degradation by sedimentation.
- The capacity of storm drainage systems is compromised by sedimentation which may flood adjacent areas.
- The contributing drainage area does not exceed 1/4 acre per 100 feet of barrier length; the maximum length of slope above the barrier is 100 feet; and the maximum gradient behind the barrier is 50 percent (2:1). If the slope length is greater, additional measures such as diversions may be necessary to reduce that length.
- Sediment barriers cannot be used in areas of concentrated flows.
- Under no circumstances should erosion control mix sediment barriers be constructed in streams or in swales.

The MDEP directs installation of sedimentation barriers as follows:

- On slopes less than 5% or at the bottom of steeper slopes (<2:1) up to 20 feet long, the barrier must be a minimum of 12 inches high, as measured on the uphill side of the barrier, and a minimum of two feet wide. On longer or steeper slopes, the barrier should be wider to accommodate the additional flow.
- Along a relatively level contour. It may be necessary to cut tall grasses or woody vegetation to avoid creating voids and bridges that may enable fines to wash under the barrier through the grass blades or plant stems.
- At toe of shallow slopes, on frozen ground, at outcrops of bedrock and very rooted forested areas, and at the edge of gravel parking areas and areas under construction. These are good

119

locations for stand-alone use without reinforcement by other BMPs.

- Locations where other BMPs should be used include low points of concentrated runoff, below culvert outlet aprons, where a previous stand-alone erosion control mix application has failed, at the bottom of steep perimeter slopes that are more than 50 feet from top to bottom (i.e., a large up gradient contributing watershed), and around catch basins and closed storm systems.

Mulch and erosion control mix for site stabilization

Each state recommends erosion control mix along with sugges- tions for its use. Depending on the site and the time of year, the mix might be winter-hardy conservation rye and other grasses, or it might be a fast-growing summer cover. The MDEP describes a conglomerate of organic matter at neutral or near neutral pH, for

Figure 8-5. Grading plan and section, labeling cut and fill and final grade. Proposed new contours are shown by a heavy solid line, contours to be altered are shown by a broken (dashed) line and unchanged contours are shown by a thin solid line.

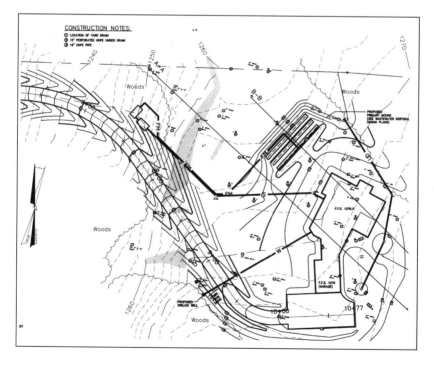

Town:	Department:	Tracking number:

Project Number_____Project Name:_____ Location: _____

Inspection date: _____Time:_____ Inspected by: _____ Signature: _____

Others present at visit: _____

Describe site conditions:_____

Note any immediate erosion control problems on site: _____

REASON FOR INSPECTION

___Permit condition ___Complaint (#:___) ___Periodic monitoring ____Request of permittee

___Stage of construction completed ___Request of _____ ___Other:_____

STAGE OF CONSTRUCTION

___ Pre-Construction Conference ___ Rough Grading ___ Final Grading ___ Clearing and Grubbing

___ Building Construction ___ Final Stabilization/Closure/Reclamation

INSPECTION CHECKLIST

Yes No N/A   Is all exposed land stabilized through seed, mulch, filter fabric or other approved means?

Yes No N/A   Are soil stockpiles adequately stabilized with seeding and/or sediment trapping measures?

Yes No N/A   Does the permanent vegetation provide adequate stabilization?

Yes No N/A   Are all required sediment traps and barriers in place?

Yes No N/A   Are earthen structures stabilized for perimeter sediment trapping measures?

Yes No N/A   Are sediment basins and stormwater detention ponds installed in the proper fashion and location?

Yes No N/A   Are finished cut and fill slopes adequately stabilized?

Yes No N/A   Are on-site channels and outlets adequately stabilized?

Yes No N/A   Is there adequate inlet protection for all operational storm sewer inlets?

Yes No N/A   Is there adequate lining, stabilization and outlet protection for all stormwater channels?

Yes No N/A   Is in-stream construction approvable and does it minimize channel damage?

Yes No N/A   Are anchored temporary stream crossings installed where applicable?

Yes No N/A   Has the water course been stabilized after completion of in-stream construction?

Yes No N/A   Are utility trenches stabilized properly?

Yes No N/A   Are soil and mud being kept off public roadways at intersections with site access roads?

Yes No N/A   Have all temporary erosion control structures been removed when no longer needed?

Yes No N/A   Is the sediment being periodically and appropriately removed from traps, barriers and channels?

Yes No N/A   Are properties and waterways downstream from development adequately protected from erosion and sediment depositing from increases in peak stormwater runoff?

Recommendation/Action:_____

Figure 8-6. Erosion and sediment control checklist for site inspection.

use on the sediment barriers, and it gives suggestions for maintenance of the sedimentation barriers and other BMPs (MDEP, 2000).
MDEP's installation suggestions are suitable for erosion control plans
and for crafting permit conditions. Other sources exist—there is no
reason for a project application to improperly address erosion control
or for municipalities not to have a good set of guidelines for erosion
control review.

Compliance monitoring

Communities may need to retain an engineering consultant to
review stormwater and erosion control plans and to check field
conditions. State agencies and the soil and water conservation district
may also review plans. Some municipalities require applicants to
cover the cost of retaining experts for the town's review. The road
commissioner, the code enforcement officer, or the planning and
zoning assistant may serve as the inspector. The project approval
process may require periodic compliance reports and certifications.
Most municipalities and reviewing agencies have their own checklist,
perhaps similar to Figure 8-6.

Stormwater management

Stormwater runoff damages property, contaminates drinking
water, endangers aquatic wildlife habitats, threatens public health by
carrying pollutants such as road salt, removes topsoil, and causes
flooding. The terrain characterizing northern New England makes
the consequences of inadequate stormwater management readily
apparent. Controlling stormwater on-site typically involves collecting
it through ditches and catch basins and directing it toward a detention
basin for partial treatment and timed release.

Most northern New England states have adopted their own
stormwater management policies and manuals, influenced by the
EPA's implementation of the Phase 2 Stormwater Rule requirements
in the Clean Water Act (CWA 4029(p)95). The Phase 2 Rule,
administered as a National Pollutant Discharge Elimination System
(NPDES) with a five-year permit life, placed additional mandates
on the states' stormwater discharge regulations.

The Clean Water Act requires each state to list waters that do
not currently meet the state's water quality standards. Many urban

and suburban watersheds are impaired principally due to stormwater runoff, which adds refuse, road salt, grease, fertilizers, oils, and other pollutants. Rural and mountainous areas are more likely to have problems with agricultural or silvicultural stormwater runoff. Under the Phase 2 Rule, communities with public stormwater conveyance systems (e.g., ditches, culverts, pipes) that discharge into surface waters must submit stormwater management strategies to the state. The strategies (BMPs) detail how to prevent pollutants such as bacteria, phosphates, nitrates, and sediment from running off the land and entering water.

Maine provides a Stormwater Best Management Practices Manual. New Hampshire posts its Innovative Stormwater Treatment Technologies Best Practices Manual on the Internet. Vermont has a Stormwater Management Handbook. These guides are helpful but do not replace the need for specific on-site designs and plans.

Stormwater management and development plan review

What does compliance with local, state and federal stormwater regulations mean for the developer of a construction site? Wording in local zoning or subdivision regulations may not help answer this question. Review of stormwater runoff may be left to the discretion of the local review board where there is no over-arching state review. If a project will disturb at least five acres, the Phase 2 Rule requires review of an erosion and sediment control plan by the state's water

---

Figure 8-7. Contents of a stormwater management plan.

· Site plan showing drainage and discharge locations.

· Grading plan showing locations of soil erosion control measures and design of stormwater control measures.

· A description of the site and of the pollution BMPs.

· A narrative describing the details of how stormwater will be managed.

· A copy of the Declaration and Covenants for any homeowners association charged with the long-term maintenance of the stormwater system.

· A copy of a Notice of Intent (NOI) for Construction Activity filled out and submitted to EPA's NOI Processing Center or to the state if it has assumed authority for administering the federal stormwater rules.

---

quality division. The Phase 2 rule also requires permits for stormwater discharges from construction sites that disturb between one and five acres of soil. A federal Multi-Sector General Permit covers many private industrial and commercial facilities such as factories, garages and treatment plants. Applicants must develop pollution prevention plans to segregate stormwater from potentially polluting substances (Figure 8-7).

Where to go for more information

Brady, Nyle C. and Ray R. Weil. (2001). *The Nature and Properties of Soils,* 13th edition. Prentice Hall: Upper Saddle River NJ.

Brown, Whitney E. and Deborah S. Caraco. (1996). *Task 2 Technical Memorandum: Center for Watershed Protection.* Silver Spring, MD.

Brown, Whitney E. and Deborah S. Caraco. (1997). *Muddy water in – muddy water out?: A critique of erosion and sediment control plans.* Watershed Protection Techniques, Vol. 2, No. 3: 57: 68.

Center for Watershed Protection. http://www.cwp.org/stormwater_mgt. htm

Geobopological Survey. http://www.geobop.com/paleozoo/Soils/ NewEngland/

Maine Association of Professional Soil Scientists. http://www.mapss.com/

Maine Department of Environmental Protection. (2000). *Interim Guideline: Erosion Control Mix-Sediment Barriers,* Augusta, ME: MDEP .

Maine Department of Environmental Protection. (1995). *Stormwater Best Management Practices Manual for the State of Maine.* November 1995. Augusta, ME: MDEP.

Natural Resources Conservation Service. http://www.nrcs.usda.gov. National Soil Survey Center. http://www.nssc.nrcs.usda.gov. Soil Quality web page. http://soils.usda.gov/sqi/

Natural Resources Conservation Service, Maine. http://www.me.nrcs. usda. gov/

Natural Resources Conservation Service, Vermont. http://www.vt.nrcs. usda.gov/soils/soil_home_page.htm

New Hampshire Association of Consulting Soil Scientists. 15 Muchado Drive, Barrington, NH 03825-3818.

New Hampshire Department of Environmental Services. (2002). *Innovative stormwater treatment technologies best practices manual.* Concord, NH: NHDES, May 2002. http://www.des.state.nh.us/wmb/was/manual/

New Hampshire Department of Environmental Services. (2001). *Managing Stormwater as a valuable resource: A message for New Hampshire communities and water suppliers.* Concord, NH: NHDES. September 2001. http://www. des.state.nh.us/desguid.htm.

Rockingham County Conservation District. (1992). *New Hampshire. Stormwater Management and Erosion and Sediment Control Handbook for Urban and Developing Areas in New Hampshire.* Concord, NH: NH Department of Environmental Services, Soil Conservation Service (now the Natural Resources Conservation Service). http://www. nh.nrcs.usda.gov/Soil_Data/

Rural Community Assistance Program (RCAP). http://www.rcap.org/

Society of Soil Science of Northern New England, USDA, Natural Resources Conservation Service, 27 Westminster St., Lewiston, ME 04240-3531

Soil Science Society of America. http://soilslab.cfr.washington.edu/S-7/

Vermont Agency of Natural Resources. (1987). *Vermont Handbook for Soil Erosion and Sediment Control on Construction Sites.* Department of Environmental Conservation, Water Quality Division. http://www.anr. state.vt.us/dec/waterq/stormwater.htm

Chapter 9
TRAFFIC

Arguably the most contentious of development issues, traffic tests the mettle of reviewers and neighbors alike. Roadway development requirements and design standards are specified in many subdivision regulations and zoning bylaws. Access permits (entrance permits in Maine) are required for driveways and connections to state roads. Traffic permits are required for large projects in the northern New England states. For example, Maine issues a "traffic movement permit" for projects generating 100 or more passenger car equivalents at peak hour (Title 23, Chapter 13, Section 704).

Traffic impacts should be examined from the following three perspectives: internal traffic (within the project), local external factors (entrances and exits, area capacities) and regional impacts (networks,

Figure 9-1. Sample checklist for applications involving transportation review or permits.

- Sufficient sets of legible, stamped plans of all project development, including landscaping, drainage, erosion control, impact mitigation, and details.
- Detailed transportation construction plans.
- Location map of the site, showing local roadways and state rights of way.
- Written description of the current and proposed use of the property.
- Estimate of the amount of traffic to be generated by the project, and the basis for this prediction.
- Discussion of access management, including efforts to use secondary rather than primary road access, maintain effective flow of traffic and the safety of state roadways, and meet the needs of the project.
- Discussion of how the project complies with local and regional plans.
- Evidence that the regional transportation system can accommodate the traffic levels associated with the project.
- Background data used in traffic study.

Figure 9-2. Sample checklist for transportation construction plans.

· Date, title, scale, north arrow.

· Legal descriptions of land, monuments and bearings.

· Labels and descriptions for state and other rights of way.

· Dimensions from the centerline of proposed roads to connection with existing roadways and public rights of way.

· Contours (existing and proposed), drainage boundaries and flow patterns.

· Existing and proposed drainage facilities.

· Drainage calculations, including stormwater runoff rates, paths, and treatment.

· Demonstration of project compliance with local comprehensive drainage plans.

· Copies of permits and approvals already obtained, including local municipalities, state agencies, watershed organizations, and U.S. Army Corps of Engineers.

· Street construction layout with dimensions and radii.

· Street cross-sections or contours and profile grades.

· Development schedule.

· Peak hour vehicle trips.

· Parking areas, including overflow parking and snow storage, as needed.

· Driveways and street access.

· Turn lanes/movements, sight distances, and geometrics.

· Number of residential units and/or square feet of commercial or industrial building space.

· Pedestrian and non-automotive traffic details.

---

regional patterns). Although people tend to feel strongly about traffic issues, particularly in their neighborhoods, the collection of data for a traffic study should be objective and scientific. Although the main focus of most traffic studies is on vehicles, the study should address pedestrian access and all the modes of transportation potentially affected by the project.

Traffic is a broad subject in impact assessment and development review. Our goal is to help reviewers make sense of basic traffic information by presenting some of the more common terms and concepts. If the traffic study is too complicated, reviewers who are not traffic engineers may have a hard time interpreting it. While there are (and must be) expert engineers to review and interpret complex studies, for public decision-making such reports must be well-written and intelligible. A good start is with a checklist of required contents in a traffic report (Figure 9-1) and in accompanying transportation construction plans (Figure 9-2).

Terms and concepts

Access

Municipalities usually have specifications for road width, grade, and construction details (Figure 9-3). If the road is a private road, it may still have to meet town specifications, making it accessible to emergency service providers and covering the possibility that the municipality may be asked to assume responsibility for the road in the future. Most municipalities have definitions for different types of streets. For example:

"**Place**" refers to a short, local road, usually a cul-de-sac, with one travel lane and an 18-foot paved or gravel width. Average daily traffic for this road is likely to be under 100 vehicles.

"**Lane**" is a short, local road that may connect several places and lead to a longer street. This road may be paved 20 feet wide and carry up to 400 trips per day.

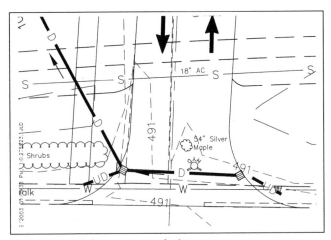

Figure 9-3. Highway access design.

"**Subcollector,**" also a local road, serves more than one parcel and leads to a larger street. A subcolleter might carry up to 1,000 trips per day.

"**Collector**" is a major residential or commercial street with two or more travelways and 36 feet in paved width, serving at least several thousand vehicle trips per day.

"**Arterials**" and "**Freeways**" are even larger public highways that convey traffic from one community to another and to major interstate highways.

Review of project entrances and exits falls under the auspices of a larger "access management" scheme in a municipality or region. Access management is the planning, design and implementation of land use and transportation strategies that control the flow of traffic between the road and surrounding land (Humstone and Campoli, 1998). Benefits of access management include postponing or preventing costly highway improvements, improving safety conditions along highways, reducing congestion and delays, providing property owners with safe access to highways, promoting desirable land use patterns, and making pedestrian and bicycle travel safer.

Average Daily Traffic

Average Daily Traffic (ADT) is determined by taking the total number of vehicles passing a point or segment of a highway facility in both directions annually and dividing it by 365. ADT is not the best basis for highway design for high volume facilities because there are seasonal, weekly, daily, or hourly variations. However, ADT is adequate for low and moderate volume facilities where only one or two lanes are needed.

Design Hourly Volume

Design Hourly Volume (DHV) is usually the 30th highest hourly volume for the design year, commonly 20 years from the time of construction completion. At resorts and other locations with high seasonal fluctuations in traffic, a different DHV may be selected. DHV is the total traffic in both directions of travel for two-lane rural highways. The directional distribution of traffic during the design hour (DDHV) is used in designing highway improvements when the road has more than two lanes or has major intersections.

The percent of ADT occurring in the design hour (h) may be used to convert ADT to DHV. To do this, use DHV = (ADT)(h).

Density

Density is the number of vehicles occupying a given length of lane or roadway in a specific time. Density is reported in terms of vehicles per mile.

Flow

Flow (q) is defined as the number of vehicles traversing a point of roadway per unit time (vehicles per hour), calculated by multiplying density (vehicles/mile) times speed (miles/hr). Flow does not give a complete picture; we do not know if the vehicles are large trucks or passenger cars.

Handicap accessibility and pedestrian flow

The Americans With Disabilities Act (ADA) and other federal regulations govern most handicap accessibility issues, especially parking spaces, sidewalk and crossing design, and wheel chair maneuverability. Sprawl and other forces are causing New England to experience traffic increase, the consequence of which is political pressure to improve the flow of vehicles. Sometimes the cost is not borne by automobile drivers but, for example, by pedestrians, who suffer reduced time to get across intersections. Unfortunately, many of our intersections and crosswalks seem to have been designed for athletic youth. However, good pedestrian flow means accommodating the least able of our population of users, just as good highway design means being able to accommodate vehicles that might be older and without brand-new tires. Consequently, there are benefits in looking beyond minimal ADA requirements.

Level of Service (LOS)

Calculating the Level of Service (LOS) is one means of evaluating traffic conditions. The LOS provides a qualitative measure based on ranges in three critical variables: average travel speed, density, and maximum service flow rate. The relationship between speed, flow, and density depends on the prevailing roadway segment and traffic conditions. LOS reads like a grade report, with A being the highest and F representing "Failing." Despite driver frustration with delays, low levels may still be safe; LOS is not quite the same thing as a safety evaluation or rating. In addition to providing standards and guidelines for design in its Highway Capacity Manual (2002), the Transportation Research Board defines levels of service (see Figure 9-4).

Figure 9-4. Level of Service (LOS) definitions.

- **LOS A**: Free flowing traffic. Drivers, passengers and pedestrians have high level of comfort and convenience. Each individual is unaffected by other users and is able to maneuver about safely.

- **LOS B**: Stable flow. Other users are noticeable because there is some affect on behavior. Less freedom to maneuver than in level A.

- **LOS C**: Still in the range of stable flow, but actions of others may significantly affect the individual. Safe speeds are determined by factoring in the behavior of others. Maneuvering about is more difficult and the levels of comfort and convenience decline.

- **LOS D**: High density traffic but still with a stable flow. Maneuverability and speed are restricted by other traffic. Users experience low levels of comfort and convenience. Pedestrians have difficulty at times with crossings.

- **LOS E**: Operations are at or near capacity level and are often unstable. All speeds are greatly reduced. Maneuverability is significantly hampered. Levels of comfort, convenience and safety are dangerously low and frustration runs high.

- **LOS F**: Forced or breakdown flow occur because the system is over capacity. Lines queue up and move in stop-and-go waves that are highly unstable. This can be considered a failing grade for the intersection or road segment. Service breaks down and gridlock can occur.

A single intersection can have various levels of service for different turns and maneuvers, and at different times of the day or year. Road segments also experience a wide range of LOS—for example, when motorists enter the Green and White Mountains during leaf peeping season or when motorists leave a ski resort or cruise through North Conway, New Hampshire or Freeport, Maine.

An analysis of a road segment Level of Service includes: number of vehicles, travel speed, travel time, ability to pass, and quality of life factors. Intersection delay can be observed in the field to help determine or verify the Level of Service. Computer simulation programs such as HCM-94, NCAP and ICU can be used for comparative analysis. The 1994 Highway Capacity Manual methods, ICU, the 1985 Transportation Research Board Circular 212 method, or newer methods can be used, depending on the preference of the reviewing agency.

Parking

Parking space dimensions and parking lot configuration depend on the local or state jurisdiction. Parking generation programs and manuals help in determining the number of spaces recommended. Usually, there will be a ratio of number of spaces per square foot of space, per number of restaurant seats, per hospital bed, per dwelling unit, etc. If local regulations require nine spaces per 1,000 square feet, this would equate to a 3:1 parking ratio.

Each project should be carefully examined for adequacy of the parking. It may help to keep in mind that the parking should be capable of supporting complete use of the site. If the parking spaces are not required to be in place prior to full build-out of the project, expect future problems with compliance and enforcement. Allowing minimal parking for a project designed as ski condominiums may lead to a problem later on when those condominiums become primary homes. Similarly, a project intended as senior citizen housing becomes locked into this low-traffic use if areas for future parking needs were not reserved. The parking should also be adequate during winter conditions when snow piles block spaces.

Different parking configurations and patterns exist, each with its advantages and disadvantages. For example, angled parking is convenient to pull into and out of but takes up more room than right-angle parking. A parking lot is not just a place to park cars, it is a place to be able to walk safely. A bare-bones parking lot may have little to commend itself except a low initial cost. Landscape and pavement islands that calm and regulate vehicle flow may be seen as a big expense but they soon pay off in safety and aesthetics (and therefore may increase business through improved customer satisfaction). The review of parking lot plans can involve many other issues, such as: stormwater runoff, pedestrian flow, handicap accessibility, snow storage, municipal services, vehicle circulation, lighting levels, public safety, aesthetics, landscaping, physical infrastructure, and neighborhood character.

Peak hour traffic

Peak hour traffic congestion, typically a major problem in most cities and suburbs, is becoming a problem in small towns. A traditional response has been to widen streets and take other steps to increase flow capacity, which in turn increases peak hour traffic volume. A new response, "traffic calming," seeks control though other means.

Road geometry

Much of road geometry—the configuration and engineering of highways—consists of the application of common sense. For example, a new intersection does not belong on a curve, and a road should seldom be intersected at anything other than a right angle (perpendicular). A four-way intersection has more potential collision points than do two T intersections separated by several hundred feet or more.

We can assume engineers want to do the right thing and design good, safe roads according to regulatory and professional standards. The American Association of State Highway and Transportation Officials (AASHTO) "Greenbook – A Policy on Geometric Design of Highways and Streets" provides commonly used standards.

Figure 9-5. Road profile.

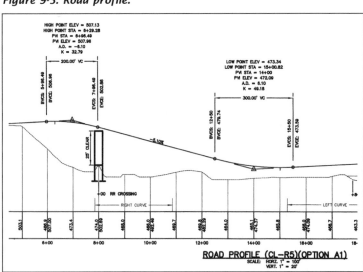

Occasionally, several factors are at work, especially in the interior of a site, that constrain good road design. These factors may be the result of client needs, site conditions, or economics. Part of making adequate findings for traffic reviews may involve delving into these factors in order to properly evaluate mitigation.

Road geometry includes road profiles. The road profile exaggerates the vertical dimension, usually by a factor of five or ten, in order to make the diagram readable (Figure 9-5). Engineers are used to this dimensional shift, but it may require explanation for better public interpretation.

A street cross-section shows how the road meets municipal or state design specifications. It may be matched to a profile drawing. A typical road might have a 12-foot travel way on either side of the centerline, plus four-foot shoulders. The road is crowned to facilitate drainage, and is built on top of a layer of crushed gravel and bank run gravel.

Signal warrants and impact mitigation

The complexity of transportation issues makes it important to plan ahead for traffic improvements such as signals, signal upgrades, and alternative transportation (Figure 9-6). A new project can accelerate the need for improvements. The state transportation agency will have already determined the conditions for which changes are warranted. The challenge for local review boards is deciding the role of the

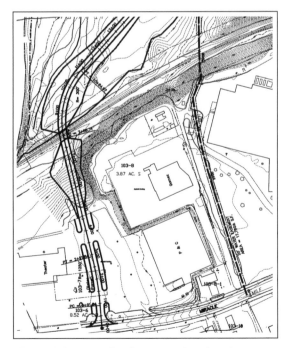

Figure 9-6. Example of proposed pedestrian walkway and bike path, with specifications noted.

135

project developer in meeting the costs of these changes. To do this, first look at thresholds for signal warrants. Then look at what level of the increased traffic is attributable to the project. If there are mechanisms for making contributions to traffic improvements (e.g., capital funds, escrows, regulatory authority), a mitigation scheme can include a schedule. The goal is to have a plan at the outset so that an acceptable solution to an anticipated problem is available.

Corner sight distance

Sight distance is the minimum distance needed for a motorist to safely make maneuvers such as entering a road or turning. A rule of thumb is to allow at least 11 feet of corner sight distance for each mile per hour of posted speed limit. For example, if the posted speed limit is 45 miles per hour (mph) then the minimum corner sight distance is 11 x 45 = 495 feet. A driver waiting to pull onto the road must be able to see vehicles approaching in all directions when they are at least 495 feet away. The risk of accidents increases if corner sight distance is less than 495 feet. Sight distance is affected by the following: posted road speed, road grade, road alignment, road condition, weather, and the speed at which drivers tend to drive. Traffic engineers use a percentile speed, commonly the 85th, as a factor in determining sight distance requirements.

Sight distances for an existing intersection are measured from the point where an automobile driver would be sitting while waiting to pull out on to the road. For a proposed intersection, the sight-distance in either direction is measured from the centerline of the intended access at a height of 3.5 feet (about 1 meter) above the proposed road surface. Even if the access is for a gravel pit and will be used primarily by trucks, it should still have safe sight distances for passenger vehicles. It would be a tragic irony if an accident were to occur during a site visit for a traffic review—if the visit includes examining sight distances or other highway conditions, two people or more should assist and they should be wearing bright orange.

Stopping sight distance

"Stopping sight distance" is a function of many things, including: road conditions, grade, weather, type of vehicle, tire condition, high-

Figure 9-7. Example of a traffic improvement when traffic grew to a level at which increased signalization or a turning lane was warranted.

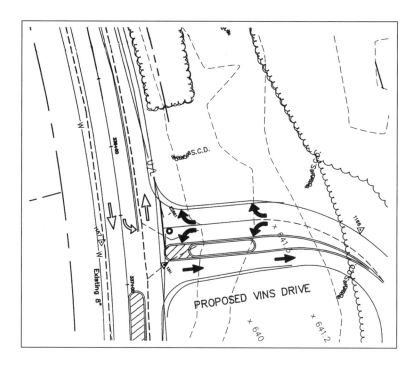

Figure 9-8. AASHTO sight distances chart for a flat, two-lane highway. These distances will vary depending on the conditions.

Metric				US Customary			
Design speed (km/h)	Stopping sight distance (m)	Intersection sight distance for passenger cars		Design speed (mph)	Stopping sight distance (ft)	Intersection sight distance for passenger cars	
		Calculated (m)	Design (m)			Calculated (ft)	Design (ft)
20	20	41.7	45	15	80	165.4	170
30	35	62.6	65	20	115	220.5	225
40	50	83.4	85	25	155	275.6	280
50	65	104.3	105	30	200	330.8	335
60	85	125.1	130	35	250	385.9	390
70	105	146.0	150	40	305	441.0	445
80	130	166.8	170	45	360	496.1	500
90	160	187.7	190	50	425	551.3	555
100	185	208.5	210	55	495	606.4	610
110	220	229.4	230	60	570	661.5	665
120	250	250.2	255	65	645	716.6	720
130	285	271.1	275	70	730	771.8	775
				75	820	826.9	830
				80	910	882.0	885

way alignment, driver reaction time, and speed of travel. AASHTO uses a brake reaction time of 2.5 seconds in its calculations. Some experts have suggested that a longer time of 3.5 seconds should be used to accommodate the elderly with diminished visual, cognitive, and psychomotor capabilities (Gordon, McGee, and Hooper, 1984).

The AASHTO calculations for stopping sight distance (SSD) assume a driver eye height of 3.5 ft (1.06 meters). Populations of elderly drivers tend to have lower driver height but the 3.5' figure is the standard for passenger vehicles.

Traffic count

The number of vehicles per hour is a consideration in designing traffic improvements. Anyone can conduct a simple traffic count to get an idea of basic conditions or to check on the data reported in a permit application. The count should begin at least a half-hour before the peak hour, the hour that likely has the maximum volume of traffic. In most areas, maximum traffic volume occurs during the morning and evening weekday rush hours—usually between 6:30-9:30 AM and 5:00-7:00 PM.

Local planning board members can do their own count using hatch marks or a clicker to record each vehicle. Most traffic counts involve two directions of flow—east/west or north/south. Record traffic flow separately for each turning movement, distinguishing between cars and trucks. A "truck" is any vehicle with 6 or more tires or 3 or more axles; everything else is a "car." Sometimes

Tale from the Trenches

QUESTIONING THE CONSULTANT

I was present at a planning commission meeting when an applicant's engineer told the board that the traffic report was very complicated and since they were just a little town board, they'd never understand it! I was outraged. As a consultant to the board, I suggested to the chair that either the engineer make a presentation so that the board could understand it, or that the board require the engineer to pay for another engineer's interpretation of the study. Consequently, the applicant's engineer withdrew that study and prepared a more suitable report.

separate counts are made of school buses and pedestrians. If counting, be sure to wear bright garments and stay well back from the flow of traffic.

Vehicle trips

A vehicle trip refers to one way—if you drive out and back, that is two trips. A rule of thumb is that the average household of today generates ten trips per day. This ensures that residential subdivisions and condominiums have adequate road design.

The traffic study

A traffic study, sometimes called Traffic Impact Analysis (TIA), addresses the ability of transportation systems to accommodate a development project. Although focusing on drivers and pedestrians, the study should include any and all modes of transportation associated with or affected by projects, such as: private roads, airports, boat docks, canals, railroads, trucks, highways, parking lots, bicycle lanes, pedestrian paths and sidewalks, bus routes, trolleys, emergency service vehicles, handicap accessibility, and helicopter pads (see Figure 9-9). In transportation planning, changes in demand can occur rapidly while changes in physical infrastructure tend to occur slowly, hence the need for strategic planning. Fortunately, traffic analysis is a well-established field and most large projects are the subject of traffic studies. However, regulatory review may not focus on all of the transportation-related aspects of a project. A comprehensive framework to understand transportation studies and plans will help ensure that all relevant elements are addressed. All aspects related to the movement of goods, services, and people are potential transportation issues.

A transportation system has a number of components for consideration in the site plan and its supporting documentation including: infrastructure (vehicles, roads, pathways, canals), resources (financial, energy, environmental), flow (levels of service, volumes), demand (desire or need for services), and land use (adjacent, population levels, employment, neighborhoods).

Figure 9-9. Outline of a typical traffic study

1. Introduction
   · Purpose of the study
   · Regulatory requirements
   · Objectives of the study
   · Authors of the study

2. Description of proposed project or development
   · Transportation uses and requirements
   · Densities
   · Location of project and access points
   · Project phasing schedule for build-out or operation

3. Background conditions
   · Limits of the study area (including rationale)
   · Land uses, current & anticipated (based on approvals and on growth projections)
   · Site access for roadway system, pedestrian, other
   · Existing traffic volumes and conditions (including LOS)
   · Transit and other traffic services
   · Any other transportation modes not previously addressed

4. Projected traffic volumes
   · Site traffic for each analysis year or phase
     · Trip generation: Sources and types
     · Trip distribution
     · Modal splits (e.g., passenger, truck, pedestrian, mass transit)
     · Trip assignment to the roadway network
   · Roadway traffic (for each analysis year or phase)
     · Method of projection
     · Area transportation plan
     · Trends and growth rates
     · Assignment of the projected trips to the roadway network
     · Total traffic volumes (for each analysis year or phase)

5. Traffic analysis
   · Site access capacity and level of service
     · Intersection of access road or driveway
     · Roadway
     · Regional
   · Site circulation and parking
     · Turning radii
     · Access widths, grades, surface
     · Emergency vehicles access
     · Loading and storage facilities (including snow loads)

   · Traffic safety
     · On-site: design standards, sight distances, widths, grades, geometry
     · Off-site: accident data, sight distances, speed limits, configurations and standards

6. Improvement analysis
   · Improvements to accommodate background (base) traffic conditions

(figure continued next page)

· Improvements to accommodate base and site traffic
· Alternative improvements
· Funding and other mechanisms for improvements
· Evaluation

7. Findings
· Site accessibility
· Traffic impacts—include noise, aesthetics, air pollution, runoff, and safety
· Necessary improvements
· Compliance with local codes or accepted standards
· Traffic safety

8. Recommendations
· Site access plans
· Internal circulation
· Roadway improvements: on-site, off-site, phasing

Figure 9-10. Checklist of questions for reviewing traffic studies.

__ Can you tell who prepared the study and what qualifications they used?

__ Is the traffic study easy to understand? If not, this indicates something is wrong with the study or the way in which it is reported, and should be a red flag about the project.

__ Is the data used in describing the background or the impacts available?

__ Does the study address accommodations for people with disabilities?

__ Does the accident history from official records mesh with local perceptions of how traffic in the area works?

__ Are the data from appropriate sources?

__ What computer model was used (e.g., TMODEL 2 or HiCAP 2000) and what assumptions were made in the model?

__ Have yearly trends, seasonal, weekly and daily variations been accounted for?

__ Are design hours, peak use and other terms clearly defined and applied in the study?

__ Are there diagrams and tables to accompany the narrative?

__ Is mass transit addressed?

__ Is the treatment on access management adequate for a project of this size?

__ Are the recommended improvements drawn on site plans?

__ How do the recommendations mesh with local planning, zoning and subdivision ordinances?

Figure 9-11. Smart growth transportation site planning principles. (Based on Growing Smarter, Best Site Planning for Residential, Commercial and Industrial Development, The Vermont Forum on Sprawl, 2001.)

- Provide options for bicycle users, pedestrians, and others not in automobiles.

- Provide connections to adjoining development and regional on and off road networks.

- Link internal roads with an existing road network to improve connectivity and accessibility instead of designing dead-end streets and cul-de-sacs.

- Include sidewalks along at least one side of the street in urban and suburban areas. Rural subdivisions should incorporate a network of on and off-road paths.

- Create recreational paths to provide access to regional trail networks and open land.

- Use traffic calming devices in high-density areas, such as: innovative road geometry (round-a-bouts, T-intersections), abrupt changes in road alignment, short blocks, on-street parking, raised crosswalks, street trees, and "bump-outs."

- Incorporate lanes or service alleys that provide rear or mid-block access to commercial lots and parking areas.

Figure 9-12. Sample traffic calming devices.

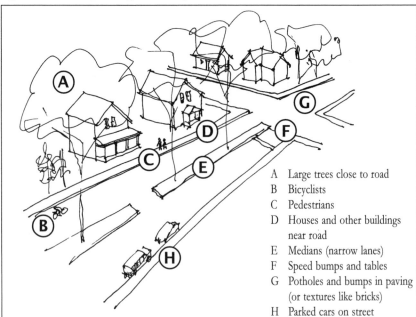

A Large trees close to road
B Bicyclists
C Pedestrians
D Houses and other buildings near road
E Medians (narrow lanes)
F Speed bumps and tables
G Potholes and bumps in paving (or textures like bricks)
H Parked cars on street

Figure 9-13. Transportation questions to ask about the overall project.

· Has the project minimized dangerous traffic movements?

· Does the project meet the standards in the current edition of the Institute of Traffic Engineers' Transportation and Traffic Engineering Handbook, and other local sources of authority as adopted by resolution?

· Does the project road configuration encourage or discourage through traffic?

· Does the project provide for pedestrians, mass transit, non-motorized vehicles and other modes of transportation?

· Is there a mechanism in place to ensure that future traffic device and road improvements caused in part by the project can be constructed or installed when they are warranted?

· Does the project design have an efficient site layout for access, parking, and open space?

· Will the project promote sprawl or poor growth management?

· How does it affect overall quality of life for the area?

· Are the rights of way in place to serve the needs of the project?

· Does the project adversely affect adjacent public investments? If so, to what degree?

· Are the layout and intended use compatible with adjacent and nearby properties?

· Does the project conserve and protect valuable natural features and amenities?

· Does the project interfere with the efficient provision of public services?

· Does the design preserve existing healthy and long-lived trees whenever possible?

· Do proposed drainage facilities promote the use and conservation of natural watercourse and patterns of drainage?

· Has the project been designed to reduce alterations to existing topography in environmentally sensitive areas?

· Are the proposed plantings compatible with the climate of the region and micro-climate conditions on the site?

· Do signs fit with local requirements and standards and do they avoid causing a distraction to motorists?

· Will the signs minimize obstructions and hazards to pedestrians?

· Does the project provide adequate and unrestricted access for fire and emergency vehicles?

Tale from the Trenches

FILENE'S DEPARTMENT STORE

When a Filene's department store was proposed for downtown Burlington, Vermont, the state review board found that the project would cause a drop from D to E in level of service at a nearby intersection— a difficult problem to remedy in a busy downtown. After reviewing the traffic study and taking testimony, the review board approved the project with conditions to "calm" traffic, including these good examples of urban growth management:

• Pro-rata participation in any future shuttle or mass transit service for the Burlington waterfront;

• A multi-modal transportation plan to manage transportation for employees;

• A north-south pedestrian/bicycle connection through the proposed development;

• Cooperation with the City of Burlington to place bicycle racks along the pedestrian/bike path;

• Cooperation with the city to design signs and place them at the pedestrian/ bike path intersections and path/street intersections.

Questions to ask about the traffic study

Some reviewing boards use a checklist of questions (Figure 9-10). Others go a step further because they make formal findings of fact and conclusions of law in which specific questions must be addressed.

Reviewing for smart growth

Patterns associated with sprawl include the proliferation of curb cuts in linear areas characterized as "strip development," and large expanses of pavement in the form of new, wide roads and parking lots. The center of town may have a coherent network of streets, but newer development in suburban areas has looping roads with dead-ends and no connection to adjacent parcels or roadways. During site plan review, regulatory boards have opportunities to guide the project in a direction that minimizes curb cuts, places parking to the rear of buildings, reduces the width of internal roads, and encourages transportation options, especially in the form of public transit (Figures 9-11 and 9-12).

Nobody knows the local traffic situation better than the people who live in the community. The locals are the ones who have to live with poor growth management; others just have to drive through it. Efficient traffic planning and the use of good traffic impact review techniques are key tools in ensuring proper growth patterns. All projects that contribute to traffic should receive a careful review of all potential issues including design, aesthetics, safety, erosion and runoff, water pollution, time and cost for mitigation, pedestrian flow, alternative transportation, and sprawl (Figure 9-13).

Where to go for more information

Conservation Law Foundation. (1998). *Take Back Your Streets: How to Protect Communities from Asphalt and Traffic*, 3rd edition. Conservation Law Foundation. January 1998. http://www.clf.org/pubs/street1.htm

Ewing, Reid. (1996). *Best Development Practices*. Planners Press, Chicago, IL: American Planners Association.

Federal Highway Administration. (1995). *Highway Traffic Noise Analysis and Abatement*. Washington DC: FHA. http://www.nonoise.org.

Federal Highway Administration. (2001). *Highway Design Handbook for Older Drivers and Pedestrians*. Publication No. FHWA-RD-01-103. Washington, DC: U.S. Department of Transportation, Federal Highway Administration. http://www.tfhrc.gov/humanfac/01103/coverfront. htm#toc

Fehr and Peers Associates, Inc. Traffic Calming (a web-based guide). http://www.trafficcalming. org/

Humstone, Elizabeth and Julie Campoli. (1998). Access management: an overview. *Planning Commissioners Journal*, No. 29. http://www.plannersweb.com/access/accintro.html

Institute of Transportation Engineers (ITE). http://www.ite.org/

Keller, Richard C. and Joe Mehra. (1985). *Site Impact Traffic Evaluation (S.I.T.E.) Handbook*. Washington, DC: U.S. Department of Transportation, Federal Highway Administration, Office of Highway Planning. http://ntl.bts.gov/DOCS/380.html

Maine Department of Transportation. http://www.state.me.us/mdot/

Maine Department of Transportation. (1994). *Access Management, Improving the Efficiency of Maine Arterials.* Augusta, ME: Maine Department of Transportation.

Mozer, David. (2002). *Calculating Multi-Modal Levels-Of-Service: Pedestrian, Bicycle, Transit, Buses.* International Bicycle Fund. http://www.ibike.org

New Hampshire Department of Transportation. http://webster.state.nh.us/dot/

Transportation Research Board. (2000). *Highway Capacity Manual 2000,* 4th edition. Washington, DC: National Cooperative Highway Research Program. http://www.highwaycapacity.com/

Vermont Agency of Transportation. http://www.aot.state.vt.us/

Vermont Forum on Sprawl. (2001). *Growing Smarter, Best Site Planning for Residential, Commercial & Industrial Development.* Burlington, VT: VFOS.

Wick, Jim. (1995). *A State Highway Project in Your Town? Your role and rights: A Primer for Citizens and Public Officials.* Burlington, VT: Preservation Trust of Vermont.

Chapter 10
MUNICIPAL SERVICES

The impacts imposed on northern New England municipalities by new development relate not only to the ability of town sewer, water, emergency service, and highway departments to do their jobs, but also to the bottom line: how much will the project cost the town in terms of revenues versus expenses? The former is a matter of review by the various departments, with the developer making needed revisions on the plans or complying with permit conditions. The latter is a mathematical exercise and one that ranges from non-existent in small towns—with limited development volume, services, and review processes—to a complex and mandatory analysis for large projects undergoing detailed state or municipal review. The impacts of new development on the school system are often considered alongside or as part of the impacts on municipal services; both kinds of impacts are linked fiscally and are included in a comprehensive fiscal impact analysis.

Development that sprawls, requiring extensions of electric utility lines or extensions of municipal sewer and water services, is especially expensive to a community in the long run. The community desirous of economic activity is placed in a difficult position: should it provide municipal services to serve development for the immediate revenue benefits, despite the costs? The best strategy is not to use the regulatory review processes as a primary defense against poor land use, but to develop a comprehensive master plan for the community that incorporates growth management goals and that gives meaning and perspective to the local zoning and planning reviews. Such reviews enable the community to do a better job evaluating the potential impact to municipal services. Three things need to match up: the plan, the regulations, and the application of both in the review and monitoring of development, beginning with accurate fiscal assessment.

A general rule of thumb is that residential units cost more for municipal services than they provide in revenues (thus, they are "tax negative"). Commercial and industrial projects are much more likely to bring in more revenue then they cost (i.e., be "tax positive"). Houses that are not primary residences may be an exception. They may not cost much in terms of services, but there is always the possibility that second homes convert to primary housing, when it is too late to re-calculate their impacts. A primary residence may cost $400,000 or more before the break-even point is reached on revenues versus cost of municipal services. Fortunately, a primary residence need not be occupied by the wealthy before its occupants can be a community asset. After all, the members of any primary household can join local boards, enlist in volunteer groups, hold bake sales, and make other contributions in ways difficult to capture by a simple cost-benefit comparison of municipal services and tax revenues.

Departmental review

In small towns without municipal sewer and water or solid waste services, departmental review typically consists of the road commissioner and fire chief passing through the planning and zoning office and taking a look at development plans prior to a hearing or administrative approval. Most towns, regardless of size, have road standards. Review includes making sure the development project complies with them. Towns may have recreation departments that work with the developer early on in the process.

Cities and large towns have formal departmental review processes in which a technical review committee consisting of department heads looks over the project after the planning staff accepts it for review, and before it goes to the planning or zoning board. The town departments scrutinize site plans for impacts to the services listed below, providing an opportunity to work out problems before the public hearing. The more these elements are addressed up front, the speedier the approval and the fewer the attached conditions.

Fire and emergency

Fire and emergency departments are primarily concerned with the adequacy of the water supply and with access to the project.

Figure 10-1. Fire and emergency department questions for project review.

- Are there sufficient hydrants?
- Do the hydrants have sufficient flow?
- Are hydrants spaced appropriately?
- If there is no municipal water, is there a cistern or pond?
- What is the static water supply volume?
- Will there be sufficient water supply for any required sprinkler systems?
- Is the water supply accessible by fire department apparatus?
- What is the expected fire flow for the structures? (Dictated by a NFPA standard.)
- If a fire pond is needed, who will maintain it?
- Are fire lanes necessary?
- Do lanes comply with acceptable NFPA standards?
- Is the road sturdy enough to carry water tankers and ladder trucks?
- Are the roads wide enough for emergency vehicles?
- Are the radii of the curves large enough?
- Are there any dead-ends or cul-de-sacs?
- Will normal traffic patterns adversely affect department response to this project?
- Are houses and commercial buildings clearly identified?
- Does the proposed occupancy present any special hazards?
- Are special resources required beyond those for typical commercial or residential use?

Issues usually addressed by these departments are summarized in Figure 10-1.

Police

Police review is very similar to fire and emergency review, with a bit more emphasis on security (Figure 10-2).

Sewer and water

The sewer and water departments may ask questions similar to those in Figure 10-3.

Figure 10-2. Police department questions for project review.

Commercial projects

- Does the driveway go all the way around the project?
- Is the lighting sufficient?
- Is visibility of the site good or do various features obscure it?
- Is the access safe for vehicles?
- What are the public safety and security issues?

Residential projects

- Is the access visible and safe?
- Are the stop signs adequate?
- Can the local highway system handle the project traffic?
- Are the streets wide enough?
- Is lighting adequate for public safety?
- Does the landscaping create a public safety problem (a particular concern in urban areas)?
- Does the project create a nuisance or other potential liability for community safety?

Figure 10-3. Sewer and water department questions for project review.

- Do the plans show profiles of proposed sanitary and storm sewers?
- Are the locations and size of existing sewer and water lines on the plans, including hydrants, gates, valves, and "blowoffs"?
- Are location and width of all sewer and water line easements shown?
- Are details of proposed connections with existing water supply services shown?
- Are required pipe widths and materials for water and sewer lines shown?
- Are service connections shown at the required minimum depth?
- Are conforming manholes shown?
- Will horizontal and vertical separation for sewer and water lines meet standards for design and installation?
- Do pump stations adhere to appropriate standards regarding materials, capacity, and force-main velocity?

Figure 10-4. Highway department questions for project review.

- Has the developer included construction drawings of all proposed public improvements?

- Are typical cross sections of the proposed grading, roadways and sidewalks shown?

- Are all proposed culverts shown?

- Are there provisions for collecting and discharging stormwater drainage?

- Do the plans show locations, widths, and names of existing and proposed roads, drives, streets, easements, and alleys?

- Do the site plans include the location and dimension of existing driveways, curb cuts, parking lots, loading areas, or any other vehicular use area?

- Are the locations of all existing access points shown?

- Do the plans include the location and dimensions of existing and proposed sidewalks, bike paths, pedestrian walkways, and other paved surfaces?

- Is the road geometry shown (including straight lines, the deflection angles, the radii, the length of curves and central angles of all road curves)?

- Are minimum sight distances based on the most current edition of the AASHTO standards?

- Are the roadways within the maximum allowed road grades?

- Are the required road widths met?

- If appropriate, is there a prospectus describing the management organization or homeowner's association?

- Is there a disclosure statement to be given to all prospective purchasers detailing responsibility for plowing and maintenance services?

Highway

Highway departments review development projects against the town's road standards or public works specifications (Figure 10-4).

Solid waste

If the project involves creation of solid waste as a result of construction or operation, what are the impacts? Are they addressed? If there are staging areas for dumpsters, these should be shown on the site plan along with landscaping and fencing details. If the project involves handling solid wastes, there might be designation of a

151

handling area with an impervious surface, possibly with a berm to protect the surrounding ground from contamination. The site design should also be able to accommodate the providers of solid waste and recycling services. If the proposed roadway can accommodate a large fire truck, it can be presumed adequate for a waste hauler.

Fiscal impact analyses for municipal and educational services

The options for development of any given parcel of land have varying impacts on a town's costs and revenues. Some projects may require expensive sewer and water line extensions, stress school capacity, and provide few tax rewards to the town. Other projects may "pay their own way" or even offer beneficial revenue consequences. The fiscal impacts of subdividing a 100 acre parcel into 5 ten-acre estate lots with 50 acres of preserved open land will vary significantly from a different proposal for the same parcel featuring a mixture of 30 small single family lots, 75 townhouses with an affordable housing component, and little open space. The location of the development affects its demand for services—compact developments are less expensive consumers compared to sprawled or low-density development of the same size. Infrastructure services (primarily sewer, water lines, and roads) do not cost as much in compact areas.

People, especially those living in high-growth areas, may want to know the financial burdens or benefits of development projects. An estimate of these fiscal issues, called a fiscal impact analysis, plays a large role in a review board's consideration of a project. To save money in assessing fiscal impacts, some review boards require developers to undertake the analyses at their own expense. These studies may be complex; developments that may be expensive to the town may also confer non-financial benefits such as preserved open space, bicycle and pedestrian trails, and affordable housing.

Every fiscal impact analysis includes a comparison of costs and revenues to determine fiscal impact. The total cost consists of operating costs and capital costs. The total revenue from a project consists of real property revenues and operating revenues (taxes and fees). The net fiscal impact is the result after subtracting the total costs from the total revenues.

The Fiscal Impact Handbook (Burchell and Listokin, 1978) describes methods to estimate the cost of growth, based on municipal services. The Per Capita Multiplier Method can be used if the municipal infrastructure is closely related to the service demand because the average costs of providing services to current users are a good approximation of the costs to provide similar services to future users. The annual town report gives the total residential and nonresidential service costs—the town budget. The Case Study Method is more suited to dynamic, changing communities, and examines the effects of population change on specific municipal and school district costs and revenues. A traditional marginal cost approach, the Case Study Method estimates the effect of population change on municipal and school district costs, but is better tailored to the individual conditions of municipal services, such as an aging sewer treatment plant that will need replacement. Another method, "Comparable City," estimates costs based on how similar projects have fared in similar municipalities elsewhere.

Fiscal impact analyses are only as good as the assumptions and information on which they are based. Disagreement over how many students will be generated by a new residential subdivision comes as no surprise; there is plenty of room to argue about community type, housing type, and new householder type. Fiscal studies often neglect the secondary impacts of development, such as residential growth induced by commercial development. There may be over-lapping jurisdictions and service districts, making it hard to apportion true service costs. The effects of a project on neighboring towns may be missed unless the regional planning commission weighs in. Despite the lack of consistently applied standards for the conduct of these studies, they remain the best tools found thus far to estimate the fiscal impacts of new development.

Schools

If the development is a residential subdivision or involves residential units, then the number of school-age children can be estimated from knowing the type of unit. Some regional planning commissions, such as Upper Valley-Lake Sunapee in New Hampshire (and including a small part of Vermont—a nice example of inter-

153

state collaboration) have generated their own estimates of children per type or unit, and figures are available for the general New England region. A project might not involve any dwellings or lots but might be large enough to attract new town residents and students and therefore burden the local school system. At some point, an estimate of the total number of school-age children is generated, either directly from the project or indirectly from the employment needs of the project, or a combination of these factors. State education departments have requirements for schools that can be interpreted on a per-child basis to get an idea of the amount of capital improvements necessary to accommodate an increase in children. If it can be shown that the local schools are at or near capacity then there may be a request for mitigation.

Windham's valuation in tax year 2001 was $1,141,981,640. The remaining amount of the six-year school bond ($4,666,425) was calculated to be $4.09 for each thousand dollars of assessed value. The tax assessor determined the average value for new construction of housing at $387,000 per single-family dwelling. Since each new house will pay taxes, a credit should be deducted from the $4157.86 in capital costs (Figure 10-5). The credit attributed to each new house based on future taxes is ($4.09/thousand) X $387,000, giving a total of $1582.83. Given a credit for past payments calculated to be $32.40, the total credit becomes $1582.83 + $32.40 = $1615.23. The net cost for new school construction costs per new single-family dwelling is therefore: $4157.86 - $1615.23 = $2542.63. An impact fee of $2542.63 could be assigned to each new house.

Figure 10-5. Example of impact fee calculation in 2001 for educational services in Windham, NH. (From: Procedure for the Computation of Impact Fees for the Windham Public School District, Revision Year 2001, Town of Windham, Windham, NH.)

The average number of new students per new single family dwelling	0.535
The average space (sq. ft.) required per student in Windham	104.74
The average cost of new school construction per square foot	$74.20
0.535 pupils / unit X $74.20 per sq. ft. X 104.74 sq. ft. / pupil	= $4157.86 capital cost per dwelling unit

Mitigation of burdens

If a town or state review board finds that the costs of a particular development exceed the revenues, mitigation is reasonable. The two most common methods are impact fees and use of a phasing schedule for construction. Some municipalities, fearful of losing a tax-revenue development to an adjacent community, may waive mitigation and may even grant tax concessions. Such an approach may be legitimate in encouraging in-fill development in a depleted downtown, or to encourage a struggling local business, but it is easy for developers to play one community against another in seeking tax increment financing or other creative venues to save developer costs.

Impact Fees

Impact fees are not new tools; the concept has been around ever since passage of the Federal Standard Planning Enabling Act of 1922. Impact fees can ensure that new development pays a proportionate share of the municipal and educational services it generates. In Vermont and Maine, towns must have certified comprehensive plans and a capital budget before they can impose impact fees. New Hampshire towns must have a capital improvement program before they can impose fees, and they cannot use impact fees for open space acquisition.

Naturally, impact fees are not popular with developers and others who, although creating a small subdivision or building a residence, do not consider themselves to be developers. However, impact fees stand up well to court challenges when correctly applied by the municipality. The courts do scrutinize whether those who pay the costs are the ones who benefit from the expenditures. If the direct connection between the fee and the benefit cannot be drawn, the fee looks more like a tax and therefore may not be legal if not applied to the entire community. Many regional planning commissions have prepared guidance documents on impact fees for their constituent communities. The state planning offices are also good sources of information and advice.

While impact fees are usually imposed on the local level, Vermont's Act 250 authorizes state review boards to impose impact fees if they find that a project will cause an unreasonable burden on the ability of a local government to provide municipal, governmental or educational services. To legally impose impact fees, a town must adopt an impact fee ordinance. The state must also have enabled this process by statute, as have all the states in northern New England (Figure 10-6).

Figure 10-6. New England States with Statutory Authority for Impact Fees

Maine	Me. Rev. Stat. Ann. Title, 30-A § 4354
Massachusetts	1989 Mass. Acts 716
New Hampshire	N. H. Rev. Stat. Ann. § 674: 21
Rhode Island	R. I. Gen. Laws § 44-22. 4-1
Vermont	Vt. Stat Ann. Title 24, § 5200-5206

Towns may adopt an impact fee ordinance for a particular service, such as recreation, or they may adopt an ordinance that applies to a spectrum of services, including schools, transportation and sewer services (Figure 10-7).

Figure 10-7. Facilities that can be financed by impact fees.

- Streets
- Bridges
- Street trees and median landscaping
- Wastewater treatment and distribution facilities
- Solid waste disposal facilities
- Placing utilities underground
- Parks and recreation facilities
- Fire protection facilities
- Harbors, ports and airport
- Mass transit facilities
- Storm drainage facilities
- Law enforcement facilities
- Public art, museums, and cultural resources
- Capital improvements to schools.

Documentation for the establishment of impact fees should be kept current and reviewed about every five years. An impact fee may be used to offset debt service payments on an already constructed school or for future expenditures on a public park and recreation area. Different fees may be imposed on the developer for single family dwellings than for multi-family dwellings. Transportation impact fees may be based on the number of peak hour vehicle trip ends a project generates and may be tied to explicit road improvements. Sewer costs are a big concern for many communities—Saco, Maine, has no fees other than for combined sewer overflow (CSO) and sewer impact.

Most impact fee ordinances contain provisions for refunds, waivers of the fee, and for a credit of in-kind contributions. Maine law is typical; it requires that: 1) the fee must be reasonably related to the developer's share of infrastructure costs attributable to the project; 2) the fee must be separately held by the town and expended only for the attributable costs; 3) the fee must be supported by the town's comprehensive plan; and 4) the fee must be refunded if not used. Fees are easier to swallow if they recognize differences among types of projects. For example, Scarborough, Maine, assesses a school impact fee of $3,200 for a single family dwelling, $1,600 for an "affordable housing unit," $1,200 per unit for a two-family dwelling, and $800 per unit for a multiplex or for a mobile home in a mobile home park.

Phasing

Communities can partially offset the costs of growth by phasing residential development—this allows a gradual absorption of impacts on municipal and educational services. The review board can exercise discretion to control the pace at which developments are constructed, or the town can enact regulations to limit the number of units to be built per year. The phasing schedule can be a condition of approval that stipulates the maximum number of housing units built in any given year, or the maximum number of commercial or residential lots to be developed. Constraints such as reduced sewer capacity may drive the need for phasing. Phasing schedules can vary depending on whether a development offers a desired benefit to the town, such as affordable housing, preservation of open space,

157

or recreational trails. Once phasing is agreed upon, the site plan should label the project phases and a narrative or set of approval conditions should explain how the phasing works.

Building Caps

Building Caps are regulations that towns can impose to limit the number of building permits issued over a specific period of time. This allows towns to pace growth, often temporarily, to allow for planning, to prevent town services from being overburdened, and to construct infrastructure. Under many state statutes, building caps may be imposed only to protect public health, safety or welfare. Accordingly, towns must identify the reason for imposition of the building cap, such as expanding facilities for schools or crafting zoning regulations that conform to newly enacted comprehensive plans. Improperly managed building caps frustrate the community and inhibit efforts to provide affordable housing and meet other growth-related needs.

Temporary Building Moratoria

This technique is used only in the most dire circumstances where communities are concerned about the pace of growth relative to their ability to provide services or to plan. In Maine this measure is allowed for only up six months, and only when a serious over-burdening of public services is anticipated that could result in significant public harm. (Me. Rev. Stat. Ann.T. 30-A §4356). In New Hampshire, moratoria are permitted for up to one year but only in unusual circumstances. (N.H. Rev. Stat. Ann § 674:23 (2000)). Towns in Vermont can adopt interim bylaws for a maximum of two years with a possibility for a one year extension. This measure does not provide for a complete moratorium on building but does allow time for the town to conduct studies, adopt comprehensive plans and zoning regulations, and install capital improvement programs.

Where to go for more information

Benfield, F. Kaid, Matthew D. Raimi, and Donald D.T. Chen. (1999). *Once There Were Greenfields*. New York, NY: Natural Resources Defense Council.

Brighton, Deb and Jim Northrup. (1990). *The Tax Base and the Tax Bill, Tax Implications of Development: A Workbook*. Montpelier, VT: Vermont League of Cities and Towns, Vermont Natural Resources Council.

Burchell, Robert W. ed. (1990). *Development Impact Analysis*. Piscataway, NJ: Center for Urban Policy Research.

Burchell, Robert W., et al. (1994). *Development Impact Assessment Handbook*. Washington, DC: Urban Land Institute.

Burchell, Robert W., et al. (1985). *The New Practitioner's Guide to Fiscal Impact Analysis*. Piscataway, NJ: Center for Urban Policy Research, Rutgers – the State University.

Burchell, Robert W. and David Listokin. (1995). *Land Infrastructure, Housing Costs and Fiscal Impacts Associated with Growth – The Literature on the Impacts of Sprawl vs. Managed Growth*. Cambridge, MA: Lincoln Institute of Land Policy.

Burchell, Robert W. and David Listokin. (1978). *The Fiscal Impact Handbook – Estimating Local Costs and Revenues of Land Development*. New Brunswick, NJ: The Center for Urban Policy Research.

Maine Municipal Association. http://www.memun.org/

National Association of Homebuilders. (1997). *Impact Fee Handbook*. Washington, DC: Home Builder Press.

Natural Resources Defense Council. (2002). *Developments and Dollars: An Introduction to Fiscal Impact Analysis in Land Use Planning*. New York, NY: Natural Resources Defense Council. http://www.nrdc.org/cities/smartGrowth/dd/ddinx.asp

Nelson, A.C., (Ed). (1988). *Development Impact Fees*. Chicago, IL: Planners Press.

New Hampshire Municipal Association. http://nhmuni.home. virtualtownhall.net/nhmuni_home/

Roddewig, Richard J. and Jared Shalaes. (1984). *Analyzing the Economic Feasibility of a Development Project*, PAS Report No. 380. Chicago, IL: American Planning Association Planners Book Service.

Ross, D.H. and S.I. Thorpe. (1992). Impact fees: practical guide for calculation and implementation. *Journal of Urban Planning and Development 18(3)*, 106-118.

Siegel, Michael L., Jutka Terris and Kaid Benfield. (2000). *Developments and Dollars: An Introduction to Fiscal Impact Analysis in Land Use Planning*. New York, NY: Natural Resources Defense Counsel

Snyder, T.P. and M.A. Stegman. (1986). *Paying for Growth: Using Development Fees to Finance Infrastructure*. Washington, DC: Urban Land Institute.

Vermont Forum on Sprawl. (2002). *Community Investments In Smart Growth: A Decision-Maker's Guide*. http://www.vt.sprawl.org

Vermont League of Cities and Towns. http://www.vlct.org/

Chapter 11
AESTHETICS

"Quality of life" is a major reason why we choose to live in northern New England. Aesthetics is a major contribution to tourism and the green image essential to our economy. Land use laws, in keeping with the picturesque image of the quaint New England village and rural landscape speckled with cows, provide for consideration of how a project will look. In part because of the controversial and subjective nature of aesthetics, project reviewers must pay particularly close attention to the regulations themselves, rather than to individual tastes or whims. Issues commonly addressed under aesthetics include landscape plans, signage, architecture, and lighting—the visual quality of both the project and its surroundings. Dust and noise can also be aesthetic concerns when they do not rise to the level of health hazards. However, these issues are addressed in separate chapters, as are historical and cultural resources, and odor.

The landscape has physical aspects (land and water, vegetation, structures) and cultural aspects (uses, values, expectations, regulations). We all make conscious or unconscious assessments of the physical conditions in a setting. Effective discussion of these assessments calls for a shared vocabulary of visual terms and concepts. For example, some towns include a viewshed[1] analysis in their town plan to identify scenic areas on a map. Such an analysis can be part of visual impact studies by developers and consultants (Figure 11-1). Computer simulations, GIS mapping, photomontages, drawings, narratives, assessment forms, demonstrations in the field, and physical models can all be used to show the environmental setting with or without the project.

---

[1] Viewshed generally refers to the landscape or scene that can be surveyed from a single point (viewpoint) or a corridor (such as a highway). Usually, a viewshed is considered to have scenic qualities.

Figure 11-1. Viewshed, showing the area that can be seen from a particular location. The photograph orientation and number ("photoangle") orients to an accompanying photograph.

Visual Impact Assessment (VIA)

A review board might ask for a Visual Impact Assessment (VIA, sometimes called Visual Impact Analysis) to help it evaluate the aesthetic impact of a development project. It is hard to get a good idea of what a project will look like when all you have is an empty field and an architect's blueprint. A VIA can assist reviewers by including a variety of techniques and materials: in-field simulations (e.g., balloons at the height of top building corners), three-dimensional models, two-dimensional models (e.g., computer-generated images, photomontages), scenic view analysis, and aesthetic ratings.

Scenic quality is more than just a function of the site. It is also based on community standards and individual perceptions. Visual sensitivity may arise from changes in scenic quality and is influenced by the visibility of a development from area roads, overlooks, parks, and neighborhoods. Municipal zoning and subdivision bylaws often incorporate visual aspects in determining the range of allowable projects. Some towns may even establish specific overlay districts or visual management zones for use when evaluating a project. In the absence of specific visual management guidelines, the impacts of projects must be determined by individual assessments based on specific site conditions.

Although formal visual impact assessment began in the 1970s, aesthetics has long been a key consideration in government decisions about how and where people can put buildings. Visual quality control can be done at a state-wide level, as in billboard laws, but is mostly accomplished through local regulations. Lighting, structural appearance, and landscaping are commonly examined, along with signs. All these aspects of a project will affect its aesthetic characteristics. Even if there are no specific checklists or regulations, there is still a logical way to understand potential visual impacts.

The following summary of visual impact assessment contains terms commonly used by governmental bodies and by experts in the field (Smarden, Palmer, and Felleman, 1986). Most visual assessment processes include an evaluation of the visual elements of the project and its setting, along with the social context. The social context includes cultural values and norms, politics, economics, and anything else used by society to understand visual quality.

Visual elements

When we look at a landscape we make a conscious or unconscious evaluation based on visual elements of color, form, line, texture, scale, and space (Figure 11-2). The visual character of an

Figure 11-2. Visual elements of form, line, texture, scale, and space.

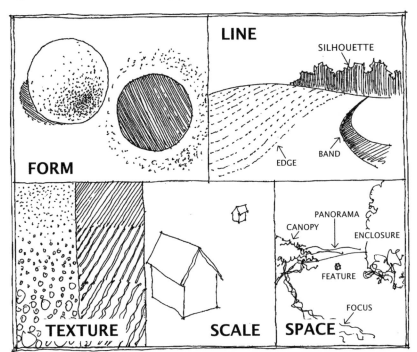

163

environmental setting is usually assessed in a glance, yet in making land use decisions we may have to analyze what occurs during that glance. Visual elements can be used to describe or rate the visual character of an environmental setting before, during, or after construction.

Color

Color is described in terms of three variables: hue, value, and chroma. The Munsell color chart (see Chapter 6) provides a standardized reference for color. Hue refers to the wavelength of visible light and is the familiar primary red, blue, yellow, or some combination. Value is the relative lightness or intensity of color and ranges from black to white. Chroma is the relative purity, brilliance, or saturation of a color, and ranges from pure (high chroma) to dull (low chroma).

The relationship between different colors in a setting affects perception. Dark colors next to light will attract the eye. Bright, warm colors look closer than dark, cooler color. Atmospheric conditions affect color. Dust particles help scatter light, reducing chroma. Clouds reduce value and chroma. The time of day is another influence; colors appear darker and redder early and later in the day, and paler in full sun.

In addition to sunshine, skylight and electrical light affect color. Some consultants may use the Color Rendering Index (CRI) to show the differences to perceived hue that are caused by using different types of lamps (e.g., mercury, high pressure sodium, low pressure sodium, incandescent). Preferences may differ markedly for these exterior and interior lamp types.

The lighting direction affects color. Objects illuminated from the front will look paler and brighter than those lit from behind (backlit).

Form

The form of an object or feature can be perceived as a two-dimensional shape or a three-dimensional mass, depending on lighting, viewing angle, atmospheric conditions, characteristics of the object, and viewer circumstances. The perception of form is affected by how the form contrasts with the setting. A geometric form in a non-geometric setting may be more noticeable. Form may also be affected by cultural values associated with shape. The most obvious example is the distinct concave shape of a nuclear cooling tower; its visual impact is affected by the perception of what it represents.

Line

There are three types of linear characteristics: edge, band, and silhouette. An edge joins two contrasting areas. A band is two edges that together divide an area, as in a road. A silhouette is the outlined edge of a mass, as in a skyline. Lines have properties of boldness, complexity, and orientation. Distance, atmospheric conditions, and lighting affect the perception of lines.

Texture

Texture is composed of small forms or color combinations in a continuous surface area. We perceive texture on the basis of color, light, and shade. We describe it in terms of grain, density, regularity, and contrast. A hayfield may appear fine-grained with dense surface variations; trees scattered on a hillside might have a coarse-grained texture, with sparse density; a cornfield would have an ordered regularity. Contrast comes from variation within the colors or values. For example, multi-colored leaves in the fall have much greater textural contrast than trees in summer. Texture, like other elements, is affected by environmental factors such as distance, atmospheric conditions, and illumination.

Scale

Scale is determined by the proportionate relationship between an object and its setting. The field-of-view and the contrast amongst objects influence the perception of scale. Scale is often described in terms of dominance: large, massive objects in a small area are more dominant than small, delicate objects in broader settings. Viewer angle, atmospheric conditions, distance, and position in the setting all influence the perception of scale.

Space

The three-dimensional arrangements of objects and empty spaces (voids) in an environmental setting define the spatial characteristics of the landscape. Landscape spatial characteristics can be described in terms of five composition types: panoramic, enclosed, featured, focal, and canopy. The backdrop of sky, water, and features or contours affects the spatial character of a landscape. An observer's position (below, above, or in the same horizontal plane) affects the perceived degree of enclosure or panorama. Longer distances tend to reduce the sense of enclosure and dominance.

Patterns

Each visual element may have a pattern, such as a row of lines, with some degree of complexity and diversity (Figure 11-3). Complexity refers to the arrangement of parts in a visual element pattern. Diversity refers to the number and variety of parts that make up a pattern of elements. A balance of these elements keeps the scene interesting, but too much of one or the other makes a feature stand out.

Assessing visual impacts

The visual elements of an object and its setting describe the object's dominance in the landscape. Visual dominance will contribute to the importance associated with specific features of a landscape. The severity of a potential visual impact is a combination of the visual compatibility of elements, especially color, form, line, and texture; the visual dominance of elements, particularly scale and space; and the relative importance of elements.

Large projects, visually sensitive or controversial projects, and projects in scenic areas all benefit from VIA. Review boards can witness demonstrations, take testimony, visit the site, rate the setting themselves, and conjure an image of the project in the setting. The review board might even use its own visual assessment form or worksheet. If the visual assessment shows that the impact is severe or undue, then the next step is mitigation. The visual elements can be used as guidelines in developing or evaluating mitigation.

Figure 11-3. Pattern diversity, complexity, and visual dominance.

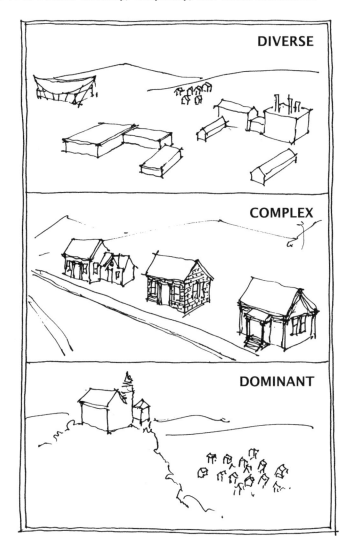

Visual screening

Visual impacts can be softened or reduced by screening the project with plants, by grading, and by adding distance (Figure 11-4). An extra deep setback can provide a buffering distance from a visual intrusion. Grading can include berms, dikes, walls, and other artificial and natural barriers. Neighborhoods may have fence or wall ordinances because perimeter barriers detract from neighborhood

167

identity. Plantings should be shown on a landscape plan and provide year-round screening. Staggered plantings may be appropriate to reduce an artificial appearance. These screening methods may also reduce light glare, noise, and other intrusions from the project.

Figure 11-4. Examples of visual screening. The trees and shrubs help hide cars and the parking lot. The berm makes the building less visible. Smaller structures blend into the background.

TREES AND SHRUBS

BERMS

SMALLER BUILDINGS

How states and municipalities address aesthetics

Maine law allows municipalities to address aesthetics in reviewing subdivisions. Particular attention can be paid to scenic areas. In adopting an ordinance and approving subdivisions, the municipality may not permit undue harm to visual access to the shoreline (Me. Rev. § 30-A-4404). To meet these requirements, review board members can require landscape plans, view the site, evaluate the height of proposed buildings, and impose conditions. Developers can protect views by entering into scenic easements that limit development of the property (e.g., see *Conservation Law Foundation v. Town of Lincolnville* 2001 [Me., 786 A. 2d 616]).

In New Hampshire, Title 64, Section 674, states that site plan review regulations can "provide for the harmonious and aesthetically pleasing development of the municipality and its environs, open spaces and green spaces of adequate proportions, [and] include such provisions as will tend to create conditions favorable for health, safety, convenience, and prosperity." New Hampshire also protects scenic views as part of reviewing coastal development.

Vermont addresses aesthetics at the state level through a variety of legislation but especially Act 250, Title 10, Chapter 151 (Criterion 8, Aesthetics), and the municipal planning law, Title 24, Chapter 117. Under Title 24, municipalities are authorized to address aesthetics in subdivision and site plan review. They can also establish design control districts in which issues relating to views and historic buildings are given special consideration. Planning commission approval is required to build, substantially alter, demolish, or move buildings within such districts (VT Rev. Stat. § 24-4407).

Aesthetic concerns are addressed in the specified format of the state or municipal approval process and may be in the form of responses to particular questions, a narrative or study, or landscape plans and building elevations, or some combination of these.

Landscape plans

Landscaping is just as much an aesthetic concern as it is one of erosion control and site utility. Approval of landscape plans is, to a certain degree, an act of faith. Two-dimensional drawings of landscapes and buildings may require a significant level of sophistication (or imagination) to interpret as real-world scenarios. Consequently, the intentions of the design should be articulated by the developer along with the actual details of the landscape and site plans. A checklist helps to ensure that the right topics are covered on the plan and narrative (Figures 11-5 and 11-6).

Figure 11-5. Checklist for reviewing landscape plans.

· Is the plan clear and easy to understand?

· Are there appropriate details on the plan?

· When will the landscaping be installed?

· What accommodations have been made to use durable indigenous species?

· Is the plan realistic in terms of the applicant's ability to carry it out?

· Is the landscape plan appropriate for the setting?

· What mechanisms are in place to ensure the plan will be implemented?

· Are the plantings of sufficient size to address aesthetic concerns?

· Is there attention to major components that make a site successful (e.g., benches, public spaces, trash receptacles, private spaces, recreational areas, navigational aides, handicap accessibility, safety, and incorporation of local scenic, historical and architectural themes)?

· Is an escrow account warranted to ensure adequate landscaping?

Figure 11-6. Sample portion of landscaping plan.

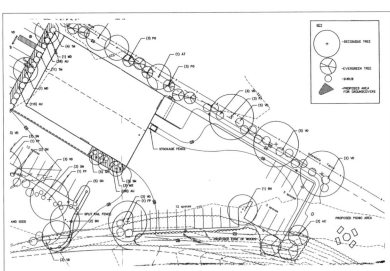

Signs

Municipalities have sign ordinances that provide guidance for the developer as well as the reviewer. These ordinances should reflect the values of the town plan. Reviewers should be cautious when reviewing architectural elements that are actually used as signs, such as gas station canopies. Many towns regulate against this use. The items listed in Figure 11-7 are common factors to consider in reviewing signs.

Figure 11-7. Sign review considerations.

- Signs should pertain only to the needs of the project (e.g., goods and services, navigation, and identification).

- Size, color, characteristics and number of signs should be appropriate to their function, the distance and speed (if to be seen from a transportation corridor) at which they are to be read, and the need for essential "first glance" information.

- Signs should not block or interfere with public space, including transportation corridors and infrastructure.

- Signs should not obstruct doors, windows, or key architectural features.

- Indirect illumination should be used rather than direct illumination if possible. The level of illumination should be in keeping with the setting.

- Avoid moving, fluttering, blinking, flashing or other garish attention-getting signs.

- Require rules for the prompt removal of temporary signs and displays.

- Have a plan for maintenance of the signs.

Structure drawings and building elevations

The built components of a project are structures, including bridges, houses, factories, storage units, towers, and outbuildings. Most towns require building elevations—a drawing showing the facade or appearance of a structure—with specific requirements for scale and detail. The compass direction of the elevation shows the perspective from which it is viewed. For example, a west elevation shows the building from the west side (see Figure 3-4).

Exterior lighting

Exterior lighting is a big part of the aesthetic review of developments. Lighting is usually necessary for security and normal work operations. Exterior light comes from light poles in parking lots and walkways; building and security lamps; signs; reflective surfaces; and interior lights that shine through windows. All should be considered in evaluating lighting. Large projects will often have lighting studies but many smaller projects rely on a brief narrative or incorporate lighting into the landscape plan. Yet even a single bulb glaring into a neighboring property can be a significant source of impact if you are the neighbor. Accordingly, good judgment and a basic understanding of exterior lighting concepts are necessary for assessing most development projects.

Lighting units and terms

Lumen: A measurement of the quantity of light flowing from a source, also called "luminous flux." A typical 100-watt incandescent bulb emits about 1750 lumens, or about 17.5 lumens per watt.

Luminance: The amount of visible light in an area. In the United States, luminance is described as "foot-lamberts" or "foot-candles" and measured in lumens per square foot. You may also see it described as "lux" and measured in lumens per square meter by scientists and others who use the "SI system."[2] A 2000-lumen streetlight produces an amount of illumination on the ground calculated by dividing the lumens by the area of brightened circle.

Efficiency: The efficiency of lighting sources can be described in terms of lumens per watt. A watt is a measure of the amount of power. Some types of light bulbs, such as sodium, are more efficient than incandescent bulbs and therefore take fewer watts to give an equal amount of lumens or light.

Light meter: A simple, relatively inexpensive device that can measure luminance. The meter can be used to determine background

---

[2] System International (*Système International d'unités*) has base units of length, mass, time, electric current, thermodynamic temperature, amount of substance, and luminous intensity. SI uses many metric terms, scientific notation, and places the unit of measurement at the end of the value with a multiplier, reducing the need for a decimal point.

Figure 11-8. Example of isochrome lighting diagram. Light is more intense in the centers by the lamp posts. The numbers show the footcandle readings taken in the field.

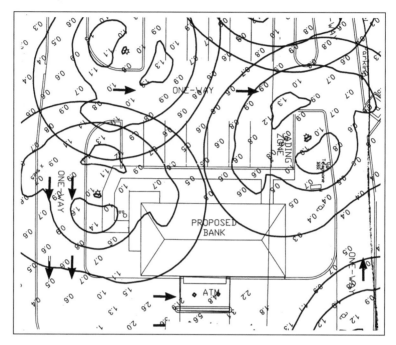

levels before a project is built and to keep track of the levels from a project. For some projects, notably correctional centers, shopping malls and airports, lighting levels may be expressed as "isochromes," areas delineated around a source and showing a change in lighting levels (Figure 11-8).

Issues for lighting review

The issues raised in reviewing illumination for a project depend on the project itself, the setting, the applicable regulations and guidelines, and the concerns of the reviewers. Certain issues continue to be raised.

In small projects, lighting might be considered only as an enhancement of the use of the project. The developer may not have considered how the light will affect others. For example, everyone has noticed unshielded bulbs designed to illuminate a sign but that also shed light onto the street and adjoining properties (Figure 11-9). This excess light should be addressed during the review and approval process, reducing the likelihood of problems in the future.

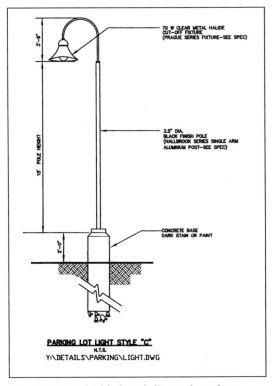

70 W CLEAR METAL HALIDE
CUT—OFF FIXTURE
(PRAGUE SERIES FIXTURE—SEE SPEC)

3'-6"

15' POLE HEIGHT

3.5" DIA.
BLACK FINISH POLE
(HALLBROOK SERIES SINGLE ARM
ALUMINUM POST—SEE SPEC)

CONCRETE BASE
DARK STAIN OR PAINT

2'-0"

PARKING LOT LIGHT STYLE "C"
N.T.S.
Y:\DETAILS\PARKING\LIGHT.DWG

Figure 11-9. Shielded and directed outdoor lighting. This type of lighting reduces trespass— the amount of light escaping off the site.

A scenic resource evaluation process

When evaluating aesthetic impacts, the Vermont Agency of Natural Resources and Vermont's Act 250 process use a two-stage aesthetic review process called the "Quechee Analysis." Part I of this process focuses on the project setting. At this stage, details of the project itself are not an issue, just the scenic values of the existing site and the context. Both are described and evaluated for significance.

Many sensitive areas dot the landscape of northern New England—ridge lines, hilltops, shorelines, agricultural districts, corridor views, panoramic views, recreational areas, historic areas, and scenic areas whether formally designated or not. If a proposed development is located in one or more sensitive areas, then identification of specific visual elements becomes critical. The area considered in determining context varies widely from a few city blocks to an entire scenic valley traversed by an interstate. The context depends on the scale of the project, the way in which it will be seen or experienced by the public, and the characteristics that define its setting.

Part II of the Act 250 process helps reviewers determine how a proposed project would adversely affect the scenic resource, and whether or not any special circumstances or considerations exist. In determining whether or not impacts are adverse, the state examines building styles, landscaping, signs, scale of project, duration of impacts, the contrast of the project with its surroundings (this can be positive or negative), and the planning decisions made at the local level. If the project creates adverse impacts, reviewers decide whether those adverse impacts are unacceptable ("undue"). In making a final determination, the three-pronged test of the Quechee Analysis for undue is used:

1) Does the project violate a clearly written community standard (local, regional or state) regarding aesthetics? Usually, if a project violates a standard, this becomes apparent through reviewing relevant planning documents and contacting local and regional officials.

2) Does the project offend the sensibilities of the average person? Decision-makers can consider themselves "average" for this purpose and need not conduct surveys or interviews. Documentation used in the Part I analysis should point to the nature and degree of aesthetic offence.

3) Has the applicant failed to take reasonable mitigation measures (including off-site arrangements) to reduce the visual impacts of the project? It can be tough to determine what constitutes reasonable mitigation measures, but they should not be limited to minor landscaping and earth-tone colors.

If a project fails to meet one or more of the above prongs, then the project does not meet the requirements of Act 250. This process is useful for other states and jurisdictions because it provides documentation and analysis for an aesthetic impact decision, reducing the likelihood of arbitrariness.

THE MULTIPLE DESIGN OPTION

Once when I was serving as interim town planner in a town with 9,000 people, I met with a potential applicant seeking guidance on filling in application forms for site plan review. He represented a national coffee/donut chain. In a very informal meeting the applicant stated that the chain was interested in locating on a particular lot. He showed me a generic sketch plan with an elevation of the building. I told him that I felt the colors and the box-style building (the chain's typical design) were totally out of character with that section of town.

He was not happy with my response to his sketch plan and left my office in a huff. I thought I would not see him again for a while. However, he immediately returned from his vehicle with a three-ring binder of pictures of different building styles that the corporation had built elsewhere.

I don't recall all of the styles that were in the book, but I do recall that some of them were actually quite attractive. I suggested one that would blend harmoniously with the New England village character. I learned that corporations might have many more building designs than they will initially admit to. Sometimes you just have to ask.

Where to go for more information

Arendt, Randall. (1999). *Crossroads, Hamlets, Village, Town, Design Characteristics of Traditional Neighborhoods, Old and New.* Chicago, IL: American Planning Association.

Berger, K.T. (1993). *Where the Sky and Road Collide: America Through the Eyes of its Drivers.* New York, NY: Henry Holt.

Campoli, Julie, Elizabeth Humstone, and Alex Maclean. (2002). *Above and Beyond, Visualizing Change in Small Towns and Rural Areas.* Chicago, IL: American Planning Association, Planners Press.

Courtney, Elizabeth. (1991). *Vermont's Scenic Landscapes: A Guide for Growth and Protection.* Waterbury, VT: Vermont Agency of Natural Resources, http://www.anr.state.vt.us/

Deen, David and Matthew Mann. (2000). *Planning for telecommunications facilities in New Hampshire and Vermont.* Easthampton, MA: Connecticut

River Watershed Council. Available online at www.rpc.windham.vt.us/
pubs/telecomm.pdf

Ewing, R. (1996). *Best Development Practices.* Chicago, IL: American Planning
Association, Planners Press.

Illuminating Engineering Society of North America. http://www.iesna.
org/

International Dark-Sky Association. http://www.darksky.org/index.html

Kelbaugh, Douglas. (1997). *Common Place: Toward Neighborhood and Regional
Design.* Seattle, WA: University of Washington Press.

Kunstler, James Howard. (1994). *The Geography of Nowhere, The Rise and
Decline of America's Man-Made Landscape.* New York, NY: Simon and
Schuster.

New England Light Pollution Advisory Group (NELPAG). http://cfa-
www.harvard.edu/cfa/ps/nelpag.html

New Hampshire Office of State Planning. Scenic and cultural byways program. http://www.state.nh.us/osp/scenicbyways/scenicbyways.htm

OnLine Conversion (provides instant conversions of various measurements, including light measurement units). http://www.
onlineconversion.com

Ryan, Kathleen, Michael Munson. (1996). *Outdoor Lighting Manual for
Vermont Municipalities.* Burlington, VT: Chittenden County Regional
Planning Commission.

Smarden, Richard C., James F. Palmer, and John Felleman, editors. (1986).
Foundations for Visual Project Analysis. New York, NY: John Wiley &
Sons.

Vermont Chapter of the American Society of Landscape Architects.
(2002).

Vermont Agency of Transportation. (June 2002). http://www.aot.state.vt.
us/projdev/Sections/Design/Design.htm

Chapter 12
CULTURAL RESOURCES

Historical, architectural, and archaeological features are all aspects of a cultural resources review. Included in the definition of cultural resources in environmental assessment are properties important to maintaining the traditions of Native American and other communities (Traditional Cultural Properties, see below). Properties of potential value must be evaluated by an agency and determined to be "significant" to be officially designated a "cultural resource." Agencies of the federal or state government designate cultural resources for identification or protection. Usually, the term "cultural resource" is used at the local level in a loose sense, referring to physical features and sites, including canals, mills, stone quarries, houses, campsites, old downtown streets, etc., without regard to regulatory or official designation. Legal or even informal designations of resources as "cultural" can be unwelcome news to landowners and developers fearful of the loss of development rights, but the process is usually meant to generate awareness of the resource.

All federal projects (i.e., done by the federal government, on federal lands, or otherwise subject to federal funds, assistance, license or permit) must be scrutinized for potential affects on cultural resources, a consideration also made by state and many local jurisdictions. In Vermont, archaeological and historical resources are considered part of the review process under Act 250, the Vermont Historic Preservation Act (22 VSA. Chapter 14) and Section 106 of the National Historic Preservation Act. Maine's Site Location of Development law (930-A MRSA 4401-4407) and Shoreland Zoning (38 MRSA 435-449) statute call for review of impacts on cultural resources. Vermont's Act 250 requires a determination of whether projects will have an adverse effect on historic or archaeological sites, and, if so, whether the adverse effect is "undue" (this two-step approach is summarized in Chapter 11, Aesthetics). New Hampshire addresses historic preservation in Chapter 32, Laws of 1974, RSA 227.

Although the presence of cultural resources such as archaeological sites and historic structures does not usually "kill" projects, it may call for some management or documentation. During project planning, potential damage ("impacts") to cultural resource sites can be reduced or mitigated through redesign of the project, designation of "not-to-be-disturbed" buffer zones, or recovery through an archaeological excavation or other documentation process. Mitigation can also include purchase of land, acquisition or transfer of development rights (TDRs), and other conservation efforts.

Every state has cemetery laws, and for obvious reasons, cemeteries are treated differently than other historical or cultural resources. Cemeteries are usually controlled at the local level.

Confidentiality and site location

Each state has laws that exempt the location of archaeological sites from the public's "Right to Know," despite the concern that local governments need to know where sites are in order to protect them from inadvertent damage (accordingly, some towns may address sensitive areas through zoning). However, the exemption is necessary to protect sites from looting. Local governments work with the state historic preservation office to strategize on how the confidentiality issue plays out in the review process.

Archaeological and historical resource management

Several interrelated statutes, along with an assortment of counterpart legislation at the state and local levels, regulate different aspects of archaeology and its performance in the United States. The most important of these is the National Historic Preservation Act of 1966 (NHPA), especially Section 106. NHPA led to the establishment of State Historic Preservation Officers (SHPO) who develop historic preservation plans for each state. It also established a forum to determine whether or not sites are eligible for listing on the National Register of Historic Places. Most states have state registers of historic places and use a cultural resource evaluation process similar to that of the federal government (Neumann and

Sanford, 2001). However, Maine uses databases and an inventory (in the Maine Historic Preservation Commission). Laws such as Site Location of Development (Title 38 MRSA, Chapter 3) drive the state-level cultural resource management process (CRM).

"Significance" is a key concept in the application of law to cultural resource assessments. In the Section 106 process, significance means being eligible for listing on the National Register of Historic Places. In determining significance, evaluators look at the condition of the site based on the amount of past disturbance (site integrity). The National Register of Historic Places is specifically intended to serve as a planning document, alerting agencies to the existence of historic properties that may come under their jurisdiction. Sites not yet listed may also be important.

If a project is being considered under state or federal law, an archaeologist or historian for the SHPO will do a "desk review" of a proposed project and determine if there is a chance that historical or archaeological resources are on the project lands or close enough for concern. Developers often arrange this review relatively early on to avoid surprises too far into the design phase. If the project has the potential to affect cultural resources, the SHPO may recommend an investigation of the property and provide a list of consultants eligible to do archaeology (the SHPO will not endorse or recommend any particular consultant). The Vermont Division for Historic Preservation posts its lists of archaeologists and historic preservation consultants on its Internet web site. The necessary qualifications for cultural resource professionals working at the federal level appear in 36 CFR 61 and in The Secretary of the Interior's Guidelines [48 FR 44738-44739] and are similar to professional standards set by the states in the Northeast; a graduate degree and significant experience is expected.

The initial cultural resource investigation is usually called a "Phase I identification process." If cultural resources are found in this first phase, the next step is to delineate them so that the potential impacts can be estimated (a Phase II investigation). If the disturbance cannot be prevented or mitigated, and if the resources appear to be significant, then the state may require a full-scale archaeological excavation (a Phase III).

Federal environmental assessment laws such as the National Environmental Policy Act of 1969 (NEPA) include archaeological

and historical evaluations as part of Environmental Impact Statements (EISs). Unlike Massachusetts and Connecticut, there is no
state NEPA equivalent in New Hampshire, Maine, or Vermont.
Federal highway improvements may require an environmental assessment that, among other things, considers the historic significance
of sites or public lands involved in a project. This accounting, known
as a "Section 4(f) evaluation," is "a major preoccupation of DOT
agencies" (King 2000:11).

Approvals for dams, federally-funded housing, and other large
projects may require cultural resource assessments under various state
and federal laws. Wetlands alterations can fall under federal Army
Corps of Engineers jurisdiction, with some of the review conducted
at the state level. The Coastal Zone Management Act of 1972
(CZMA) includes scenic, cultural, and historic values in addition to
natural and economic resources.

While procedures may vary by state, the regulations are quite
accessible. Usually, the regulations and permit applications are provided
on an Internet web site. The SHPOs and state government Internet
pages have descriptions and links to state archaeological laws and
assessment procedures. Agencies such as the National Park Service
and professional societies such as Society for American Archaeology
(SAA) and Register of Professional Archaeologists (RPA) provide
standards, resources, and training. State historical and archaeological
societies are other sources of information.

The common forms of archaeological or historical properties,
as identified by the federal government, are the following: object,
site, building, structure, and district (Neumann and Sanford 2001).
Objects include monuments, mileposts, statues, fountains, and similar
location-specific items the significance of which is related both to
where they were placed and the purpose they served. Usually, objects
are fixed, but a boat or airplane can also count. Sites represent
locations of significant events, prehistoric or historic occupations
or activities, buildings, or structures. Petroglyphs, battlefields, ruins,
settlements, burial mounds, and any other physical remnant of
human activity might also qualify as a site. Buildings refer to structures that shelter human activities, including houses, barns, out-
houses, businesses, churches, and farm compounds. Structures refer
to elements of the built environment that are not buildings: bridges,
highways, railroad tunnels, ships, railroad stock, military fortifications,

aqueducts, fire towers, and canals, among others. A stone wall itself would not be an historical structure unless it was part of an historic landscape or a contributing feature to an archaeological site or district. A district is a collection of buildings, sites, structures, or even objects—all with a unifying theme.

Traditional Cultural Property (TCP), as defined for National Register purposes, is a property eligible for inclusion in the National Register because of its association with the cultural practices or beliefs of a living community that are rooted in that community's history, and are important to maintaining the continuing cultural identity of the community. For example, a place used by a Native American community to gather herbs for medicinal use or to get rushes for basketry may be a TCP.

State surveys

State surveys are a frontline tool in cultural resource management. The historical resources in northern New England date back more than 10,000 years and range up to the past 50 years. They include all kinds and types of resources, ranging from early Paleo-Indian campsites to pre-Contact agricultural villages, from European fur trading posts to nineteenth-century canals and logging camps. Surviving buildings and structures range from colonial fortifications to Greek Revival mansions, from slate and granite quarries to village centers, from CCC camps to classic American roadside diners. Each state has an active survey program to identify historical resources (including archaeological, architectural, and other physical cultural resources). The individual assessment requirements for projects in the state are influenced by the results of these on-going surveys and the reports in turn contribute to the knowledge base of the surveys.

Certified Local Government (CLG)

The National Historic Preservation Act established a nationwide program of financial and technical assistance to local governments through the Certified Local Government (CLG) Program. Eligible municipalities have their own historic preservation commissions, inventories of historic structures, surveys of prehistoric and historic archaeological sites, programs for public education, and design guidelines. CLG municipalities have greater access to funding and greater control in planning and regulatory decisions concerning the cultural resources in the community. A CLG community does local review of historical and architectural resource assessments, thanks to local expertise on volunteer Design Review Boards. As of 2003, Maine has eight CLGs: Bangor, Castine, Hampden, Kennebunk, Lewiston, Saco, Topsham, and York. New Hampshire CLGs are Concord, Derry, Durham, Gilford, Goffstown, Hollis, Jaffrey, Nashua, Newington, Newport, Sanborton, and Sommersworth. Amherst and Wakefield, NH, will soon be on the list too. In Vermont, the CLGs are: Bennington, Brandon, Burlington, Hartford, Rockingham, Shelburne, Stowe, Williston, Windsor and the Mad River Valley.

State cultural resources plan

Each state also has a written plan for its cultural resources, which can be obtained from the appropriate state agency or office. The plan will be familiar to the consultants who prepare reports. Survey and research strategy are provided in the plan along with a discussion of resources that are important to the state. Current practice is to require that the cultural assessments in a state address potential resources in light of research questions provided in the state plan. The eligibility criteria for State or National Register listing should be referenced in the cultural resource assessment report.

The cultural resource assessment report

This report should provide the information necessary to meet the applicable regulations and a stand-alone documentation of site investigation. The confidential site location information might be removed so that there are two versions of the report, one edited for public consumption that does not reveal where sites are, and another version with the complete information available to regulatory reviewers and bona fide researchers. All cultural resource assessment reports should provide the history and prehistory from a literature review, in addition to the actual results from the fieldwork and laboratory analyses. Figures, maps, and photographs should illustrate the points made in the report.

Each state has guidelines for how an archaeological resource assessment is conducted, who conducts it, and how it is reported.

These guidelines are found at official state web sites or obtained by request from the state agency. A scoping process should be used so that the assessment and its report focus on the important information to be used in making decisions about the resource. Figure 12-1 shows a typical report outline (Neumann and Sanford 2001).

Figure 12-1. Outline of a typical cultural resource assessment report.

- Cover, title page (with an appropriately descriptive title), documentation page.

- Table of Contents.

- List of Tables and List of Figures.

- Abstract/Summary: The abstract is a brief orientation to the report. The summary is more detailed than the abstract and may be in the form of a "letter from the field" (as in Vermont). Likely the only portion of the report that many people will read, the summary should present a clear announcement of the contents.

- Chapter 1: Introduction and Statement of Problem. This section describes the project; the laws and regulations mandating the cultural resource assessment; the people who directed or supervised the work; the history of the undertaking and reason for the field investigation; research design and objectives; a summary of project impacts; and an overview of the contents of the report.

- Chapter 2: Environmental Background. The local environmental history is described along with the present environmental setting (including surface waters, soils, geology, land forms, and plant and animal species).

- Chapter 3: Prehistoric and Historic Background. The state of knowledge about existing prehistoric and historic cultural resources in the area is summarized. This section provides a cultural context for understanding any existing or potential cultural resources.

- Chapter 4: Field and Analytical Methods. Field methods include strategy, number, depth, and location of excavation units or transects (lines across the project land used for sampling data); the strategy for surface and subsurface inspection; mapping strategies; and sampling strategies. The analysis methods include how artifacts and other materials from the site were processed, catalogued, labeled, studied, and prepared for curation.

- Chapter 5: Results of Investigations. The data is analyzed and interpreted in the context of basic compliance issues. A site or project map shows where excavations or surface collections were done. Features and diagnostic artifacts are drawn or photographed.

- Chapter 6: Summary and Recommendations. This short section addresses the next steps for the client. The recommendations can range from a finding

(Figure continued next page)

Figure 12-1 (continued)

that nothing is present, to a finding that further testing or mitigation is warranted. Sites that appear to satisfy the criteria for listing on the state or National Register might need a Phase III data recovery process or to have the project be redesigned.

- References. Complete references are given in a standard format for all sources of information: books, Internet sites, interviews, and artifact collections.

- Appendices. Included are the artifact inventories, site forms, original Scope of Work (SOW, setting forth the framework for the investigation), the Request for Proposals (RFP, a solicitation for contract services), and various correspondence and communications, including summaries of all interviews.

Where to go for more information

Albers, Jan. (2000). *Hands on the Land: A History of the Vermont Landscape*. Rutland, VT: MIT Press/Orton Family Foundation.

Advisory Council on Historic Preservation. (1991). *Treatment of Archeological Properties: A Handbook*. Washington, DC: Advisory Council on Historic Preservation.

Cronon, William. (1983). *Changes in the Land: Indians, Colonists, and the Ecology of New England*. New York, NY: Hill and Wang.

King, Thomas F. (2000). *Federal Planning and Historical Places: The Section 106 Process*. Walnut Creek, CA: AltaMira Press.

Maine Archaeological Society. http://www.mainearchsociety.org/

Maine Historic Preservation Commission. http://www.state.me.us/mhpc/

Maine Olmsted Alliance for Parks and Landscapes. http://www.maineolmsted.org

Maine Preservation. http://www.mainepreservation.org/

Massachusetts Archaeological Society. http://webhost.bridgew.edu/mas/

National Park Service. (1995). *How to Apply the National Register Criteria*. National Register Bulletin 15. Washington, DC: National Park Service. (http://www.cr.nps.gov/nr/nrpubs.html)

National Trust for Historic Preservation. http://www.nthp.org/

Neumann, Thomas W. and Robert M. Sanford. (2001). *Cultural Resources Archaeology: An Introduction*. Walnut Creek, CA: AltaMira Press.

New Hampshire Archaeological Society. http://www.nhas.org/

New Hampshire Division of Historical Resources (DHR). http://webster. state.nh.us/nhdhr/

New Hampshire DHR, State Conservation and Rescue Archaeology Program. http://www.mv.com/ipusers/boisvert/.

New Hampshire Department of Cultural Resources. http://webster.state. nh.us/nhculture/

New Hampshire Historical Society. The Tuck Library, 30 Park Street, Concord, NH 03301-6384. Telephone: 603/228-6688. Fax: 603/224-0463.

Parker, Patricia L., and Thomas F. King. (1995). *Guidelines for Evaluating and Documenting Traditional Cultural Properties*. National Register Bulletin. Washington, DC: National Park Service. (http://www.cr.nps.gov/nr/ nrpubs.html)

Sagadahoc Preservation Inc. Box 322, Bath, ME, 04530. http://www. sagadahocpreservation.org/index.html

Thorson, Robert M. (2002). *Stone by Stone: The Magnificent History in New England's Stone Walls*. New York, NY:Walker & Co.

Vermont Archaeological Society. http://www.vtarchaeology.org/

Vermont Division for Historic Preservation (DHP). Agency of Development and Community Affairs. http://www.historicvermont.org/

Vermont Division for Historic Preservation (DHP). (2002). *Vermont Historic Preservation Office's Guidelines for Conducting Archaeology in Vermont, working draft*. Division For Historic Preservation. Montpelier, VT. July, 2002. (Available at http://www.historicvermont.org/)

Vermont Historical Society. Vermont History Center. http://www.state.vt. us/vhs/

Chapter 13
PLANTS AND WILDLIFE

The first step when reviewing a development plan for potential impacts to plants and wildlife is to determine the precise location of the tract for comparison with habitat and wildlife maps. Then the plans and narrative are interpreted to check for accuracy. Next, the plant and wildlife impacts are summarized in accordance with applicable regulatory schemes. Local or state hearings may be held to determine whether the project is going to imperil significant plants and wildlife. Figure 13-1 shows key plant and wildlife factors commonly addressed in the review of subdivision and development plans.

Figure 13-1. Potential plant and wildlife effects from project development.
- Habitat destruction
- Population density decline
- Loss of species diversity
- Reduction in the land's carrying capacity
- Reduction of breeding and nesting sites
- Imperilment of natural animal corridors
- Effects on migratory game birds
- Impacts to wildlife refuges and sanctuaries
- Consequences to endangered and threatened species

The environmental consequences of a project are not always negative. Development can create opportunities, including off-site and on-site mitigation, enhancement programs, stewardship and land management, and reclamation.

The federal government and all New England states have lists of threatened and endangered species. An endangered species has a high likelihood of being wiped out in the state (extirpated), while a threatened species teeters on the brink of endangerment (usually as a result of the pressures of development). State regulators review projects by comparing them to these lists and to the federal lists prepared by the U.S. Fish and Wildlife Service in accordance with the Endangered Species Act (42 USCA §§ 4321-4370c). Regulators also check to see how development affects wildlife that is not threatened or endangered. Good wildlife management means not waiting until the population of a species is depleted. For example, the northern New England states actively manage bear, moose, deer, turkey, and other species and take an avid interest in conserving wildlife habitat. Plant species are less likely to get special management if they are not on a specific list, but they still get the benefit of wildlife management, which tends to be habitat based. Forests and agricultural lands—important habitat resources in northern New England—are discussed in Chapter 15.

In addition to endangered species protection, legislation that enables municipalities to review site plans and subdivisions allows for protection of plant and wildlife habitat. State-wide legislation such as Act 250 in Vermont (10 VSA 151), Maine's Natural Resources Protection Act 38 MRS § 480), coastal laws in Maine and New Hampshire, and the states' regulation of their own activities all consider the plant and wildlife consequences of land use development. State Natural Area Programs use GIS tools to map habitats for plant species. The Maine Office of GIS is rapidly expanding its services for environmental planning. The Maine Natural Area Program will provide comments on projects through a comparison with its GIS and other records of botanical areas. Vermont's Nongame and Natural Heritage Program is similar. The Vermont Center for Geographic Information contains GIS maps of deer wintering areas and other wildlife and natural area documentation. The New Hampshire Geographically Referenced Analysis and Information Transfer System (NH GRANIT) is a cooperative project to create, maintain, and make available a statewide geographic data base, as well as maps and infrared photographs of protected areas and other documented plant and wildlife critical areas.

Most municipalities conduct a natural resource inventory when they develop their comprehensive plans. Some communities have done the inventory even if they do not have a comprehensive plan. The inventory addresses threatened and endangered plants and animals as well as game animals and other species valued by the community. This inventory is usually mapped and forms the basis for the evaluation and comparison of development plans with the natural resource goals of the town. Responsibility for the development and stewardship of these inventories and maps may fall to a local conservation commission, as in Vermont, where they have certain statutory duties.

A project might also involve plant and wildlife habitat enhancement as mitigation for other impacts, such as the loss of open space, or because the enhancement is part of the goals of the project (e.g., nature center, green-space in a commercial development park, recreational space in a residential subdivision). Most commercial and industrial projects have a landscaping component. Individual lots in residential subdivisions are usually landscaped as well. Landscape plans provide more than aesthetic improvement. They can enhance native species of plants and animals by creating or improving green-space buffers and other land management areas.

Plants

The two approaches to considering plants in development review are the following: 1) What plants already exist on or adjacent to the development site?, and 2) What is proposed for new landscaping? Dealing with the first approach means a check on whether the site contains rare, threatened or endangered species. If the town or city has a conservation commission or board, this group may have a plant inventory and provide advice. Regional Planning Commissions often provide useful GIS mapping services including natural resource areas and inventories. State district biologists are available for consultation. The project developers should have already addressed the likelihood of botanical and wildlife impacts when preparing their application because, as a primary source of "red flags" for the project, it is a logical first step.

Each state maintains a list of plants to be protected or conserved. Maine has a list of over 300 rare, threatened, and endangered plants. The list is maintained by the State Natural Area Program in accordance with the Maine Endangered Species Act (12 MRS § 7751-7759). New Hampshire has a Native Plant Protection Act (NH RSA

217-A, passed in 1987) that lists approximately 289 plants. New Hampshire Natural Heritage Bureau (in the Division of Forests and Lands) keeps records on rare and imperiled plants. Vermont has over 150 threatened or endangered plant species on its state list, in accordance with its endangered species legislation (10 VSA. Chap. 123). The list can be accessed from the Vermont Agency of Natural Resources Internet web site.

Invasive species

The New England states have a number of invasive species that out-compete native plants, usurping their place in the landscape. Some of these invaders were introduced as part of past economic enterprises. For example, Japanese Knotweed *(Falopia Japonia)* was imported to provide blossoms for bee production. Others spread by accident or by following corridors of disturbed land. Some native species such as Poison Ivy *(Toxicodendron radicans)* are notorious colonizers. Fragile habitats such as wetlands and beach dunes are particularly vulnerable to invasive species. Eurasian Milfoil *(Myriophyllum spicatum)* is a common invader. In Maine, it is illegal to transport or introduce eleven invasive water plants (Maine is one of two or three states to, as of 2004, not have Eurasian Milfoil).

Invasive plant species abound in northern New England, especially in disturbed areas where they out-compete local species as early colonizers. Some common plants of concern in reviewing developments are: Multiflora Rose *(Rosa multiflora)*; Common Reed *(Phragmites australis)*; Common Buckthorn and Glossy Buckthorn *(Rhamnus cathartica* and *Rhammus frangula alnus)*; Purple Loosestrife *(Lythrum salicaria)*; Shrubby Honeysuckles—Tartarian, Morrow, and Belle's Honeysuckle *(Lonicera spp.)*; Japanese Knotweed / Mexican Bamboo *(Fallopia japonica / Polygonum cuspidatum)*; Asiatic Bittersweet *(Celastrus orbiculata)*; Japanese Barberry *(Berberis thunbergii)*; and Morrow and Tertarian honeysuckle *(Lonicera morrowii* and *Lonicera tatarica)*.

Types of projects and conditions that might entail invasive species include: waterfront development; wetlands enhancement as part of a project impact mitigation; gravel pit and other open tract reclamation; and development in or near a known ecologically vulnerable site (which will usually be listed on municipal or state natural resource maps). Occasionally, a new fragile area or critical ecological site will be discovered through the local review of a proposed development or subdivision. In such cases, state assistance is usually sought.

Landscape plans

Most review processes encourage landscaping plans that include native species, or at least species that will blend with the surrounding neighborhood and environment (see Chapter 11, Aesthetics). A landscape plan should be accompanied by planting details (Figure 13-2) listing the amount, size, and species, along with a diagram to show the proper method for installing them. The time of year

Figure 13-2. A typical detail of the plant specifications.

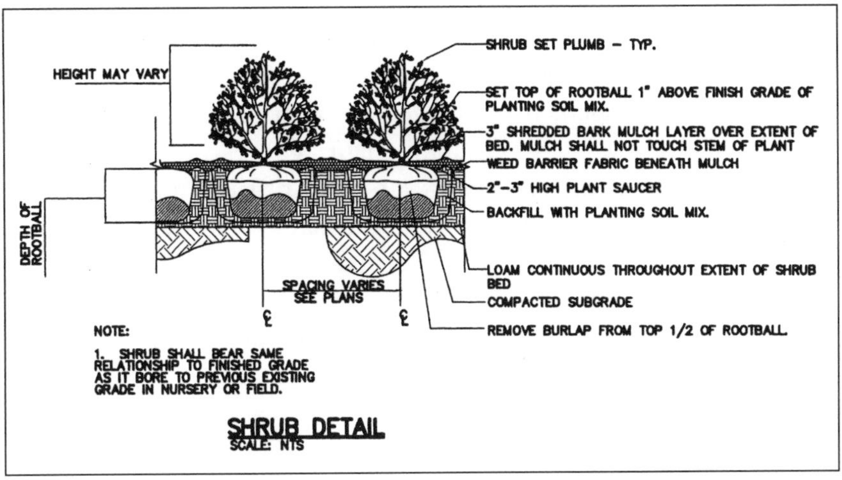

for the planting should be specified. The plan should disclose a procedure to evaluate the plantings and replace any failed or diseased plants. If the plants are intended to provide visual screening or to improve aesthetic viewing, then attention should be paid to how the site will look in winter as well as summer. Staggered placement in the field should be used if the plants are intended to simulate natural conditions. Straight, precise rows ("soldiers") may look great on a site plan but appear uninteresting or too manicured in the field.

The landscape plan may specify plantings for windbreaks and hedges–important sources of food and shelter for birds and small animals. There will be a list of the species and some discussion of their hardiness and appropriateness. Wildlife enhancement plantings may be proposed. Plants such as Switchgrass *(Panicum virgatum)*, Chokecherry *(Prunus virginiana)*, Flowering dogwood *(Cornus florida)* and other dogwoods *(Cornus* spp.), Crabapple *(Malus* spp.), Elderberry *(Sambucus canadensis)*, Winterberry *(Ilex verticillata)*, and American cranberrybush *(Viburnum trilobum)* are good for wildlife food and cover, but the actual species are best derived through specific recommendations from state biologists or local community experts.

Wildlife

Reviewing projects for effects on wildlife has three components: the potential consequences to any threatened or endangered species; the presence of critical wildlife habitat such as vernal pools, deer wintering yards, wetlands, shorelands, beech stands (for bear), and designated natural areas; and the proposed wildlife mitigation, enhancement, management, or usage. For most projects, state wildlife officials will review all three components either on request or as part of the permit process. However, state officials may not know of small, local, or new wildlife resources and critical areas. Not all critical habitat has been mapped. Further, wildlife areas can change, and maps can become outdated. Fortunately, wildlife resources are valued in northern New England and communities generally recognize their importance in the resource base. Maine, New Hampshire, and Vermont are among the top five states in terms of the percentage of the population that appreciates wildlife (Maine Audubon Society, 1999) and each state has endangered species legislation to consider along with the federal list (US Fish & Wildlife Region Five). The loss of habitat is a major concern in northern New England—songbirds are fast disappearing from loss or disruption of forest habitat—and piecemeal development across the landscape has done little to promote consistent planning for cumulative impacts.

If threatened or endangered species such as the bald eagle *(Haliaeetus leucocephalus)*, piping plover *(Charadrius melodus)* or tiger beetle *(Cicindela puritana)* are found on the tract, then the state and federal officials will review the impacts and decide what to do. Their choices include recommending avoidance, minimization, rectification (correction), preservation, and compensation. Rectification can be a form of minimization that also requires corrective or restorative actions. Preservation is a form of avoidance that also has a protective land management component.

Wildlife impact measurement involves consultation with appropriate agency officials and field assessments. Town records may also contain maps. Field assessments are usually conducted by a biologist (who need not necessarily hold an advanced degree). Frequently, the consulting biologist has a peer-reviewed professional designation as a Certified Wildlife Biologist. Assessment procedures include use of computer modeling such as VORTEX, Management Indicator Species (MIS), Population Variability Analysis (PVA) and Habitat Viability Analysis (HVA). Several models for habitat evaluation are available, notably, the Habitat Suitability Index (HSI), Habitat Evaluation System (HES), and Habitat Evaluation Procedure (HEP). The Gap Analysis Program (GAP) uses LANDSAT Thematic Mapper and ARC/INFO geographic information systems to integrate satellite imagery with data analysis and mapping. Assessment may include preparing a values matrix, a species habitat matrix, and accompanying maps. Maine has a Habitat Consultation Area Mapping Project that identifies grid cells of areas with natural features and characteristics for critical or important wildlife—"Essential Habitat" maps. New Hampshire and Vermont also have mapping projects for critical habitat areas. All three states provide consultations with state wildlife and fisheries biologists.

Corridors and critical mass

Historically, wildlife management focused on species. Current practices focus more on the habitat and on ecological concepts to maintain a balance of species. However, we still largely regulate projects on a case-by-case basis. A consequence is the tendency to fragment habitats through lack of a comprehensive plan or management of natural resources on a local or regional level. Strategic planning is needed to maintain wildlife corridors necessary for breeding, migration and other critical wildlife functions. Thus, the critical factor in maintaining wildlife is not the total size of the wildlife areas conserved but rather where and how they are located.

Large species such as the Black Bear *(Ursus americanus)* need access to vernal areas in early spring so they can offset the consequences of winter hibernation. They also need an undisturbed home range of more than a square mile (usually between 8 and 60 square miles) and access to other bears for reproduction. If the bear population in a region gets below a certain number due to the reduction of the land's carrying capacity, or due to the encroachment of development, then there will not be enough critical mass for survival of the species. Similarly, a certain critical mass of deer is necessary for the species to survive the winter. They need a deer wintering yard (places where deer hole up to get through the winter) which is why the states protect southern-exposed hemlock stands and other suitable habitats.

The Maine Land Use Regulation Commission (LURC) uses zoning and land use standards to protect deer yards and wildlife corridors in land under its jurisdiction. Vermont's Act 250 protects deer yards and other critical habitat under Criterion 8(A). New Hampshire, Maine, and Vermont all use zoning and land use standards for protection at the municipal level.

A species must be managed for survival at its most vulnerable point. For deer, it is the winter. Disturbance of these animals by predators, dogs, or humans, can jeopardize their survival. Wildlife buffers are needed to allow the deer and other species to use the corridors, vernal pools, wintering yards, dens, and other areas without being disturbed. Remoteness is an important factor for the survival of songbirds, large predators, and large herbivores. A wilderness tract may lose its quality of remoteness if several building lots are scattered among it, whereas clustering the units might avoid impairing the habitat quality.

According to the Patterns of Development Task Force of the Maine Environmental Priorities Project (1997), land can be considered as "tiers" that have differing thresholds for wildlife accommodation. Tier I represents undeveloped landscape, usually large forests, and can contain moose, bear and bobcats along with animals that can exist in the higher tiers. Tier II consists of large blocks of land 500 to 2500 acres in size; Tier III contains 100 to 499 acres; Tier IV contains 20 to 99 acres; and Tier V contains 1 to 19 acres and represents a suburban landscape. The number of species that can exist drops significantly in each tier.

Figure 13-3. Sample list of wildlife mitigation actions.

· Protection of an existing wildlife travel corridor.

· Designation of a naturally vegetated undisturbed buffer with sufficient width and length.

· Timing (day and season) sequence for explosives and other earth-disturbing activities.

· Enhancement of existing habitats by management, including culling invasive plant species.

· Use of conservation easements.

· Use of transferable development rights programs.

· Participation in site and land banking programs.

· Prompt re-vegetation of disturbed sites.

· Prohibited use of snowmobiles and trails within the habitat.

· Posted, fenced or otherwise marked land as protection for wildlife.

· Requirements for dogs to be kept on leash during winter and early spring months.

· Wildlife barrier installation.

· A vegetative cover on stockpiled topsoil and other stored earth materials.

· Site illumination and noise levels designed to accommodate wildlife.

· Preservation of den trees, snags, brush piles, stone walls, fallen trees, and other sheltering habitat.

· Avoidance of lawn care chemicals, especially near wildlife areas.

· Incorporation of the project lands into Critical Habitat Conservation Plans.

· Involvement in programs for captive breeding, species reintroduction, and other enhancements.

· Specification of plans for monitoring and upkeep of mitigation.

State wildlife biologists, consultants, and individual organizations provide recommendations for municipalities to use in determining requirements for effective wildlife management and plan review. For example, the Maine Audubon Society (2000) suggests acreages required for individual species of forest birds, grassland birds, turtles, and large mammals. The shape and size of habitat has much to do with its viability. Maine Audubon recommends consideration of size, shape, proximity, barriers, corridors, and habitat type in evaluating the conservation of open space for wildlife.

Site and development plans should contain appropriate wildlife and open-space habitat protection. Tailoring the mitigation package to the site is more effective than a "cookbook" approach, which may miss differences in sites, projects, conditions, and regulatory goals. Mitigation can entail a broad range of strategies and options developed upon consultation with experts and reviewers (Figure 13-3). After the land use decision is made, the site should be visited to inspect buffers and other mitigative measures.

Where to go for more information

Beattie, Molly, Charles Thompson, and Lynn Levine. (1993). *Working with your Woodland: A Landowner's Guide.* Hanover, NH: University Press of New England.

Environmental Protection Agency. (1997). *Community-based environmental protection: A resource book for protecting ecosystems and communities.* Washington, DC: US EPA (# 230-B-96-003).

Gerhold, Henry D., Willet N. Wandell, and Norman L. Lacasse (editors). (1993). *Street tree factsheets.* Municipal Tree Restoration Project. University Park, PA: Pennsylvania State University.

Kashanski, Catherine. (1994). *Native Vegetation for Lakeshores, Streamsides and Wetland Buffers: What you need to know to re-establish or enhance a buffer strip along waters and wetlands in Vermont.* Waterbury, VT: Division of Water Quality, Agency of Natural Resources.

Maine Audubon Society. (1999). *Watching out for Maine's Wildlife.* Falmouth, ME: Maine Audubon Society.

Maine Audubon Society. (2000). *Conserving Wildlife in Maine's Developing Landscape.* Falmouth, ME: Maine Audubon Society.

Maine Natural Areas Program, Maine Department of Environmental Conservation. http://www.state.me.us/doc/nrimc/mnap/home.htm

New Hampshire Fish and Game Department. http://www.wildlife.state.nh.us/index.htm

Patterns of Development Task Force. (1997). *A Response to Sprawl: Designing Communities to Protect Wildlife Habitat and Accommodate Development.* Augusta, ME: Report of the Patterns of Development Task Force, Maine Environmental Priorities Project.

Regan, Ronald J. and Ginger Anderson. (1995). *A Landowner's Guide: Wildlife Habitat Management for Vermont Woodlands.* Waterbury, VT: Vermont Agency of Natural Resources.

Stone, Amanda J. Lindley. (2001). *Natural Resources Inventories: A Guide for New Hampshire Communities and Conservation Groups.* University of New Hampshire, Cooperative Extension.

US Fish and Wildlife Service. List of threatened and endangered species can be found at http://endangered.fws.gov/wildlife.html

Vermont Agency of Natural Resources. http://www.anr.state.vt.us/

Vermont Agency of Natural Resources. (1998). *Vermont Invasive Exotic Plant Fact Sheet Series.* Waterbury VT: Agency of Natural Resources.

Chapter 14
ENERGY

One of the most important impacts of new development, especially when viewed from larger statewide, national, and even global perspectives, is energy use. Unfortunately, it is also one of the least understood and most underutilized areas of development review. If taken seriously by review boards and given the level of scrutiny of, say, traffic impacts, our states would start to see energy savings in the tens of millions of dollars. Even the smallest impacts are cumulative; we don't need high stack industrial emissions in our communities to contribute to global warming—cars lined up in congested commuter traffic play their own roles.

We can review development projects for energy usage from two perspectives, that of site configuration or layout, and that of structures. Energy review in northern New England has mostly evolved into a codes-based system for residential building standards and commercial/industrial building standards.

Site design can lead to energy savings if attention is paid to the solar sky. Some communities encourage development that accommodates solar access to rooftops, southern walls, south-facing slopes and "detached collectors" (used for solar heating systems). Designers can calculate shadow patterns for winter (when the shadows are longest during hours of useful solar radiation) to determine conditions for solar access on the development tract. The latitude and slope of a tract can be used to determine a morning, noon, or afternoon multiplier for determining shadow length—necessary to determine how much of a site or structure gets sun and for how long. For example, a 5% slope at a latitude of 45° has a multiplier of 2.9 for noon. If a tree is ten feet, then its shadow will be 2.9 x 10 = 29 feet. In urban design, "solar trespass" (blocking of sun by a structure) is a hot issue, and regulations may require the calculation of a shadow pattern based on how the shadow area changes over time of day and season. Solar access can also be a factor in the creation of subdivisions and resorts.

Energy concepts and terms

Review boards are likely to encounter the following terms and concepts in development applications submitted at the local or state level:

AFUE: Annual Fuel Efficiency refers to the measure of the efficiency of the main heating system in a building, such as a furnace, as well as space heaters and boilers. The AFUE is determined by a standard U.S. Department of Energy test method for both gas and oil equipment

ASHRAE: The American Society of Heating, Refrigeration and Air Conditioning Engineers. This group, along with the Illuminating Engineering Society (IES) developed a national design standard to promote the efficient use of energy resources in new commercial and high-rise construction.

Building envelope[1]: This includes all components of a structure with enclosed spaces to which heating and cooling are applied. Building envelope components distinguish conditioned spaces from unconditioned spaces or from outside air. For example, walls and doors between an unheated garage and a living area are part of the building envelope; walls separating an unheated garage from the outside are not.

Energy rating: This is a uniform method of ranking houses based on energy efficiency. Energy ratings range from 1 to 100 points and from 1 to 5 stars. Eighty points, the beginning of the 4 star range, is considered "energy efficient."

HVAC equipment: The equipment and distribution network that provides heating, ventilating, or air conditioning to a building.

Life cycle costing: A comparison of initial costs with total costs for the duration of the product or unit. Energy conservation measures may cost more at the beginning of a project but will pay for themselves over the long run. One way to evaluate trade-offs and determine the point of least cost is a life-cycle cost analysis. The

---

[1] Building envelope in this sense is different from the use of the term in site design as an indicator of an area in which a building's footprint or foundation can be placed.

analysis usually yields a prudent approach for investment in conservation measures. Taking the energy costs expected over time and applying them to the initial construction costs will result in a total cost for each option. The option that costs the least over a period of years is the most cost-effective and energy efficient choice. Some common choices such as residential electrical heat as a primary source are made because the up-front cost is low, despite resulting in a net energy inefficiency. Actions by state utility boards and the utilities themselves are helping to promote more energy-efficient developments.

R-value: This is a measurement of thermal resistance, or how well a material resists the flow of heat. Insulation materials are commonly rated and labeled using an R-Value. Higher numbers indicate superior performance. R-Values are additive, meaning adding an R-19 layer to an R-11 layer creates an R-30 value.

Solar gain: This represents the energy benefit from the sun. A structure oriented towards the south benefits from increased solar gain. A super-insulated house balances out heat loss with solar gain through efficient design and mechanisms of thermal storage.

Thermal values: A reference to the insulation levels in the roof, foundation and exterior walls.

U Value: A measurement of how well a material conducts heat. Windows and doors are typically rated using the U-value rather than the R-value. Lower numbers mean better performance and less heat loss.

Factors for energy-efficient site design

Many factors can be used in reviewing development plans for energy efficiency. Figure 14-1 is a sample checklist of some common things to look for when examining the site and the plans.

Energy codes

Energy codes have a hierarchical nature that covers residential, commercial, and industrial construction, as well as individual appliances. At the top level sits the International Code Council (ICC), which represents the consolidation of BOCA (Building Officials and Code Administrators), ICBO (International Conference of Building

Figure 14-1. Sample checklist for energy-efficient sites.

__ Lot orientation is north-south to extent possible.

__ Highest structure density is on south-facing slopes.

__ Little or no development is proposed for north-facing slopes.

__ There is appropriate distance between structures for effective solar access.

__ Berms and/or conifers are located to the north of structures to help block wind.

__ Colors are selected for ability to absorb (or reflect) sunlight.

__ Orientation of streets is east-west rather than north-south.

__ Buildings are near north lot lines to allow yard space to the south.

__ Tall buildings are north of shorter ones.

__ Mature height and canopy size of trees has been considered.

__ Deciduous trees are placed strategically for summer cooling.

__ Energy codes for structures are used.

Officials) and SBCCI (Southern Building Code Congress International). More than 97% of U.S. cities, counties, and states that adopt model codes choose building and fire codes created by these building groups. The objective of the ICC is to develop a single set of comprehensive, coordinated model construction codes that can be used throughout the country and around the world.

The International Energy Conservation Code (IECC) is recommended by the ICC to conserve energy in all communities by addressing the design of energy-efficient building envelopes and the installation of energy-efficient mechanical, lighting and power systems through performance requirements. It is a comprehensive code that establishes minimum regulations for energy-efficient buildings using prescriptive and performance-related measures. In 2000, substantial changes were made to the IECC in the area of commercial buildings, although the Code has not yet been updated to incorporate the provisions of ASHRAE/IES Standard 90.1-1999, except in the area of lighting.

At the encouragement of the federal government, states in the northeast region and around the country are starting to adopt IECC

2000 as a model code in an effort to standardize the requirements for builders, and to help build a healthier economy and a cleaner environment. This code has largely been welcomed by the construction industry seeking consistent, up-to-date building standards.

The Federal Energy Policy Act of 1992 directs states to adopt a statewide Commercial Building Energy Standard based on ASHRAE/IES Standard 90.1-1989, Energy Efficient Design of New Public Buildings Except Low-Rise Residential Buildings. The ASHRAE Standard 90 is a general term that includes present and previous iterations of the standard and is perhaps the most commonly referenced and adopted energy standard in the country, forming the basis for energy codes adopted in over 40 U.S. states, including Maine, New Hampshire, and Vermont.

Sample energy standards

When evaluating the energy impacts of new development there are some standards and terminology review boards can expect to see in applications and regulations, or hear in testimony. Figure 14-2 shows common energy standards, although they can vary by many other factors, including state or jurisdiction, square footage of an area, type of framing and foundation, and voltage.

Similarities and differences in energy codes and review in the three northern New England states

Federal Title XII, Public Safety and Welfare, Chapter 155-D, Energy Conservation in New Building Construction, eff. 6/18/90 (The Energy Conservation Act), provides funds to the states for the development of a comprehensive energy conservation plan. New Hampshire has created two statewide energy codes: The New Hampshire Commercial Energy Building Code (essentially ASHRAE 90.1-9189, and conforming with IECC 2000) and the New Hampshire Code for Energy Conservation in New Building Construction, PUC 1800, also known as the Residential Energy Code. The codes cover many areas of construction, including mechanical, architectural, and lighting systems.

All but one percent of New Hampshire's transportation energy demand is met by petroleum. Commercial and industrial energy use

Figure 14-2. Residential and commercial energy standards:

Residential

- Heating system: By federal law, a minimum efficiency of 80% AFUE for boilers and 78% AFUE for furnaces.

- Windows: U-Value of .35 (Low-E windows). Varies depending on the area involved and the level of other energy conserving features such as the use of other Low- E windows.

- Ceiling flats: Minimum total R-value of 38

- Ceiling slopes: Minimum total R-value of 30

- Basement walls: Minimum total R-value of 10

- Glazing percentage: 12% or less

- Domestic hot water: Minimum total R-value of 14

- Recessed lighting fixtures: Type IC rated, manufactured with no penetration between the inside of the recessed fixture and ceiling cavity.

Commercial

- Walls, above grade, metal buildings: Minimum U-value of 0.057

- Air-cooled air conditioners: Split system with a minimum efficiency of 10.0 SEER

- Air-cooled heat pumps: Split system with a minimum efficiency of 10.0 SEER

- Warm air furnaces (gas-fired): A minimum efficiency of 78% AFUE

- Condensing units (air-cooled): A minimum efficiency of 9.9 EER

- Pipe insulation: 1 inch on circulating water–heating systems.

- Vapor retarders: A perm rating of 1.0 or less, installed in all unvented framed areas in ceilings, walls and floors.

in New Hampshire costs about $900 million on an annual basis and residential energy use runs as high as $798 million. The state is undertaking initiatives to curb this trend. The Governor's Office of Energy and Community Services provides technical assistance to the localities for energy efficiency. The New Hampshire Alliance for Clean Transportation Systems seeks to improve the state's air quality through two programs promoting alternative vehicles that reduce air emissions through the use of more efficient and cleaner-burning vehicles.

Electricity customers in New Hampshire can take advantage of "core" energy efficiency programs established by the New Hampshire Public Utilities Commission, including the Energy Star® Lighting Program; rebate programs for energy efficient lights and fixtures; the Energy Star® Appliance Program; the New Hampshire Energy Star® Homes Program; the Small Business Energy Efficiency Program; and the Building Energy Conservation Initiative (BECI).

In towns where building codes have been adopted, the building code official or similar municipal representative reviews the plans and specifications to determine conformance with the code. The building inspector may request assistance from the state's public utilities commission. If no building codes have been adopted in a town, it is the responsibility of the owner-builder or the general contractor to submit plans and specifications to the state public utilities commission for review.

There is no state-wide land use regulatory regime in New Hampshire that reviews the energy impacts of new development. Compliance is left entirely to the code officers or administrators in municipal offices. Municipalities can require engineers and architects to certify that their buildings meet or exceed the requirements of the energy code (RSA 155-D:4, VUI and VII). In Hanover, NH, the comprehensive plan and planning/zoning regulations only minimally address energy efficiency for new development. In towns with no building inspectors or code officials, the only option for builders or architects is to have the plans reviewed by state officials in Concord or do it with the assistance of a state web site. Only the larger towns such as Concord, Lebanon, Keene, and Nashua have adequate local staff available to evaluate compliance with state energy codes. Even in these larger towns, there is little language in zoning or subdivision regulations for use by review boards to evaluate the energy impacts of new development.

Vermont created the 2001 Vermont Guidelines for Energy Efficient Commercial Construction to serve as a statewide commercial building energy code. These guidelines adopt IECC 2000 as the model energy code for the State of Vermont, with amendments to suit Vermont's climate and special needs and to meet ASHREA/IES Standard 90.1-1999. Under the guidelines, a qualified design professional submits a set of construction documents, including plans and specifications, to the local code official. These documents should include all building envelope, mechanical, lighting, and electric power distribution system plans. The specifications should contain enough information to identify and verify thermal and solar ratings; all mechanical system components, capacities, and efficiency ratings; and all lighting system arrangements and ratings. Subsequently, the consultant certifies to the code official that the project has been designed and specified to meet the requirements and that all the systems have been installed in substantial accordance with the construction drawings.

The Vermont Residential Energy Code, also known as the "Residential Building Energy Standards" (RBES), is based on the Model Energy Code adopted by the Council of American Building Officials. It provides a minimum standard of energy efficiency for all new residential construction. The RBES encompass a technical requirement and a certification requirement in which the builder self-certifies compliance. The RBES covers building envelope, air exchange, ducts, HVAC, temperature controls, fireplaces, hot water, swimming pools, and electric systems.

Builders certify in writing that the building complies with the law. Methods to determine compliance include use of the Home Energy Rated Method, and the Systems Analysis Method developed by the Council of American Building Officials. If the home meets the technical requirements of the Energy Code, a Vermont Residential Building Energy Standards Certificate must be completed and permanently posted in the home.

In a random telephone survey of Vermont towns, we found that compliance by builders with the certificate provision is spotty at best. Several town clerks report that this practice is non-existent to occasional, with the highest levels of compliance found in the larger, more urbanized areas. Several of the municipalities reported that there is very little done with energy efficiency on the local level. Even some larger towns claim that while their comprehensive plans and supporting regulations have a few paragraphs about energy, the local permit application forms do not ask energy questions, and the subject is rarely raised at public hearings. Not many towns in Vermont have code officials, although the Vermont Department of Public Service does receive the certificates routinely. Three towns in Vermont have adopted the BOCA Code for building construction as of 2003 but only one, Burlington, has adopted and is enforcing its own energy guidelines.

The Vermont Department of Public Service reviews and comments on each Act 250 land use permit application under Criterion 9(F) Energy Conservation and 9(G), Public Utilities. With regard to residential projects, if the developer can demonstrate that the project complies with the RBES, then the code creates a "presumption of compliance" with Criterion 9(F) and the review is a relatively simple matter. Electric space heating is prohibited unless special approval is given by the review board. All Act 250 applicants must demonstrate compliance with the Vermont Consolidated Act 250 Energy Guidelines for Typical Commercial and Industrial Buildings. These guidelines provide minimum performance standards for commercial projects and meet the IEEC 2000. The state established an organization, Efficiency Vermont, to help builders comply with codes and standards. Meeting the minimum guidelines has become an acceptable way to address the "best available technology" component of Criterion 9(F). On larger projects, the applicant may also find the best choice by using a life-cycle cost analysis.

The Maine Public Utilities Commission has established a number of programs for energy efficiency under the Conservation Act. The state uses the ASHRAE 90.1 (1999) standard for commercial energy efficiency. Title 10 Commerce and Trade, Part 3, Chapter 214 (Energy Efficiency Building Performance Standards) apply to all but single family residences. Maine has an Energy Council to coordinate energy activities. Additionally, the Maine Department of Economic & Community Development, Energy Conservation Division, and the Maine State Planning Office take lead roles in energy efficiency issues and measures similar to those in New Hampshire and Vermont.

Core Enforcement Officials in each town apply standards to the review of structures. Some towns such as Rockland have adopted the BOCA Code, which has some energy efficiency aspects. The Natural Resources Council of Maine has called upon the state to regain its former energy leadership role.

Raising the bar

Energy codes usually represent the minimum energy efficiency standards that new construction must meet. States' efforts to codify even the minimum standards can be fraught with controversy between interest groups. When minimum standards are in place, that is exactly what the designers will provide. Energy codes are certainly better than nothing but in many cases they are a low hurdle. The engineering, architectural, and construction practices gravitate toward minimum standards but, in fact, there is a lot of upside potential. Review boards genuinely interested in controlling the energy impacts of new development may accept evidence of code compliance and then go a step further.

Some measures to improve energy efficiency may involve minor tweaking in the building orientation or installation of a more efficient furnace, but some involve taking a much broader look at issues such as scattered development involving greater automobile dependency and electric utility line extensions. Sprawling development should be reviewed carefully in a regulatory context because its energy use is comparatively higher than compact development. The type of land cover makes a significant contribution to the chemical composition of the atmosphere. Mixed uses, transit-friendly development, and efficient use of building space and materials help reduce energy demand. Environmental ills such as deteriorating urban air quality, acid rain, global warming, ozone depletion, nuclear waste, and disastrous oils spills can be decreased through careful management of our energy demand one project at a time.

On a planning level, communities can plan for future growth to occur in areas close to public transit and that allow pedestrian access to town centers where amenities, schools and services are found. Sprawled and decentralized development bleeds into "greenfield" areas, increasing automobile dependence. Planning measures to provide housing for all income levels and mixed uses in our downtowns throughout northern New England include concentrated development and allow us to become less dependent on fossil fuels. However, regulators are not always planners. They must make decisions within a fixed framework and consider development projects on a case-by-case basis, on a specific parcel of land that may or may not make sense from an energy efficiency standpoint. Therefore, it is important to ask questions and encourage developers to think creatively about what more they can do to cut energy costs.

The renewable energy resources most commonly thought of in northern New England are wood, hydroelectric, solar, and wind energy. Emerging and renewable energy technologies merit consideration and research today, as shown by the growth of New England businesses that provide energy efficiency services.

Energy issues affect transportation review, architectural design, and site planning itself. A good overall question to ask is "What further steps can be taken, customized to your project, to increase energy efficiency?" The responses might include looking at street alignment to see if it optimizes structure location for solar gain and prevailing winds. Or perhaps decreasing space heating costs through passive solar design. Landscaping can help cool in the summer and block wind in the winter. Houses can receive increased space for thermal insulation; significant caulking; life cycle costing analyses; sealing and gaskets; double-glazed, gas-filled windows; and heat ducts within the interior walls. Although some of these measures may go beyond state or local code requirements, the concepts may be expressed in comprehensive municipal plans. Anyway, it never hurts to ask.

Sources of information on sustainable energy practices for residential and commercial construction are given below. Recommendations range from "green lighting" to encouraging greater solar access, to construction of "eco-industrial parks."

Where to go for more information

American Society of Heating, Refrigerating and Air Conditioning Engineers, Inc. (ASHRAE). www.ashrae.org

Consumer Federation of America Foundation. http://www. buyenergyefficient.org

Efficiency Vermont. http://www.efficiencyvermont.org

Energy and Environmental Building Association. http://www.eeba.org

Energy Information Administration. http://www.eia.doe.gov/

Federal Transit Administration. http://www.fta.dot.gov

Local Governments Commission. http://www.lgc.org/economic/centers

Maine Department of Economic and Community Development, Energy Conservation Division, 59 State House Station, Augusta ME 04333

Maine Department of Environmental Protection. http://www.state.me.us/dep/index

Maine Public Utilities Commission. http://www.state.me.us/mpuc/homepage

New Hampshire Code for Energy Conservation in New Building Construction (PUC 1800). http://www.puc.state.nh.us/rules/puc1800

New Hampshire Governor's Office of Energy and Community Service. http://www.state.nh.us/governor/energycomm/

New Hampshire Public Utilities Commission. http://www.puc.state.nh.us/

Northeast Energy Efficient Partnerships, Inc., 5 Militia Drive, Lexington, MA 02421. http://www.neep.org

Northeast Sustainable Energy Association. http://www.nesea.org

Renewable Energy Policy Project/Center for Renewable Energy and Sustainable Technology. http://www.crest.org/index

U.S. Climate Change Science Program/U.S. Global Change Research Program. http://www.usgcrp.gov

U.S. Department of Energy. http://www.energy.gov/

U.S. Environmental Protection Agency Energy Star ® Programs, US EPA, Region 1. http://www.epa.gov/region1/

Vermont Department of Public Service, Energy Efficiency Division. http://www.state.vt.us/psd/ee/ee

Vermont Residential Building Energy Standards. http://www.state.vt.us/psd/rbesupdt/act20sum.htm

Chapter 15
FORESTRY AND AGRICULTURE

Much of northern New England history is tied to forestry and agriculture. In some floodplains, agricultural fields were being cultivated well before the advent of European settlers, although not as early as in the southern United States. The characteristics that first made those fields desirable still apply today: deep soils, relative flatness, large size, good drainage, good nutrients, and adequate water for irrigation. Modern agricultural operations also depend on the ability of the land to support mechanized equipment through adequate drainage, gentle slopes, and good soil structure. However, agriculture and forestry are more than economic pursuits; they are part of our cultural fiber.

Subdivision and development projects may affect forestry and agriculture because the project lands contain or adjoin these resources, or because these activities are already occurring on them. About 75% of northern New England's land base is forested and almost 10% is farmland—almost the exact reverse of what it was in the late 19th century. Both the forestry and agricultural industries sustain local businesses, and are important to the region's overall economy. They provide shelter for wildlife and add to the beauty of the landscape, which is vital to the tourism industry. Some studies have shown that undeveloped land is less of a financial burden to municipalities because it doesn't require schools, roads, and sewer and water infrastructure. Undeveloped land kept in agriculture or forestry is often a community benefit. According to the Maine Department of Agriculture, Food and Rural Resources, agriculture has a $1.2 billion impact on the Maine economy. Maine is increasingly diverse in agriculture, despite the decline of the dairy industry. It is the largest producer of brown eggs and wild blueberries in the world, not to mention ranking eighth in the country for the production of potatoes.

Maine, Vermont, and New Hampshire all have a host of governmental and non-profit entities working to strengthen the agricultural and forestry industries. Vermont has a "current use" program that lightens the tax load for owners of both agricultural and forest land in production, as well as a "right-to-farm law." Vermont also has a Forest Resource Plan 1999-2008 that identifies opportunities for foresters, along with a Forest Legacy Program that provides funding to help conserve important forestland threatened with conversion to non-forest uses. Vermont's Municipal and Regional Development Act (24 V.S.A. § 117) stipulates that all local comprehensive plans must include provisions that encourage and strengthen the agricultural and forest industries. The New Hampshire Department of Agriculture, Markets and Food brings producers and consumers together through marketing programs and promotional incentives. Maine prohibits "inconsistent development" within 100 feet of a farm (7 M.R.S.A. §56). There are also states, including Maine, that ensure that farms with operations meeting "Best Management Practices" (BMPs) are not considered a "nuisance." In Vermont, operations implementing BMPs are eligible for financial assistance awards. Many state planning and environmental protection programs in all three states work on agricultural and forestry issues.

Yet, the issue of maintaining vital farm and forest industries is complex and difficult. Maine, New Hampshire, and Vermont lost about ten percent of prime farmland to development between 1982 and 1997 (Heart *et al*, 2002). Prime forest and agricultural land is often the development land of choice; keeping land in production has never been harder for New England farmers. Encroaching suburbanization; low milk prices; competition from mid-western and western mega-farms; a short growing season; problems with subsidies; questions about generational transfer; mountainous debt loads; and long, arduous work days all conspire to make the future of farming in the region a constant source of debate and concern. Many communities no longer have the feed stores, farm equipment stores and other necessities for a true agricultural economy, making farming no longer viable. Suburbanization of the countryside has led to concern about the adverse effects of farming on housing development rather than the other way around. Maine has had to pass laws to protect farms from being considered a "nuisance." In spite of the regulatory and social difficulties, reviewers increasingly sense an obligation to preserve agricultural land for future generations. According to The American Farmland Trust (1996), growth itself is not the problem; the real culprit is wasteful land use. In the US, urbanization has increased at more than double the rate of population growth. Marking a trend found across northern New England, the Vermont Forum on Sprawl (VFOS, n.d.) found that from 1982 to 1992, Vermont's population grew by 8.8% while developed land grew by 25.3%—almost 40% as much. In many municipalities, zoned lot sizes are too big in both village and rural areas; and land is being used inefficiently and with little regard for open spaces. Market choice drives this land use pattern, notably, individual desires for large residential lots in the countryside; the popularity of 1-3 acre lots in subdivisions with cul-de-sacs and private roads; and higher development costs for land, parking, etc. in town centers compared to outlying areas. If a community response to growth management is merely to zone for big lots, then the result will be sprawl, and natural resource lands will be fragmented and dotted with residential housing. Other strategies are needed in addition to regulating lot sizes, such as agricultural or forestry use restrictive zones. Growth can be pursued and accommodated, but retaining open space should also be a goal.

Agricultural and forestland protection

Strengthening the agricultural economy in northern New England and ensuring that forestry land is not fragmented beyond economically productive use are complex, seemingly intractable objectives that can't be met on a parcel-by-parcel, piece-meal basis by local or state development review boards. However, regulatory review boards can capitalize on any municipal planning and zoning mechanisms that are in place, and any legal tools, conservation schemes, and management plans that make sense for the project under review. The review board must ensure that it is not creating any impediments to agricultural or forestry use by the location and configuration of the development plans it approves and the conditions it imposes. Additionally, even agricultural soils that are less than prime (i.e., not of statewide significance) may still be needed

215

at some time in the future. It is not possible to accurately predict agricultural methods and needs 100 years from now.

Mapping is an essential tool. Most New England soils have been mapped by the Natural Resources Conservation Service (NRCS, formerly Soil Conservation Service). NRCS soil data are usually accompanied by an accuracy rating or other information to guide the reader. Given the huge nature of NRCS soil-mapping efforts, it is easy to see how the field conditions might vary from the mapped conditions. When making a land use decision, field reports are best for individual projects, and the NRCS maps are best for general planning and zoning. Soils maps are often reproduced on an aerial photograph, with open fields and features easily visible. A mapping scale of 1 inch = 1,000 feet is often used. Most forestry occurs on land that was formerly logged and used for pasture or other agriculture. These woodlands now play a very significant role in wildlife protection. If the land is forested or has only recently been logged, the quality of the soils for forestry should be apparent without soil testing. Like many forms of agriculture, forestry requires large tracts to be viable. The size of the parcel remains debatable and often depends on what kinds of wildlife are to be protected. An economically viable parcel for logging purposes is usually at least 25 acres in size (the Natural Resources Council of Maine suggests 50 acre minimum lot size zoning for forestry). This is primarily a planning concern and not something that can be solved in reviewing one tract, however the development of a large tract of land may affect adjacent forest operations as well as the on-site resources. Similarly, the subdivision of a tract may fragment ownership of forest resources, making comprehensive forest management almost impossible.

Agriculture, too, is dependent on sufficient land resources and a supportive rural community; good soil is not enough for viable agriculture. The land characteristics (configuration) must also be suitable and the land must be able to contribute to an agricultural operation. If an adjacent farmer is to use the land it must be accessible from his or her farm. Many tracts of agricultural land become isolated through subdivision or through suburban development of the surrounding area. In either case, isolation may remove the agricultural viability of a tract even though it contains suitable soils and land configuration.

Language to protect agriculture and forestry in local comprehensive plans, and in zoning and subdivision regulations, varies from town to town. Local review boards vary in how creatively they use the planning techniques available to them. Agriculture usually gets more attention than forestry, but both can benefit from the same strategies.

The Planned Residential Development (PRD) is a zoning mechanism that allows the review board to decrease the lot size from what would normally be allowed in the district and allow more units, as long as they are clustered, in order to retain a reasonable amount of open space. This technique, which also allows for decreasing the size of set-backs from lot boundaries, is provided for by law in New Hampshire and Vermont, and by practice in Maine.

Another consideration is in the definition of "farming." Farming is going to look more diverse in the future than it does today, with many sorts of niche products produced and marketed. Review boards may find that "farming" is defined broadly in their town's regulations and that they have considerable discretion when considering projects. Right-to-farm laws and programs can be used to encourage agricultural conservation.

Municipal open-space plans are a powerful tool. In conjunction with its comprehensive plan, a municipality may undertake an open space planning process that inventories and maps open spaces, describes their values, and suggests strategies and recommendations for implementing the plan. These strategies may range from changing zoning regulations and subdivision bylaws to working with local land trusts and advocacy groups.

A tree growth tax law or "current use" appraisal program can be an incentive for clustering development and for conserving forestlands. The review board can encourage working with state foresters in promoting this program. To this end, Maine requires any municipality attempting to regulate forest harvest activities to use definitions of forestry terms consistent with those adopted by the Commissioner of the Department of Conservation (12 M.R.S.A. § 8869). However, the municipality has individual discretion on regulating forestry. All states have community or county foresters that can offer advice.

Superimposing a resource area over an underlying zoning district with special requirements and certain extra review procedures can create agricultural and forestry overlay districts. An overlay district is mapped, included as part of the comprehensive plan, and is applicable to development review.

Transferable Development Rights (TDR) represent a market-based technique to identify a section of a municipality that the community wants to protect from growth (the sending zone) and a section where the municipality would like to encourage growth (the receiving zone). TDR programs can be voluntary or mandatory and allow the sending zone landowners to sell the development rights to owners in receiving zones. A conservation easement is often placed on the sending zone land. TDR programs are complicated and do not work unless the market conditions are right, but in some places they are a technique that works well for review boards and towns wishing to take an active role in directing the location of growth. TDRs are allowed by law in Vermont and New Hampshire and in Maine because of the "home rule" authority of the towns.

Sewer and water service areas are boundaries established by the municipality beyond which no further sewer and water infrastructure may be extended. This delineation serves to concentrate development in already developed areas and limit new and large developments at the fringe or beyond the service area. Urban growth boundaries accomplish some of the same goals but are considered more controversial and draconian.

Zoning districts are a front-trench method to conserve agricultural and forested land. Zones should be derived from the comprehensive plan. In agricultural and forestry zoning districts, the lot sizes are usually larger in order to support viable operations. Typically, forestry and farming are the primary land uses allowed in the district. Residential uses are also allowed, but PRDs may be required in order to keep more land open. Housing for farm labor should be allowed in these districts. In some states, only seasonal camps and forest-related development are allowed in forestry zones. Forestry, agricultural and rural zones, when viewed on a map, often define an "edge" for the town in terms of built-up and rural areas. What is permitted in such zones is often the first thing local review boards take into consideration when reviewing a development project.

Single use zoning for forestry and agricultural purposes is permitted by law in New Hampshire. In Vermont it is permitted along with residential lots of more than 25 acres. State law in Maine allows such zoning districts and includes broad provisions for the protection of natural resources. If single-use policies exist, they may prevent land speculation and inflated prices.

Vermont's Act 250 review of agricultural and forestry soils

The Vermont approach may be useful to other states. Agricultural and forestry soils in Vermont can receive an additional review beyond the local level if a proposed development is subject to Act 250 jurisdiction. This review contains a rationale for allowing development that "significantly" reduces the potential of agricultural and forestry soils under the following conditions: 1) if there is no other reasonable "return on the fair market value" in the tract; 2) if the applicant owns no other more suitable soils; 3) if the project has been designed to minimize the reduction of agricultural or forestry potential; and 4) if the project will not unduly interfere with adjacent agriculture or forestry. For success in reducing impacts, the statute requires: "providing for reasonable population densities, reasonable rates of growth, and the use of cluster planning and new community planning designed to economize on the costs of roads, utilities and land usage." [10 V.S.A. Section 6086(a)(9)(B) and (9)(C)].

"Primary agricultural soils" and "forest and secondary agricultural soils" are defined by the statute, but the definition for the latter is less precise. Considerable case law has been built up around the interpretation of these criteria. Savvy developers conduct the analysis early in the feasibility stage of the project. An impact fee or suitable off-site mitigation can be used to meet the criteria. Debate has intensified in recent years about allowing the development of primary agricultural soils when they occur in town centers or in designated growth areas. In these instances, mitigation may be required. Most communities do not have sophisticated agricultural or forestry soils analyses and mitigation programs at the local level.

Local protection of farming and forestry

A drive through the areas of northern New England experiencing the most growth pressure suggests that, despite a number of laws to protect forestry and farming, a better job could be done at the local review level. Debate over the conversion of agricultural land can be some of the most fractious and contentious dialogue at public development review hearings. Reviewers have a broad array of choices and tools; these must be used frequently and wisely (Figure 15-1).

Figure 15-1. Checklist for review boards to evaluate site plans for agricultural and forestry impacts.

___ Are the prime and non-prime agricultural soils mapped, as well as areas suitable for commercial forestry?

___ How much of the prime agricultural soils will be consumed by the project?

___ If the loss of these soils is significant, has an impact fee been proposed or is there a plan for off-site mitigation?

___ Have appropriate buffer zones and setbacks from farming / forestry areas and residential uses been incorporated into the site plan? Has the potential for incompatible uses been minimized?

___ Has land conservation in the form of the purchase of development rights through a state organization or private land trust been considered?

___ Has a PRD been designed or have the housing units or commercial project been clustered to preserve the bulk of the agricultural or forestry resource? Has the development, including the road, been sited along the edge of fields rather than in them? Has a "conservation design" been considered that minimizes impacts on natural areas to the greatest extent possible?

___ Who is going to own the residual agricultural land? Has an agricultural management plan been prepared?

___ Has an easement been provided for access for farming equipment for the land that will remain productive? In a forested area, has an easement for a logging road and a landing area been reserved?

___ Have specific building locations ("envelopes") been designated for residential subdivisions to further discourage encroachment into forest or agricultural land?

___ If the project is a residential subdivision, does it provide community or individual garden spaces?

___ Does the site plan minimize fragmentation of the natural resource land?

___ If there are significant forestry resources, is there a forest management plan?

Where to go for more information

American Farmland Trust. Farmland Information Center, *Right-to-Farm Laws Fact Sheet*. http://www.farmlandinfo.org/fic/tas/tafs-rtfl.html

Arendt, Randall, 1994. *Rural by Design*. Chicago, Planners Press.

Brady, Nyle C. and Ray R. Weil. (2001). *The Nature and Properties of Soils* (13th Edition). Upper Saddle River, NJ: Prentice Hall.

Daniels, Thomas L. (1991). Do tax breaks on farmland help protect it from conversion? *Farmland Preservation Report, Special Report*.

Daniels, Thomas L. (1991). The purchase of development rights: preserving agricultural land and open space. *Journal of the American Planning Association*. 57, No. 4: 421-431.

Daniels, Thomas L. (1999). *When City and Country Collide–Managing Growth in the Metropolitan Fringe*. Washington, DC: Island Press.

Daniels, Thomas L. (1997). Where does cluster zoning fit in farmland protection? *Journal of the American Planning Association*, 6663, no. 1 : 129-137.

Heart, Bennet, Elizabeth Humstone, Thomas F. Irwin, Sandy Levine, Dano Weisbord. (2002). *Community Rules – A New England Guide to Smart Growth Strategies*. Burlington, VT: Conservation Law Foundation and the Vermont Forum on Sprawl.

Lapping, Mark B. (1982). *Toward a Working Rural Landscape in New England*. Carl Reidel, ed. Prospects: Critical Choices in a Time of Change. Hanover, NH: University Press of New England.

Lapping, Mark B., Thomas L. Daniels, and John Keller. (1989). *Rural Planning and Development in the United States*. New York, NY: Guilford Publications.

Maine Association of Professional Soil Scientists. http://www.mapss.com/

Maine Department of Agriculture, Food and Rural Resources. (2002). *Maine Food and Farms Resource Guide: Handbook for Maine Agricultural Businesses*. August, ME: Maine Dept. of Agriculture, Food and Rural Resources. (Also available on CD.)

National Small Flows Clearinghouse. http://www.estd.wvu.edu/nsfc/nsfc_
homepage.html

National Soil Survey Center. http://www.nssc.nrcs.usda.gov

Natural Resources Conservation Service. Primary web site for national
soils information. http://www.nrcs.usda.gov

Natural Resources Conservation Service. (1992). *Stormwater Management and
Erosion and Sediment Control Handbook for Urban and Developing Areas in
New Hampshire.* Rockingham County Conservation District, NH
Department of Environmental Services, Soil Conservation Service
(now the Natural Resources Conservation Service).

Natural Resources Conservation Service, Maine. Primary web site for
Maine soils information, including mapping, services, and links. http:/
/www. me.nrcs.usda.gov/

Natural Resources Conservation Service, New Hampshire. http://www.nh.
nrcs.usda.gov/Soil_Data/

Natural Resources Conservation Service, Vermont. http://www.vt.nrcs.
usda.gov/soils/soil_home_page.htm

Natural Resources Council of Maine, n.d., *Working Landscapes: Are we zoning
our farmland, forestland, and wildlife habitat out of existence?* Augusta, ME:
Natural Resources Council of Maine.

New Hampshire Association of Consulting Soil Scientists. 15 Muchado
Drive, Barrington, NH 03825-3818.

NRCS & SSSA. (2002). *Soil Planner 2002: State Soils and Protecting Important
Farmlands.* Natural Resources Conservation Service, Soil Science Society of America.

Rural Community Assistance Program (RCAP). http://www.rcap.org/

Russell, Howard S. (1982). (Abridged and edited by Mark Lapping.) *A Long
Deep Furrow: Three Centuries of Farming in New England, and Rural Planning
and Development in the United States.* Hanover, NH: University Press of
New England.

Society of Soil Science of Northern New England, USDA, Natural Resources Conservation Service, 27 Westminster St., Lewiston, ME 04240-3531.

Soil Science Society of America. http://soilslab.cfr.washington.edu/S-7/.

Sundquist, D. and Michael Stevens. (1999). *New Hampshire's Changing Landscape, Population Growth, Land Use Conversion, and Resource Fragmentation in the Granite State.* Concord, NH: Society for the Protection of New Hampshire Forests and the New Hampshire Chapter of the Nature Conservancy. www.spnhf.org

U.S. Department of Agriculture, Natural Resources Inventory, December 2000. http://www.wi.nrcs.usda.gov/nri/nri.asp

Vermont Agency of Natural Resources. (1987). *Vermont Handbook for Soil Erosion and Sediment Control on Construction Sites.* Waterbury, VT: Department of Environmental Conservation.

Vermont Department of Agriculture, Food and Markets. (1994). *Sustaining Agriculture: A Handbook for Local Action.* Supplement to the *Planning Manual for Vermont Municipalities.* Montpelier, VT: Vermont Dept. of Agriculture, Food and Markets.

Vermont Forum on Sprawl. *Exploring Sprawl Number 3, The Causes and Costs of Sprawl in Vermont Communities.* Burlington, VT: Vermont Forum on Sprawl. See also http://www.vtsprawl.org

COASTAL AREAS

The waters off the coast of New Hampshire and Maine are part of the Gulf of Maine, a semi-enclosed sea with tall underwater land forms ("banks") as a partial barrier to the North Atlantic Ocean. The coastlines of Massachusetts, New Hampshire, Maine, New Brunswick, and Nova Scotia are the western and northern boundaries of the gulf and the banks are to the south and east. The gulf is served by a large watershed area of 69,115 square miles (179,008 square kilometers), containing all of Maine and much of Nova Scotia, New Brunswick, New Hampshire and Massachusetts, and a small portion of Quebec. The gulf defines our coastal identity and it is influenced by development along its shoreline.

The federal Coastal Zone Management Act (CZMA) of 1972 led to the Maine Coastal Program hosted in the Maine State Planning Office and the NH Coastal Program within the NH Office of State Planning. Various other federal laws, including the Clean Water Act; Marine Protection, Research and Sanctuaries Act; Water Pollution Control Act Section 404; and the Rivers and Harbors Act, apply to coastal areas. The federal Army Corps of Engineers exerts regulatory jurisdiction over construction and fill activities under federal law.

In Maine, the Natural Resources Protection Act, Site Location and Development Law, and Mandatory Shoreland Zoning Law govern coastal areas, in addition to local municipal regulations. At least half of all Mainers live near the mostly rocky 4,342 miles of coast. New Hampshire has only about 18 miles of seacoast.

In New Hampshire, the Comprehensive Shoreland Protection Act (CSPA), establishes "protected Shoreland" as the area of land existing between the "reference line" and 250 feet from the reference line. The reference line for coastal waters is the highest observable tide line defining the furthest landward limit of tidal flow (exclusive of storm events). To detect the reference line, look for a line of stranded flotsam and debris, the landward margin of salt-tolerant vegetation, or a physical barrier that blocks further flow of the tide. Certain activities are restricted or prohibited within the protected Shoreland; others require a permit from the New Hampshire Department of Environmental Services (DES). The CSPA has jurisdiction over all coastal waters subject to the ebb and flow of the tide, including the Great Bay Estuary and the associated tidal rivers. The DES Internet web site includes information on the allowable activities and standards in the Shoreland Protection Act.

A basic understanding of coastal marine processes and environmental conditions helps in proper assessment of development projects. Most projects that affect coastal resources will have to endure several permit processes and reviews, meaning that these project proposals are likely to be accompanied by a significant amount of information and detail on the nature of the construction as well as the nature of the environmental setting and anticipated impacts.

Perhaps the most important concept to keep in mind is that coastal environments are dynamic systems, with all kinds of changes occurring from sea level rise to alterations in basic landforms. Coastal erosion is a constant issue, as are development pressures with their attendant septic discharge, urban runoff, and habitat loss. Communities are faced with the need to entrench Best Management Practices (BMPs) along with adequate regulatory and physical infrastructure systems. Upland communities are also involved because coastal water quality is influenced by activities throughout entire watersheds. NOAA, Maine, and New Hampshire have created coastal non-point pollution control programs to reduce non-point source pollution.

Maine and New Hampshire coastal programs have broad-based Coastal Plans to help state agencies and local communities. Large municipalities such as Portland, Maine, and Portsmouth, New Hampshire, have well-developed site plan and subdivision regulations for coastal development, as do communities that have undergone population and resort pressures (e.g., Kennebunk, Maine). The regional planning commissions that encompass coastal areas are also prepared to assist, notably through the use of GIS in planning, and through refinement of comprehensive plans. However, a continual problem for coastal communities is preserving the community way of life amid pressure to allow more development and to provide more services. Historically, strip development has been a major coastal response to growth pressure. Fortunately, communities are now much more careful of the need to guide growth and to account for the cumulative effect when they review site plans.

Common types of coastal environments

Mud flats

Mud flats, also known as tidal flats, lack vegetation and consist of mud, sand, or gravel. Formed by the deposition of fine sediments coming out of suspension in the sea or estuary, mudflats are regularly exposed and flooded by the tides. Mud flats occur in estuaries, inlets, and sheltered areas where the wave-action is low. The primary concerns from shoreline development in these areas are the potential change in water patterns and the introduction of contaminants (e.g., heavy metals, hydrocarbons, wastewater discharge, and stormwater runoff).

Sand and pebble beaches

Beaches are dynamic and diverse habitats. Most of Maine and New Hampshire shoreline is not beach; what little we do have is highly valued. Yet the quality of Maine's sand beaches are declining due to encroachment by development and sea level rise. The public may not notice this decline until a building or landscape feature is in danger of collapse. In Maine, buildings that are destroyed by a storm must be removed. New engineering structures cannot be built to protect existing property on a shoreline. The options for property at risk are "beach nourishment" and relocation of structures. Yet the nourishment of beaches by adding sand typically costs between one and five million dollars per mile.

Rocky shoreline

Most of the coast of northern New England consists of rocky shoreline characterized by high wave action, constant submersion and exposure, and changing salinity and temperature—a high-energy situation. The tidal pools along the shoreline and the other shoreline features serve protective functions, particularly in absorbing or reducing wave energy. Potential impact from shoreline construction includes changes in water patterns, increase of discharges, changes in sunlight levels, introduction of contaminants and debris, habitat loss, and the alteration of energy flows.

Dunes

Dunes, relatively uncommon in northern New England, are comparatively temporary or migratory mounds, hills, and ridges of sand located above the tidal area, Trapped sand over many years builds up into dunes. Dunes are anchored by grasses and may seem stable but can change rapidly with a single storm event. Adjacent beaches depend on dunes for sand supply and storage. Dunes also absorb storm energy, protecting inland areas, and provide valuable habitat, notably for nesting birds such as the Least Tern *(Sterna antillarum)* and Piping Plover *(Charadrius melodus)*. Highly vulnerable to impacts from hiking and other relatively minor human activities, dunes are particularly at risk from the construction of nearby beachfront dwellings. Sand transport rates and directions can be greatly affected by other construction, especially jetties and wave barriers up and down the coast. The loss of dunes has the potential to affect upland houses and other structures, increasing the need for storm surge and erosion control. In response, the Maine NRPA has specific sand dune regulations.

Coastal wetlands

Estuaries and salt marshes are among the most productive habitats on earth. Approximately 70% of all marine species use coastal wetlands at some point in their life cycles. Estuaries are critical watershed areas that played an historic role in the settlement of New England. Salt marshes were important in early New England farming as a source of salt hay. They also provide flood storage, animal habitat, and perform other critical coastal functions. Development pressures threaten the ability of wetlands to carry out their functions. A particular concern is the construction of roads or other barriers across or adjacent to wetlands. In the past, undersized culverts have been a problem because people did not realize the importance of minimal impedance to water flow patterns.

Seagrass beds

Seagrasses are flowering plants that live in shallow saline waters, usually in an estuary or protected bay environment. The only seagrass found in the Gulf of Maine is eelgrass. Seagrasses require a soft muddy substrate and plenty of sunlight and nutrients. In return, seagrass beds provide homes for many estuarine plants and animals, buffer nonpoint source pollution, and reduce the effects of erosion. These highly productive habitats are vulnerable to brown tides, dredging, shoreline development, boat propeller scarring, and decreases in water volume and quality.

Coastal hazards and shoreline change

Like elsewhere, coastal areas in Maine and New Hampshire undergo environmental processes such as climate change, sea level rise, river discharges, wind, currents, tides, and storm events, that are not inherent hazards. These things become hazards only when they are a potential human harm. Hazards occur when sea level rise threatens stability of structures, bluffs and other formations. Sea level may be the number one hazard because it is slowly rising. A long time ago, sea level rise was high, but for the past few millennia it has been less than half a millimeter per year. Things have changed; since 1912, sea level has been rising at about 2.0 mm/year—almost a foot a century. As a rule of thumb, each foot of vertical increase causes a horizontal increase of at least ten times that: a 100 to 150-foot (30.5 to 45.7 meters) migration inland of the shoreline. As seawater warms, the molecules expand, increasing volume and raising sea level. Thus, sea level change correlates with climate change. The Intergovernmental Panel on Climate Change (2001) estimates sea levels could rise another 4 to 34 inches (10.2 to 86.3 cm) before the end of the century, depending on the rate of climate change (i.e., global warming). An increase in sea level will mean a reduced buffering effect from wetland areas in addition to the obvious loss of coastal land and structures. The rise in sea level can be tracked from analyzing historical air photographs, comparison with beach markers, and by looking at the edges of shoreline vegetation. Although sea level rise is only part of the erosion concerns for coastal areas, it is potentially the biggest part.

Communities in New England have responded to coastal erosion by intervention, largely through an engineering disruption of natural processes. Seawalls are used to protect coastal structures and property from storm surges and a potential rise in sea level. Jetties are used by the U.S. Army Corps of Engineers to protect navigational channels and to shelter harbors from destructive wave action. Construction of groins (long rock structures placed perpendicularly to the shoreline) and other artificial features represent attempts to control the force of waves and prevent loss of sand at beaches. But the last groin in a system will cause soil scouring for the next area below, shifting the sand 'budget." Thus, what one project or community does will affect the next one. Other factors demonstrate this connection. Long shore drift, the zig-zag effect of waves arriving at an angle, also shifts the forces acting on one shore line to another, as part of the dynamics of a coastal system. Intruding jetties and groins concentrate wave action and redirect it. The results can be compounded without intent. For example, doubling the height of a wave quadruples the wave energy. Wave reflection off of fortifications has a scouring effect that increases erosion and undermines the fortifications. The other policy choice besides intervention is retreat. However, increased development pressures mitigate against retreat from use of shorelines. Figure 16-1 shows some environmental changes that can occur as a result of development in coastal waters.

Many resort communities are struggling to maintain their sand beaches and are concerned about the effects of any shoreland development. Sand enters the coastal system from rivers, shoreline bluffs, and from off-shore. Sand leaves the system via estuaries, long shore drift and off-shore currents and forces. Erosion rates up to 2.5 feet per year are fairly common. Erosion is very site-specific, although the effects can be quite scattered. The varying coastal environments further ensure a tremendous variety of developmental impacts throughout the region.

Climate change coupled with an increase in sea-level will likely lead to greater destruction from storm surges. Projects located within these areas are at increased risk. Mapping programs from New Hampshire and Maine GIS offices as well as the NOAA C-CAP program can be used to help determine and manage high-risk areas.

Figure 16-1. NOAA matrix of habitat factors compared with human coastal activities. This matrix, showing estimated environmental impacts of shoreline and near-shore construction, is based on National Oceanic and Atmospheric Administration (NOAA) data and the NOAA approach to impact assessment. "D.O." means dissolved oxygen, "cover" refers to organic and inorganic protective cover for organisms, "access" refers to potential ability of organisms to move into or out of the habitat, "flow" means affect on the velocity of water, and "area" is a size measurement.*

Habitat factor	Dredge project	Fill	Pier	Float	Culvert	Discharge source	Bulkhead
Temperature	low	med	low	low	low	high	low
Water quality	high	low	low	low	med	high	low
D.O.	high	low	none	none	med	med	low
Ocean bottom	high	high	low	low	med	med	med
Aquatic plants	high	high	med	med	med	high	med
Cover	med	high	low	med	low	med	low
Food sources	med	high	low	med	low	med	low
Access	low	high	low	low	high	low	high
Flow	med	med	low	low	high	low	low
Area	high	high	med	med	med	med	low

Numerous coastal engineering projects exist along the coasts of Maine and New Hampshire. However, the long term effects of coastal engineering projects include the following: disrupting the longshore drift that distributes sand and sediment along beaches; eroding beaches on the low energy side of jetties (an example of this can be seen in the Camp Ellis/Saco River area in Maine); nurturing a false sense of protection; interrupting the natural responsiveness and adaptation of natural systems; and misleading the true cost of property and structures.

Public access to coastal areas

Most of Maine's coastal lands are privately owned. Approximately 75% of the New Hampshire coast is owned by the public. Public access points to the water and beaches are an issue and can play a role in project mitigation. There are access points available including walkways (e.g., Marginal Way, Ogunquit, ME; Cliff Walk, York, ME), municipal, state and national parks and beaches (e.g., Acadia and Scarborough Beach in Maine, Odiorne Point State Park, NH, Wagon Hill Farm, Durham, NH); fishing Piers, commercial and municipal docks; boat ramps/launches; refuges (Rachel Carson, ME); and existing rights of way (public and established private). Improving public access and increasing public lands remains a viable option for mitigation in coastal development. The intertidal zone is also a public area, although public rights in it are not unlimited.

Aquaculture

Aquaculture is an expanding industry. Conditions are especially favorable in Maine (Downeast), due to tidal flushing, which helps in prevention of diseases. However, problems such as conflicts of interest, genetic contamination of native stock, and private lease of public resources, can lead to contentious reviews. A major goal is to ensure that water quality is not degraded. Any approved aquaculture project should be compatible with adjacent land uses and with protection of coastal wetlands.

Islands

Coastal islands are feeling the pressures of development. Groups such as the Maine Island Trail Association work to conserve resources. Historically, the islands were important for agriculture and the fishing industry. A long tradition of aesthetic enjoyment of the islands prevails. Primary concerns for development center on the need for septic system accommodation, preserving traditional lifestyles, shoreline protection, archaeological site protection, and conservation of natural resources.

Links to organizations along the coast of Maine and New Hampshire that have a role in planning, coastal research, and resource management are provided at the end of this chapter. Some of the more active groups include: Maine and New Hampshire state planning offices, Maine Casco Bay Estuary Project, Friends of Casco Bay (and other Friends organizations), local and regional planning commissions, land trust organizations, Wells National Estuarine Research Reserve, Great Bay National Estuarine Research Reserve, Seacoast Science Center in Rye, NH, and Sandy Point Discovery Center, Stratham NH.

Where to go for more information

Gulf of Maine Council on the Marine Environment. http://www. gulfofmaine.org/index.html

Intergovernmental Panel on Climate Change. (2001). *Third Assessment Report*. Union of Concerned Scientists. http://www.ucsusa.org/ environment/TARscippt26.html

Maine Coastal Program. (2001). *Coastlinks: A resource guide to Maine's coastal organizations*. Maine Coastal Program, Maine State Planning office. Available on-line at the Maine Coastal Program internet site (see below).

Maine Coastal Program (MCP). State Planning Office. http://www.state. me.us/mcp/

Maine State Planning Office, Maine Coastal Program. (1997). *The Waterfront Construction Handbook: Guidelines for the Design and Construction of Waterfront Facilities*. August, ME: MSPO.

National Oceanic and Atmospheric Administration (NOAA), Coastal Services Center. http://www.csc.noaa.gov/CID/

National Oceanic and Atmospheric Administration, U.S. Department of Commerce. http://www.noaa.gov/coasts.html

New England Floodplain and Stormwater Managers Association. http:// www.nefsma.org/

New Hampshire Coastal Program (NHCP). http://www.state.nh.us/ coastal/home.htm

Office of Response and Restoration, National Ocean Service, National Oceanic and Atmospheric Administration. http://response. restoration.noaa.gov/cpr/cpr.html

US Army Corps of Engineers. (1994). *Shoreline Protection and Beach Erosion Control Study, Phase 1: Cost Comparison of Shoreline Protection Projects of the U.S. Army Corps of Engineers*, by Shoreline Protection and Beach Erosion Control Task Force.

Vestal, Barbara A., Alison Rieser, Joseph Kelley, Kathleen Leydon, and Michael Montagna. (1994). *Anticipatory Planning for Sea-level Rise along the Coast of Maine.* Augusta, ME: Maine State Planning Office.

Wells National Estuarine Research Reserve. http://www.wellsreserve.org/

GLOSSARY

A horizon: Layer of mostly decomposed organic soil and dark, organic-rich soil above the B horizon or subsoil. The "A" horizon is known informally as the "topsoil."

Accessory use: A secondary use of land subordinate or incidental to the principal use allowed on a lot by the zoning law. A garage is incidental to the principal use of a single-family residential lot.

Access point: A new road cut onto a state or town highway.

Alteration: Any change to the exterior or structural elements of a building or structure, excluding maintenance or repairs.

American Cultural Resources Association (ACRA): A professional association of consulting archaeologists.

Architectural elevations: Drawings depicting the geometrical projections of a building's architectural features as seen from various angles, typically north, south, east and west. These viewpoints refer to the direction from which the viewer is looking at the building.

B horizon: The soil horizon usually below the A or E horizons, and having less organic content because it is more weathered. The B horizon is known informally as the "subsoil."

Bedrock: Solid ledge or loose weathered rock.

Best Management Practices (BMPs): A procedure recommended for a given set of field conditions, intended to maintain environmental quality. BMPs exist for logging, stormwater management, erosion control, and other environmental actions.

Biological diversity: A measure of the quality of an environmental setting, based on the variety of life and its organization. Diversity includes richness (number of organisms) and evenness (how the organisms are distributed).

Bioremediation: The use of oil-eating or other pollutant-consuming organisms such as bacteria and fungi for environmental cleanup.

Biosolids: Solid materials from wastewater treatment process that meet government criteria for beneficial use, such as for fertilizer.

Block: An area bounded by streets.

Blue line map (blue line drawing): Architectural or engineering rendering of a project, used for planning purposes.

BMP: See Best Management Practices.

Boring log: Record of drilling and similar subsurface testing done by engineers to determine the physical properties of the area.

Boundary adjustment: The adjustment of a boundary line between two contiguous lots such that the adjustment does not create any new lots or substantially change any previous subdivision of land.

Brownfields: Abandoned or underused properties known or suspected to be contaminated with hazardous waste from past commercial or industrial uses.

Building coverage: The percentage of a lot occupied or covered by buildings and other structures.

Building envelope: The area on a site plan designated for construction of a building or other structure. To allow for choice in placement on a site, the building envelope may be larger than the actual building footprint.

Building height: The vertical distance measured from the average elevation of the finished grade to the highest point of the roof for flat and mansard roofs, and to the average height between eave and ridge for other roof styles.

Capacity study: An inventory of natural and human-made resources on a site, based on detailed data collection, which identifies the capabilities and limitations of those resources to accommodate the development of land.

Carcinogenic: A substance that causes cancer.

Catch basin: An excavated sedimentation area designed to remove pollutants from runoff before being discharged.

CLG: see Certified Local Government.

Certified Local Government (CLG): As defined in 36 CFR Part 61.2, CLG is a local government certified to carry out the purposes of the National Historic Preservation Act, in accordance with section 101(c).

Check dam: Small dams, usually temporary and often made of hay bales or stones (preferred), constructed across a swale or drainage ditch to reduce the velocity of concentrated stormwater.

Cluster development: A development design technique that concentrates buildings in a specific area on a site to allow the remaining land to be used for recreation, common open space, and the preservation of natural areas.

Comprehensive plan: The coordinated land use map and policy statement of a government, usually a municipality, that inventories and interrelates all functional and natural systems and activities relating to the use of lands.

Community sewage disposal system: A shared, non-municipal sewage system for domestic, commercial, industrial or institutional uses.

Community water system: A shared, non-municipal water system that supplies water for domestic, commercial, industrial, or institutional uses.

Confined aquifer (artesian aquifer): An aquifer with a dense layer of compacted earth material over it that prevents passage of water.

Conservation easement: A legal agreement in which the landowner continues to own and manage the land, but certain natural or cultural resources on the property are protected.

Compliance project: A particular environmental assessment or reconnaissance response to government regulations, usually in the form of a Phase Assessment or other formal process.

Cone of depression: The cone-shaped area formed in the ground when the spaces in the rock or soil are emptied as water is withdrawn from a well.

Contour line: A line on a map or plan connecting points of equal elevation.

Corridor: A narrow strip of land associated with the movement of people, wildlife, goods, services, and utilities in a right-of-way.

Covenants: A legal agreement between parties or persons regarding mutual rights and responsibilities, such as those binding members of a homeowners association to maintain roads.

Cul-de-sac: a street terminating with a vehicular turn-around area.

Cultural resource: A generic term for archaeological, historical, and built-environment properties.

Cut-off angle: The angle between the vertical axis of a lamp fixture (luminaire) and the first line of sight at which one can no longer see the light source.

CRM: Cultural Resource Management (See below).

Cultural Resource Management (CRM): The research, conservation, and management of archaeological resources within a regulatory framework.

dbh: See Diameter at Breast Height.

DEIS: Draft Environmental Impact Statement (see Environmental Impact Statement).

Design flow: The flow, set by regulation, that establishes the size of water supply or wastewater disposal systems serving a lot, site, or building.

Density: The number of acres or square feet of land required for a given number of units, uses or structures. Road rights-of-way and public easements are typically not included in calculations of density.

Design review: A process by which development within a specific zoning district, designated to encompass an area containing historical, architectural or cultural merit, is subject to formal review or approval.

Design speed: A traffic engineering term typically referring to the posted speed limit for automobiles.

Diagnostic: A term typically used in reference to an artifact or feature distinctive of a particular culture or cultural period.

Diameter at Breast Height (dbh): The diameter of a tree taken at 4.5 feet above average ground level.

Discoverable document: A document entitled to review by an opposing party in a legal proceeding. This is generally everything in subdivision or development applications, including materials associated with their preparation and review.

Downshielded luminaire: A hooded or angled feature of a luminaire (lighting fixture) that prevents glare or reduces excessive luminance.

Dwelling unit: A separate or attached structure containing sleeping, kitchen, and bathroom facilities, designed or used for occupancy by one or more individuals living together as a single housekeeping unit.

Easement: A grant of one or more property rights by a property owner to the public, a corporation, a municipality, or another person or entity, or designated for their use.

EIS: see Environmental Impact Statement (EIS).

Environmental Impact Statement (EIS): A formal written report in response to an environmental assessment activity required under federal legislation (NEPA).

FEIS: Final Environmental Impact Statement (see Environmental Impact Statement).

Final subdivision plat: The final drawings of a subdivision presented to a review board and submitted for recording with the town clerk.

Findings of Fact: Written or oral statement of factual determinations made by a review board relating to regulatory criteria and justifying the imposition of conditions on a development project.

Floodway: The land lying between a lake, river, stream or watercourse and the high water mark of the 100-year storm event, typically shown on municipal maps, as derived from FEMA (Federal Emergency Management Agency) maps.

Fluvial deposits: Materials deposited by flowing water.

Footcandle: A measurement of light falling on a given surface. One footcandle is equal to the amount of light generated by one candle shining on a square-foot surface one foot away.

Footprint: The surface area that will be covered by a building.

Frontage: The side of a lot abutting on an approved town road or street.

Gabion: A compartmentalized rectangular container of galvanized steel hexagonal wire mesh, filled with stone and used to stabilize a construction site.

Geographic Information System (GIS): A system of computer hardware and software used to store, retrieve, map and analyze geographic data. All spatial data is geographically referenced via an earth coordinate scheme.

GIS: See Geographic Information System.

Groins: Long rock structures placed perpendicular to the shoreline.

Ground truth: Verification of remotely sensed (or externally supplied) data by on-site measurements.

Groundwater: Water found underground in porous rock strata and soils.

High and good agricultural soils: Soils classified by the U.S. Soil Conservation Service as having high or good potential for agriculture.

Historic property: A regulatory term meaning a property eligible for listing on the National Register of Historic Places.

Homeowners association: A residential community organization, other than a condominium association, in which individual homeowners share common interests in open space, facilities, or infrastructure, and the maintenance and repair of facilities.

Indigenous: Produced, growing, or living naturally in a region or climate; native.

Impact fee: A charge assessed against newly-developing property that attempts to partially recover the cost incurred by a local government in providing the public facilities required to serve the new development.

Integrity: Degree to which a site, structure, feature, or collection is undisturbed or unaltered relative to currently known examples.

Intervener: A person or other entity allowed to participate in a hearing or similar regulatory or judicial process. The intervener has certain rights by statute or assigned by the court or reviewing authority.

Isochrome: A line on a map joining points associated with a distinguishing variable such as noise or lighting levels from a source.

Land development: Division of a parcel into two or more parcels; the construction, conversion, relocation or enlargement of any building or other structure; any mining, excavation or landfill; and any changes in the use of a building or land.

Latitude: Distance in degrees measured north and south from the equator.

Leachfield: That portion of an on-site septic system that discharges wastewater into the soil. May include absorption trenches, beds, mounds, and other designs.

Level of Service (LOS): A term in the field of traffic engineering that refers to the operating conditions, including frequency of stops, speed, travel time, and traffic density.

Longitude: Distance in degrees measuring the portion of the equator intersected between the meridian of a given place and the prime meridian, as in Greenwich, England.

Lot: Any undivided interest in a parcel of land having boundaries established by deed records in the land records of a town or county.

Lot coverage: The percentage of a lot area covered by buildings, structures, parking areas, loading areas, driveways, or impervious surfaces.

Lumen: A measure of light energy generated by a light source.

Luminaire: A complete lighting unit, often referred to as a fixture.

Mitigate: To offset the effects of development by actions that avoid, minimize, rectify, reduce, or compensate for adverse impacts.

Mixed use development: The development of a tract of land or building with two or more different uses, specifically those permitted in a particular zoning district.

Monument: A permanent concrete or stone marker or metal pipe placed in the ground to identify changes in property lines.

Mylar®: A trademarked polyester film, but generally refers to use of the film to contain a site plan. The film is durable and can be used to make copies of the plan. Many municipalities require filing of a final plat or development plan on Mylar.

NAGPRA: Native American Graves Protection and Repatriation Act of 1990 (25 USC 3001-3013).

Natural area: An area of land or water that has unusual or significant flora, fauna, geological, or similar features of scientific, ecological, or educational value.

National Register of Historic Places: Defined in CFR Part 61.2 as the national list of districts, sites, buildings, structures, and objects significant in American history, architecture, archeology, engineering, and culture, maintained by the Secretary of the Interior under authority of Section 101.(a)(1)(A) of the NHPA.

NHPA: National Historic Preservation Act of 1966 as amended (16 USC 470-470t, 110) and subsequent modifications. The basic historic preservation legislation requiring agencies to check for properties eligible for the National Register prior to a federally enabled project (undertaking).

Non-complying structure: A structure or part of a structure not in conformance with the zoning regulations covering building mass, dimensions, height, area, yards, density, or off-street parking requirements, but which conformed to previous laws, ordinances and regulations.

Non-conforming use: Use of land or a structure that does not comply with all zoning regulations but which met prior regulations or laws governing the tract of land. This term may be specifically defined in local ordinances.

Nonpoint source: Source or discharge of pollution picked up by runoff as when rain, melting snow, or flowing water picks up contaminants and carries them to lakes, rivers and other surface waters or to groundwater.

Open space: The undeveloped portion of any development parcel, unoccupied by any construction (e.g., buildings, rights-of-way, parking spaces, recreational facilities, private, individual yards) and which is set aside, designated, or dedicated for the use of owners, adjoiners, or the general public.

Off-site mitigation: Reduction of the impacts of development (e.g., environmental, municipal, economic, social) though some action, augmentation, or protection on a different tract of land.

Pathogen: An organism causing disease.

Party: A person, agency, property owner, or other entity granted the right, by statute or by permission, to participate in a hearing, regulatory review, or formulation of a government undertaking.

Perimeter: A measurement of the whole outer boundary of a piece of land, structure, or feature.

Planned Residential Development: See PRD.

Planned Unit Development: See PUD

Plat: A map or representation on paper of land subdivided into lots and streets, drawn to scale.

Point source: A discharge of pollution from a specific source such as a pipe or chimney.

ppm: Parts per million; a measure of concentration.

PRD (Planned Residential Development): A specific type of residential project that, by reason of design or other factors, qualifies for an increase in density or for placement in an area where it might not otherwise be allowed.

Primary area: In septic design, the land area designated for the original wastewater system including a leachfield or mound.

PUD (Planned Unit Development): A parcel of land to be developed as a single entity for mixed residential and commercial or industrial uses. A PUD is usually defined in municipal regulations and may qualify for regulatory concessions.

Off-road parking: Parking space outside the road right-of-way or at least 25 feet off the centerline, whichever is greater.

Overlay district: A zoning district that encompasses one or more underlying districts and that imposes additional standards or requirements than otherwise required by the underlying district.

Remote sensing: Non-invasive reconnaissance and surface survey techniques to determine the extent and nature of subsurface conditions and buried environmental features.

Renewable energy resource: Energy available for collection or conversion from direct sunlight, wind, running water, organically derived fuels including wood, agricultural sources, waste materials, waste heat, and geothermal sources.

Request for Proposals (RFP): An invitation to respond to the articulated need for research or professional services. Usually in the form of a bid for a contract.

Right of Way: A right of passage over another person's lot; often, the strip of land over which a private driveway, public road or electric transmission line passes.

RFP: See Request for Proposals

Scope of Work (SOW): The range and details of professional services and activities to be provided by the contractor.

Section 106: That portion of the NHPA requiring agencies to identify then take into account any adverse effects on properties eligible for listing on the National Register that may be located within the area of an agency-enabled undertaking.

Section 106 process: Procedure set out in 36 CFR 800.3 - 800.13 in response to NHPA Section 106, meant to identify and resolve any adverse effects likely to be caused by a project.

Sedimentation basin: An excavated area that collects and holds sediments deposited by runoff.

Set-back: A designated distance between a lot boundary or feature such as a road or watercourse, and allowable construction or other land alteration. Lots may have setbacks for development, in accordance with local municipal regulations.

Shadow analysis: Determination of the exposure of a site or structure to sunlight. The shadow of a building can be calculated from its height and orientation and by determining the slope of the land. Some ordinances require a shadow analysis be done for solar access at mid-day on December 21.

SHPO: see State Historic Preservation Officer.

Sight distance: In traffic studies, refers to visibility of other traffic, usually from the perspective of a passenger car driver.

Silt fence: A temporary fence made of plastic or similar material, which is placed during construction near streams and along areas vulnerable to soil erosion.

Site plan review: A primary tool in local land-use management for ensuring that the development of a particular parcel follows the municipality's land-use objectives. The review process is usually concerned with the development of lands intended for non-residential or multi-family housing purposes, and addresses a broad range of issues, including traffic, noise, landscaping, erosion, compatibility with surrounding land uses, parking, and public services.

Sketch plan review: An informal review of a drawing of a proposed subdivision. The process helps the board get acquainted with the project and helps the developer get acquainted with applicable regulations.

Slope: Ratio between distance and elevation. Percentage slope can be calculated by dividing elevation by distance, then multiplying by 100.

Solar Access: The sunlight that is allowed to reach the site or to reach buildings on the site. Solar access is often determined by a shadow analysis.

SOW: see Scope of Work

Spaghetti lot: A lot that is much longer than it is wide (usually a 5:1 or more ratio), and may meander. Usually created to obtain minimum road frontage at the expense of good land use.

Spot zoning: The rezoning of a single parcel or a small land area to benefit one or more property owners.

Sprawl: Low density, automobile-dependent development located along roads and in the country outside compact urban and village centers.

State Historic Preservation Officer (SHPO): The state official that administers the State historic preservation program.

Strip development: A linear pattern of commercial, residential, commercial, or mixed-use development along a roadway, often characterized by auto-dependent, single-story structures with parking in the front, and un-shared curb cuts.

Structure: Any construction, erection, assemblage or other combination of materials on the land, including, in general, swimming pools, satellite dishes, tennis courts, and utility sheds.

Subdivision: A parcel of land, vacant or improved, which is divided or proposed to be divided into two or more lots for the purpose of offer, transfer, sale or development.

Survey: The process of determining boundaries and areas of tracts of land. Also a map prepared as a result of that process.

Swale: A low-lying linear area of land providing natural or artificial drainage. Design specifications for the use of swales to treat storm water generally call for a broad, shallow, vegetated channel with erosion-resistant and flood-tolerant grasses.

Telecommunication facility: A support structure, often a tower, used primarily for communication or broadcast.

Traditional Cultural Property (TCP): A property eligible for inclusion on the National Register of Historic Places because of its association with cultural practices or beliefs of a living community.

Viewshed: The appearance of a landscape, view or physical feature that can be seen from a particular vantage point.

Well-head protection area: The zone around the source of a well designated for protection from contamination or harm.

Wetlands: Land areas inundated by surface water or groundwater sufficient to support vegetation or aquatic life. Includes marshes, swamps, mud flats, bogs, ponds, and surface water overflow areas.

Wildlife habitat: The natural living area of an animal species, especially the particular location where it normally lives, grows, and reproduces, as in a desert, softwood forest or seacoast.

Where to go for more information

Buyer's Resource Real Estate. *Glossary of Real Estate Terms.* http://www.buyersresource.com/Bglossary.html

Environmental Protection Agency. (1993). *The plain English guide to the Clean Air Act.* EPA-400-K-93-001. Includes a glossary of terms. http://www.epa.gov/oar/oaqps/peg_caa/pegcaain.html

Kelso, David and Al Perez. (1983). *Noise control terms made somewhat easier.* Noise Pollution Clearinghouse. http://www.nonoise.org/library/diction/soundict.htm

Land Use Law Center, Pace University School of Law. *Universal glossary of land use terms and phrases.* http://www.pace.edu/lawschool/landuse/zoning%20school/glossary.html

BIBLIOGRAPHY AND INTERNET REFERENCES

Note: Additional sources of information are provided at the end of each chapter.

Bibliography

American Association of State Highway and Transportation Officials (AASHTO). (2001). *A Policy on Geometric Design of Highways and Streets* (AASHTO "Greenbook"). Washington, DC: AASHTO.

American Farmland Trust. (1996). *Farming on the Edge.* Washington, DC: American Farmland Trust.

Argentine, Cindy Corlett. (1998). *Vermont Act 250 Handbook – A Guide to State and Regional Land Use Regulation,* 2nd edition. Newfane, VT: Putney Press.

Benfield, F. Kaid, Matthew D. Raimi, and Donald D.T. Chen. (1999). *Once there were Greenfields.* New York, NY: Natural Resources Defense Council.

Brighton, Deb and Jim Northrup. (1990). *The Tax Base and the Tax Bill, Tax Implications of Development: A Workbook.* Montpelier, VT: Vermont League of Cities and Towns. Vermont Natural Resources Council.

Brown, Whitney E. and Deborah S. Caraco. (1997). Muddy water in – muddy water out?: A critique of erosion and sediment control plans. *Watershed Protection Techniques,* Vol. 2, No. 3: 57- 68.

Brown, Whitney E. and Deborah S. Caraco. (1996). *Task 2 technical memorandum.* Silver Spring, MD: Center for Watershed Protection.

Burchell, Robert W., ed. (1990). *Development Impact Analysis.* Piscataway, NJ: Center for Urban Policy Research.

Burchell, Robert W. and David Listokin. (1978). *The Fiscal Impact Handbook—Estimating Local Costs and Revenues of Land Development*. New Brunswick, NJ: The Center for Urban Policy Research.

Conservation Law Foundation v. Town of Lincolnville 2001 [Me., 786 A. 2d 616]

Courtney, Elizabeth. (1991). *Vermont's Scenic Landscapes: A Guide for Growth and Protection*. Waterbury, VT: Vermont Agency of Natural Resources.

Cronon, William. (1983). *Changes in the Land: Indians, Colonists, and the Ecology of New England*. New York, NY: Hill and Wang.

Daniels, Thomas L. (1999). *When City and Country Collide – Managing Growth in the Metropolitan Fringe*. Washington, DC: Island Press.

DeChiarra, Joseph, and Lee Koppleman. (1978). *Site Planning Standards*, New York, NY: McGraw Hill.

Delogu, Orlando E. (1997). *Maine Land Use Control Law*, 2nd edition. Standish, ME: Tower Publishing, Standish.

Ewing, Reid. (1996). *Best Development Practices*. Chicago, IL: American Planning Association.

Gordon, D.A., H.W. McGee and K.G. Hooper. (1984). Driver characteristics impacting on highway design and operations. *Public Roads*, June, pp. 12-16. Washington, DC: Federal Highway Administration.

Heart, Bennet, Elizabeth Humstone, Thomas F. Irwin, Sandy Levine, and Dano Weisbord. (2002). *Community Rules – A New England Guide to Smart Growth Strategies*. Burlington, VT: Conservation Law Foundation and the Vermont Forum on Sprawl.

Humstone, Elizabeth and Julie Campoli. (1998). Access management: an overview. *Planning Commissioners Journal*, No. 29.

Intergovernmental Panel on Climate Change. (2001). *Third Assessment Report*. Washington DC: Union of Concerned Scientists.

King, Thomas F. (2000). *Federal Planning and Historical Places: The Section 106 Process*. Walnut Creek, CA: AltaMira Press.

Maine Audubon Society. (2000). *Conserving Wildlife in Maine's Developing Landscape.* Falmouth, NH: Maine Audobon Society.

Maine Audubon Society. (1999). *Watching Out for Maine's Wildlife.* Falmouth, ME: Maine Audubon Society.

Maine State Planning Office. (2000). *Noise.* Technical Assistance Bulletin #4. Maine State Planning Office.

Moulton, David G., Amos Turk, and James R. Johnston, Jr., eds. (1975). *Methods in Olfactory Research.* London: Academic Press.

National Resources Defense Council. (2002). *Developments and Dollars: An Introduction to Fiscal Impact Analysis in Land Use Planning.* Washington, DC: NRDC.

Neumann, Thomas W. and Robert M. Sanford. (2001). *Cultural Resources Archaeology: An Introduction.* Walnut Creek, CA: AltaMira Press.

New Hampshire Code for Energy Conservation in New Building Construction (PUC 1800).

Patterns of Development Task Force. (1997). *A Response to Sprawl: Designing Communities to Protect Wildlife Habitat and Accommodate Development.* Report. Augusta, ME: Maine Environmental Priorities Project.

Rapoport, Amos. (1977). *Human Aspects of Urban Form.* Elmsford, NY: Pergamon Press.

Ryan, Kathleen and Michael Munson. (1996). *Outdoor Lighting Manual for Vermont Municipalities.* Burlington, VT: Chittenden County Regional Planning Commission.

Thorson, Robert M. (2002). *Stone by stone: The magnificent history in New England's stone walls.* New York, NY: Walker & Co.

Schultz, T. J. and N. M. McMahon. (1971). *HUD Noise Assessment Guidelines.* Washington DC: US Government Printing Office.

Seigel, Michael L., Jutka Terris and Kaid Benfield. (2000). *Development and Dollars: An Introduction to Fiscal Impact Analysis in Land Use Planning.* Washington, DC: Natural Resources Defense Council.

Smarden, Richard C., James F. Palmer, and John Felleman, eds. (1986). *Foundations for Visual Project Analysis*. New York, NY: John Wiley & Sons.

Transportation Research Board. (2000). *Highway Capacity Manual 2000*. 4th edition. Washington, DC: National Cooperative Highway Research Program.

USDA Natural Resources Conservation Service. (1996). *Soil Quality Information Sheet*. Washington, DC: USDA NRCS.

Vermont Agency of Natural Resources. (1987). *Vermont Handbook for Soil Erosion and Sediment Control on Construction Sites*. Waterbury, VT: Department of Environmental Conservation, Water Quality Division.

Vermont Agency of Natural Resources. (2002). *Report on Options for Municipal and Responsibilities in Stormwater Management*. Waterbury, VT: ANR.

Vermont Department of Housing and Community Affairs. (1999). *History of Planning in Vermont*. Montpelier, VT: VDHCA.

Vermont Department of Public Service. (2001). *2001 Vermont Guidelines for Energy Efficient Commercial Construction, State of Vermont Amendments to the International Energy Conservation Code 2000*. Montpelier, VT: Vermont Department of Public Service.

Vermont Department of Public Service. *Vermont Municipal and Regional Planning and Development Act, Title 24, Chapter 117* (with additional sections including Act 250 and the Downtown Development Act). Reprinted from Vermont Statutes Annotated and 2000 Cumulative Supplement. Montpelier, VT: Lexus Publishing.

Vermont Department of Public Service. (1998). *Vermont Residential Energy Code Handbook, A Guide to Complying with Vermont's Residential Building Energy Standards*. Montpelier, VT: Vermont Department of Public Service.

The Vermont Forum on Sprawl. (2001). *Growing Smarter, Best Site Planning for Residential, Commercial and Industrial Development*. Burlington, VT: VFOS.

Vermont Forum on Sprawl.(1998). *Exploring Sprawl No. 3, The Causes and Effects of Sprawl*. Burlington, VT: VFOS.

Internet Resources

Agriculture Network Information Center - provides access to agriculture-related information, subject area experts and other resources. http://www.agnic.org/

A Guide to Wastewater Treatment. http://www.gurd.bc.ca/sewers/bro/wwguide. html

Agroecology Homepage. http://www.agroecology.org/principles.htm

American Forests Homepage. http://www.amfor.org

Center for Excellence in Sustainable Development: Transportation. http://www.sustainable.doe.gov/transprt/trintro.htm

Coastal Information Directory – NOAA website providing links to a wide range of coastal interests. http://www.csc.noaa.gov/CID/

Energy Efficiency and Renewable Energy Network – The US Department of Energy's web site on renewable energy and efficiency. http://www.eren. doe.gov/

Groundwater Protection Council Homepage. http://gwpc.site.net/

Gulf of Maine Council on the Marine Environment. http://www. gulfofmaine.org/council/

Maine Coastal Program. http://www.state.me.us/spo/mcp/mcp.htm

Maine DEP Air Quality Home Page. http://www.state.me.us/dep/air/home.htm

Maine Preservation – non-profit organization dedicated to preserving and protecting architectural heritage, historic sites and communities of Maine. http://www.mainepreservation.com/home1.htm

Maine Rural Water Association. http://www.mainerwa.org/index.html

Maine Woodlot Assistance Homepage – provides information on sustainable forestry and other aspects of forestry to landowners in Maine. http://www.ume.maine.edu/~woodlot/woodlot.htm

National Forest Foundation. http://www.nffweb.org/

National Small Flows Clearinghouse – provides information on wastewater treatment to small communities. http://www.estd.wvu.edu/nsfc/nsfc_homepage.html

Natural Resources Conservation Service – Soil Quality web page. http://soils.usda.gov/sqi/

New England Floodplain and Stormwater Managers Association. http://www.Seacoast.com/~nefsma/

New England Interstate Water Pollution Control Commission – creates water quality standards throughout New England. http://www.neiwpcc.org/

New Hampshire Air Resources Division. http://www.state.nh.us/des/ard/homepage.htm

New Hampshire Coastal Program. http://www.state.nh.us/coastal/

Noise Pollution Clearinghouse – provides information relating to noise pollution and control. http://www.nonoise.org/

Noise Control/Pollution Terms – this site provides a glossary of terms commonly used in noise control and assessment. http://www.nonoise.org/library/diction/soundict.htm

Northeast Sustainable Energy Association. http://www.nesea.org/

Rural Community Assistance Program. http://www.rcap.org/

Smart Growth Network – information on development relating to economy, community and environment. http://www.smartgrowth.org/

Solstice – provides information on sustainable energy. solstice.crest.org/index.shtml

Sprawl Watch Clearinghouse – provides information related to sprawl, smart growth and livable communities. http://www.sprawlwatch.org/

State Natural Resources Conservation Service
Maine. http://www.me.nrcs.usda.gov/
New Hampshire. http://www.nh.nrcs.usda.gov/
Vermont. http://www.vt.nrcs.usda.gov/

Sustainable Communities Network. http://www.sustainable.org/

Sustainable Farming Connection. http://www.ibiblio.org/farming-connection/

Transportationion for Livable Communities Network. http://www.tlcnetwork.org/

The Plain English Guide to the Clean Air Act – EPA site that provides a glossary of terms commonly used in air quality control. http://www.epa.gov/oar/oaqps/peg_caa/pegcaain.html

U.S. EPA Office of Ground Water and Drinking Water. http://www.epa.gov/OGWDW/

U.S. EPA Office of Wastewater Management. http://www.epa.gov/OWM/

U.S. EPA Wetlands information hotline. http://www.epa.gov/OWOW/wetlands/wetline.html

Vermont Air Pollution Control Division. http://www.anr.state.vt.us/dec/air/index.htm

Vermont Fish and Wildlife Department Homepage. http://www.anr.state.vt.us/fw/fwhome/index.htm

Vermont Forum on Sprawl. http://www.vtsprawl.org

Vermont Heritage Network – site dealing with historic preservation in the State of Vermont. http://www.uvm.edu/~vhnet/

INDEX

Transferable Development Rights
(TDR)   180, 218
Transportation Research Board   132
true north   29

U

U Value   203
U.S. Bureau of Mines standards   57
U.S. Department of Housing and Urban
Development (HUD)   65
United States Geological Survey (USGS)
maps   28, 34–35
Universal Transverse Mercator
(UTM)   29, 34–35

V

vehicle trip   139
Vermont Business Roundtable   25

Vermont Forum on Sprawl   25, 215
vibration   57
viewshed   161–162
Visual Impact Assessment (VIA)   162–163
visual screening   167

W

watershed   101
well head protection areas (WPAs)   107
wetlands   15, 97–100
mitigation   98–100
wetlands, coastal   228
wetlands hydrology   98
wood smoke   54
worst condition analysis   51

Z

zoning   15

About the Authors

A former resident of Vermont and New Hampshire, Rob Sanford lives in Gorham, Maine with his wife Robin and children Corey, Dan, and Morgan. Rob has been an environmental consultant and a land use regulator. He received his PhD from the State University of New York College of Environmental Science and Forestry in 1989 and is an Associate Professor of Environmental Science and Policy at the University of Southern Maine.

Active professionally for many years in the fields of land use planning and regulation, Dana Farley lives with her family in Charlotte, Vermont. She received a MA degree from Georgetown University in Government and Public Policy in 1982. She is a principal of LaPlatte Land Planning, LLC, and is completing Vermont's Four Year Law Office Study Program in the Law Offices of George T. Faris IV, both in Shelburne, Vermont.

PUTNEY PRESS
Publications

Vermont Act 250 Handbook, by Cindy Corlett Argentine – A detailed analysis of the Act 250 process, including jurisdictional questions, an explanation of the hearing and appeal process and a comprehensive discussion of each of the Act's 10 criteria. Fully indexed and referenced. Cost: $34.95 (Add $3.75 to cover shipping and handling, and applicable sales tax for delivery to Vermont addresses.)

Site Plan and Development Review: A Guide for Northern New England, by Robert M. Sanford and Dana H. Farley – This handy guidebook helps both professionals and citizen volunteers make informed decisions on development projects. Cost: $34.95 (Add $3.75 to cover shipping and handling, and applicable sales tax for delivery to Vermont addresses.)

Vermont Environmental Monitor Newsletter – A monthly report on Vermont's environmental regulatory and permit process, including information on Act 250, ·municipal planning, hazardous waste, water pollution, air toxics, landfills and recycling. Published 12 times per year. Cost: $89 per year ($74 for not-for-profit entities). Free sample issues available.

New Hampshire Government Directory – A comprehensive directory to demystify the workings of New Hampshire State Government. The directory contains phone numbers, addresses, department classification and the names of political appointees and civil servants. Cost: $25.95. (Add $3.75 to cover shipping and handling.) Quantity discounts available.

Vermont Government Directory – Like the New Hampshire Government Directory, it contains phone numbers, addresses, department classification and the names of political appointees and civil servants. Cost: $25.95. (Add $3.75 shipping and handling, and applicable sales tax for delivery to Vermont addresses.) Quantity discounts available.

To order any of the above,
or to request further information, contact:
Putney Press, PO Box 430, Newfane, VT 05345,
800/639-6074 or 802/365-7991. Fax: 802/365-7996,
E-mail: ppress@sover.net

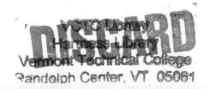